I0800494

IMAGES
of America

ALONG THE ROUTE 100 CORRIDOR REVISITED

On the cover: Seen here is the family of Elam and Rosa Benfield, who are the great-grandparents of the author, Patricia Stompf Blackwell. The photograph was taken at their home, along South Sixth Street in Bally, a location known to Bally residents as "the church path." As the name suggests, it was the dirt pathway leading to the Catholic church, school, and cemetery, used by parishoners and school children walking to their destination. (Courtesy of Patricia Stompf Blackwell.)

IMAGES
of America

ALONG THE ROUTE 100 CORRIDOR REVISITED

Patricia A. Stompf Blackwell

ARCADIA
PUBLISHING

ISBN 978-0-7385-3844-0

Published by Arcadia Publishing
Charleston, South Carolina

Printed in the United States of America

Library of Congress Catalog Card Number: 2005925430

For all general information contact Arcadia Publishing at:
Telephone 843-853-2070
Fax 843-853-0044
E-mail sales@arcadiapublishing.com
For customer service and orders:
Toll-Free 1-888-313-2665

Visit us on the Internet at www.arcadiapublishing.com

Contents

ACKNOWLEDGMENTS

My sincere thanks to so many people who have made the first book so successful. It totally surpassed my expectations. First, I could not have done it without my deep Christian faith and my husband and soul mate, Bill Blackwell.

Due to the overwhelming interest, many Berks Countians have supplied me with ancestral information, photographs, and historical books they had in their possession.

Richard Hoffman of Barto, a fellow historian, supplied a wealth of information dating back centuries. Through this venture, Richard and his wife, Karen, have become not only dear friends, but I have found that as they say in this area, "everybody is related to everybody." Yes, looking back we have found such a family relationship.

Others are Maria and Julia Calandra from the Padre Pio Center; Jane and Jerry Stahl, formerly of Bally; Luanne Zambanini (née Riegner); Sharon Boyer (née Benfield); Lindsay Davenport of the Boyertown Historical Society; and Mark and Carole Shearer of Shearer Technical. These are just a few, and my thanks go out to all.

INTRODUCTION

Along the Route 100 Corridor hardly touched the rich historical legacy of this beautiful rural area of Berks County. This second book, *Along the Route 100 Corridor Revisited*, includes many additional views of the towns.

The addition of the views of surrounding villages such as Clayton, Niantic, Eshbach, Landis Store, Forgedale, and Gilbertsville again revives historical interest. Travel back to the various industries that thrived in past centuries. The faces of the early settlers of the area depict the strength and tough character that was needed at the time. The educational transition from early beginnings of the one-room schoolhouses in villages, such as Heydt's School, Rehr's School, and Oberholtzer School, just to name a few, as we look back at the faces of the students and teachers from these schools that closed in the mid-1900s. Time moved forward through Boyertown High School, Most Blessed Sacrament School, which opened in 1953.

Religion in the communities began with the early Jesuit missionaries arriving in the once-known area of "Goshenhoppen," and also to the Mennonites, Schwenkfelders, and Lutherans arriving and building their churches and congregations.

At least 30 potteries once operated in Berks County alone during the 19th century. Many are familiar with the Isaac Stahl family pottery, but many are not aware that there was a Passmore Pottery (named after the village known as Passmore) founded by Sebastian Glaes, a native of Pike Township, Berks County, in 1828. After Glaes's death in 1869, the pottery continued under the operation of his eldest son, John. What was known as Passmore during the 19th century is now known as the home of Grandview Speedway. This is a perfect example of the transportation revolution—from the horse and wagon used to deliver products to fast-paced race cars at Grandview Speedway.

What were wages during these times? Working for the Glaes family at Passmore Pottery, apprentices David Huber, John Frey, Nathan Reigner, Edwin and Albert Fox, and Henry Schoch received 8¢ an hour, and they had to pay their board and lodging out of this.

The many cigar manufacturing companies are no longer operating. The area no longer has the wealth of the industrial companies that for years employed the majority of the residents along the Route 100 corridor.

Time moves ahead along Route 100, but the rich German influence that laid the groundwork for this picturesque landscape should never be forgotten.

One

Bally Revisited

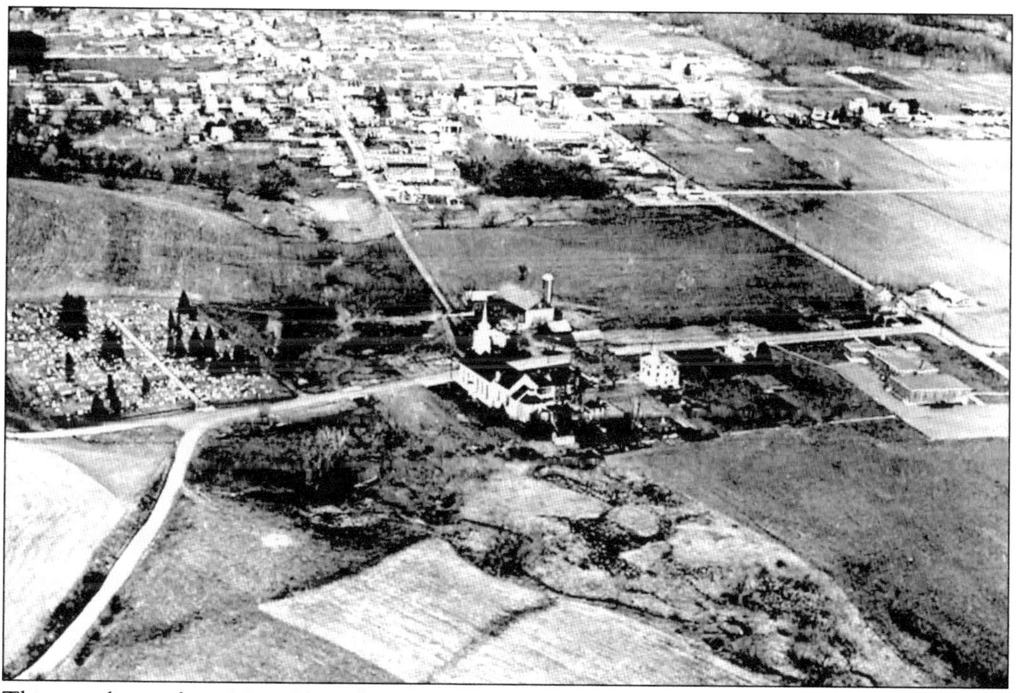

This aerial view from Most Blessed Sacrament Church looks toward the residential area of Bally.

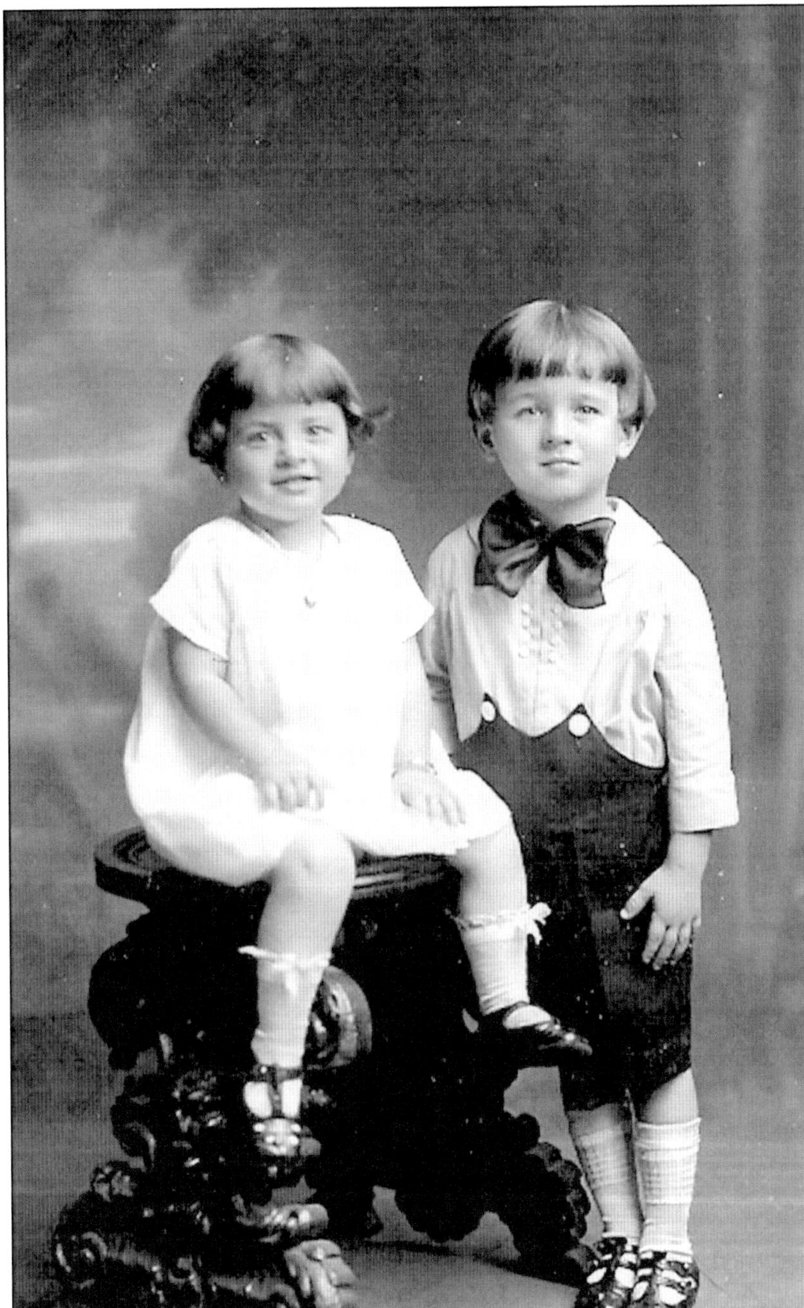

These two children lived on North Seventh Street in Bally. They are siblings Edith Fronheiser (née Weller) and Paul Weller.

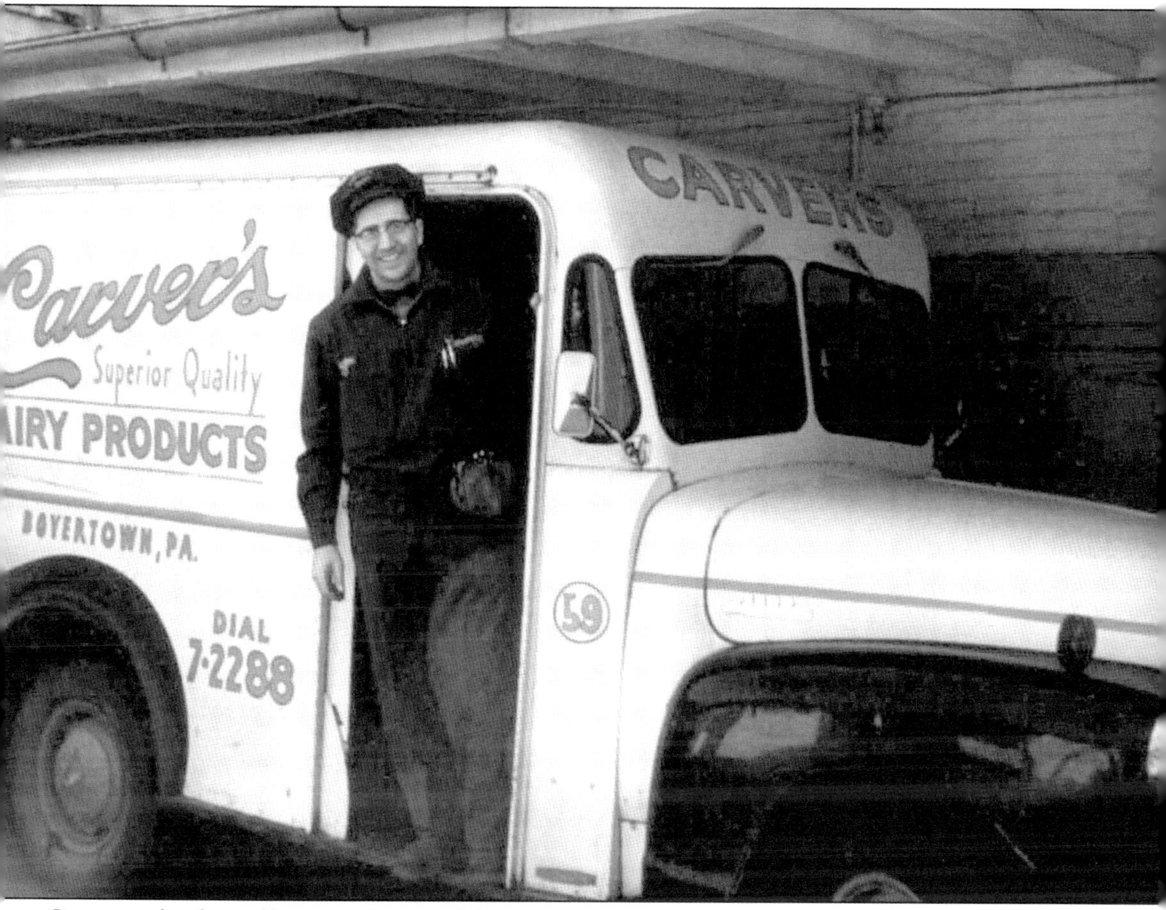

Gone are the days of having groceries delivered to one's home by the milkman, baker, huckster, or the butcher. Joe Riegner from Bally spent many years delivering milk when he drove the milk truck for Carver's Dairy.

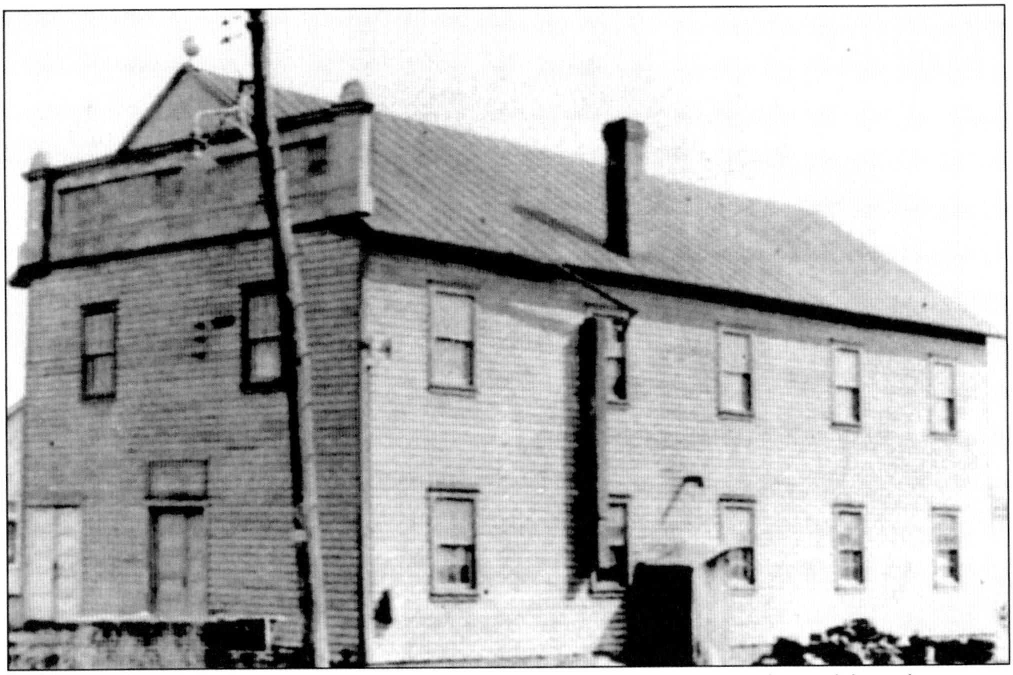

This frame building was company headquarters of Bally Novelty Works and later known as Bally Case and Cooler when George Prince joined the firm in 1934. The old Band Hall, as it was known, was located on North Seventh Street, opposite the Bally Ribbon Mill.

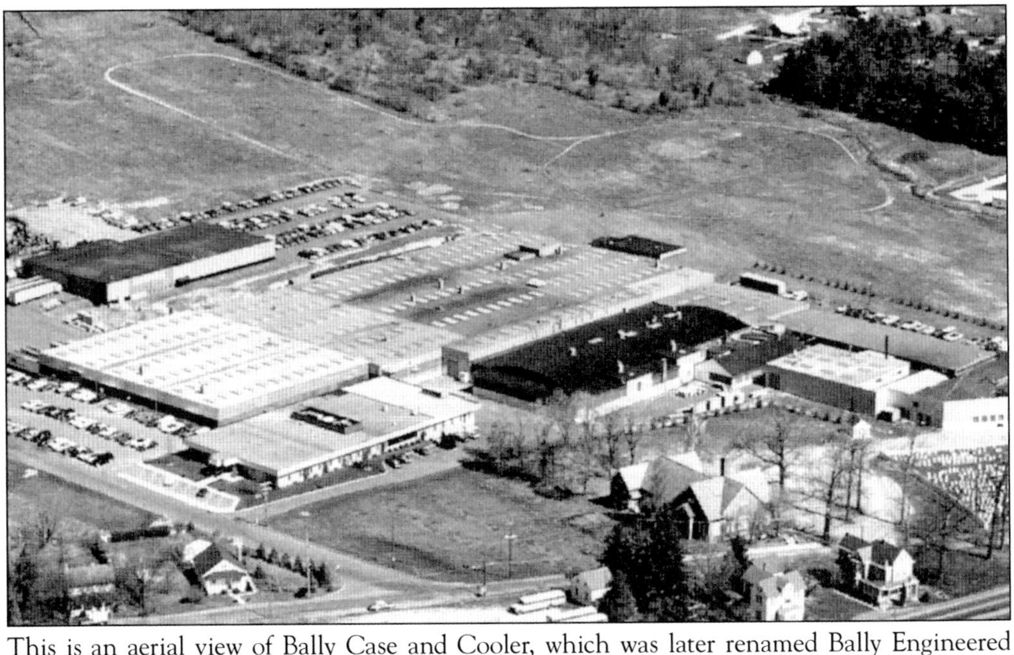

This is an aerial view of Bally Case and Cooler, which was later renamed Bally Engineered Structures. Bally Case and Cooler became the world's largest manufacturer of walk-in coolers and freezers. In the early days of the company, it specialized in ice-cream cabinets and meat display cases. The company was owned by brothers Leonard and George Melcher and brothers George and Leon Prince of Pottstown.

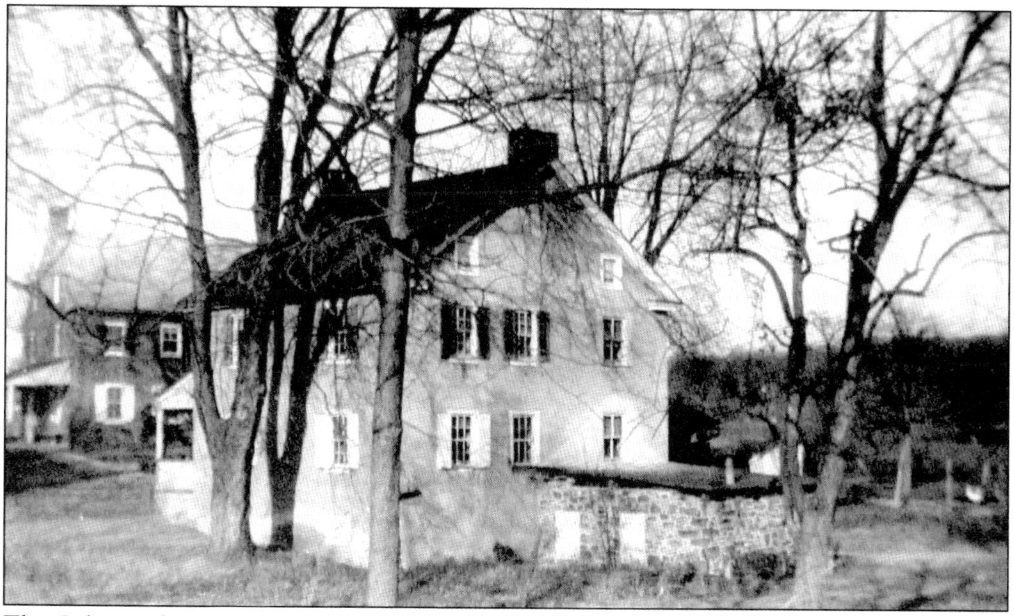

The Gehman farm was located in the Butter Valley area below Bally. This area is now known for the Butter Valley Golfport built by John Gehman.

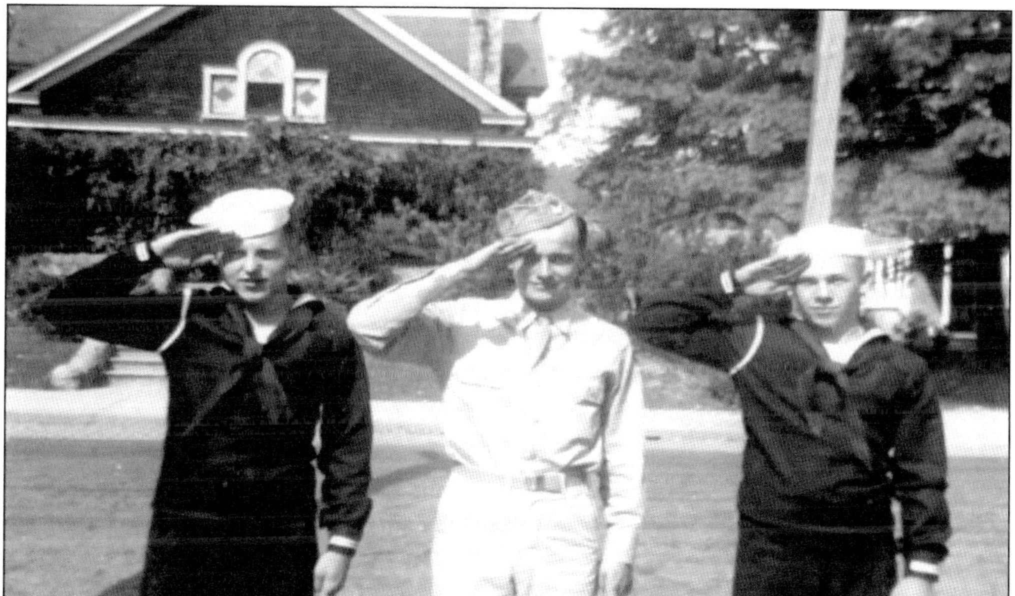

World War II Bally GIs are seen here on leave, enjoying their visit on Main Street. From left to right, they are LeRoy Stengel, Norbert Reichart, and Eddie Melcher.

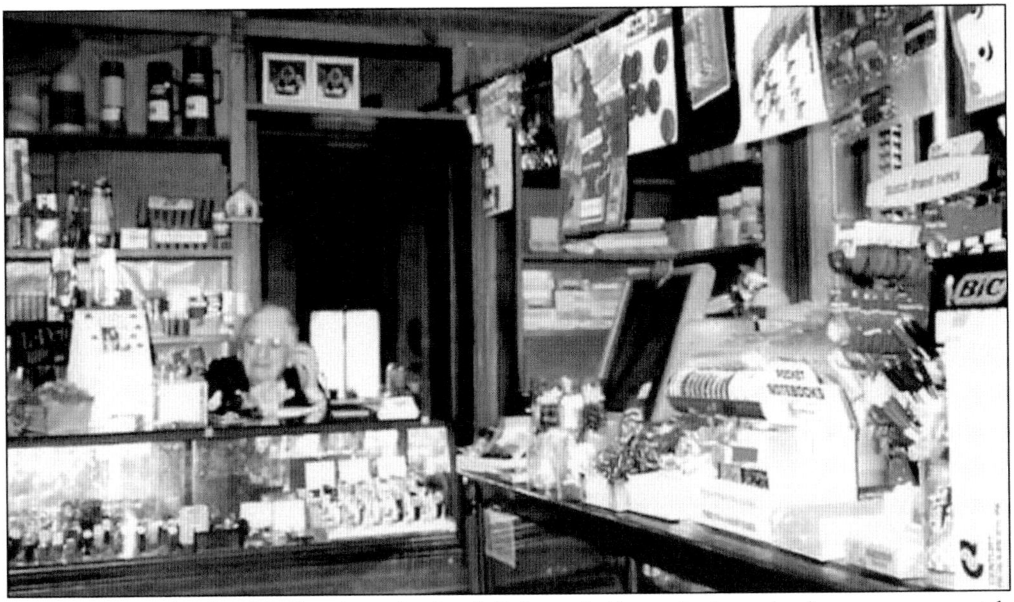

When people think of Bally, they think of Gehman's Store. It dates back many years with remembrances of Mary and her daughter, Sarah, standing behind the counter with cheerful greetings to those entering the store. Sarah is shown in this photograph. Gehman's Store today still remains in the Gehman family, and LuElla Gehman (owner of the store, granddaughter of Mary, and Sarah's niece) has kept the store almost identical to its appearance years ago. LuElla's cousin Patricia works in the store and is the new friendly face of Gehman's Store.

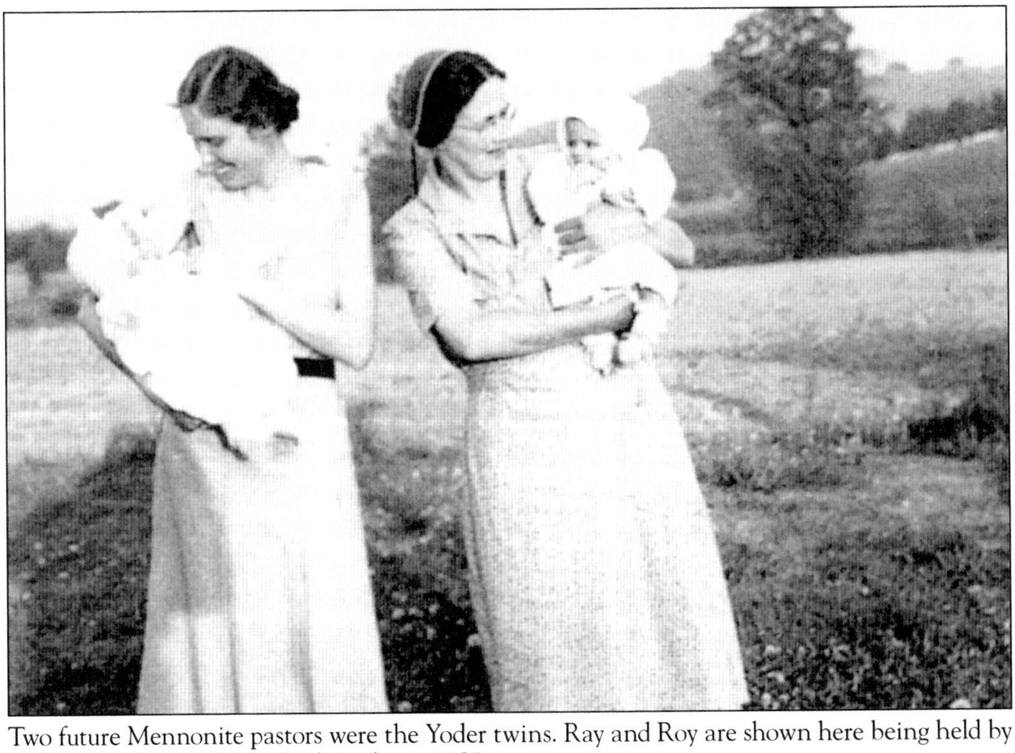

Two future Mennonite pastors were the Yoder twins. Ray and Roy are shown here being held by Mildred Gerhart and Elizabeth Yoder in 1938.

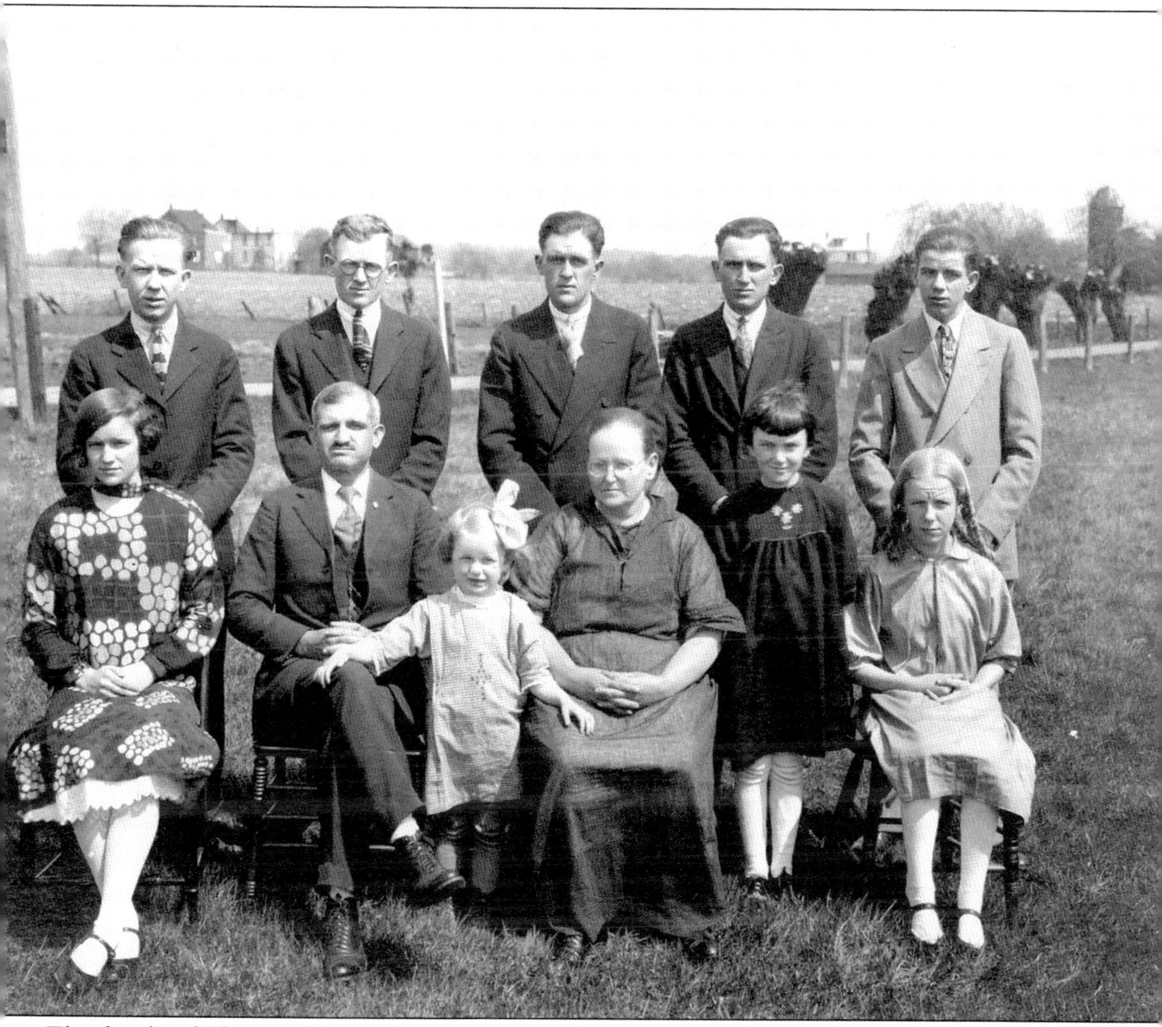

The family of Elam and Rosa Benfield dates back to the early 1900s. They are the author's great-great-grandparents and resided at 155 South Sixth Street in Bally. Pictured here from left to right are the following: (first row) Rosa Miller (née Benfield), father Elam, Matilda Conrad (née Benfield), mother Rosa, Grace Minner (née Benfield), and Emma Campbell (née Benfield); (second row) Warren, William, George, Charles, and John Benfield. Elam was the street supervisor in the 1920s, earning 33¢ per hour. He also performed the duties of auditor at a wage of $5 per month.

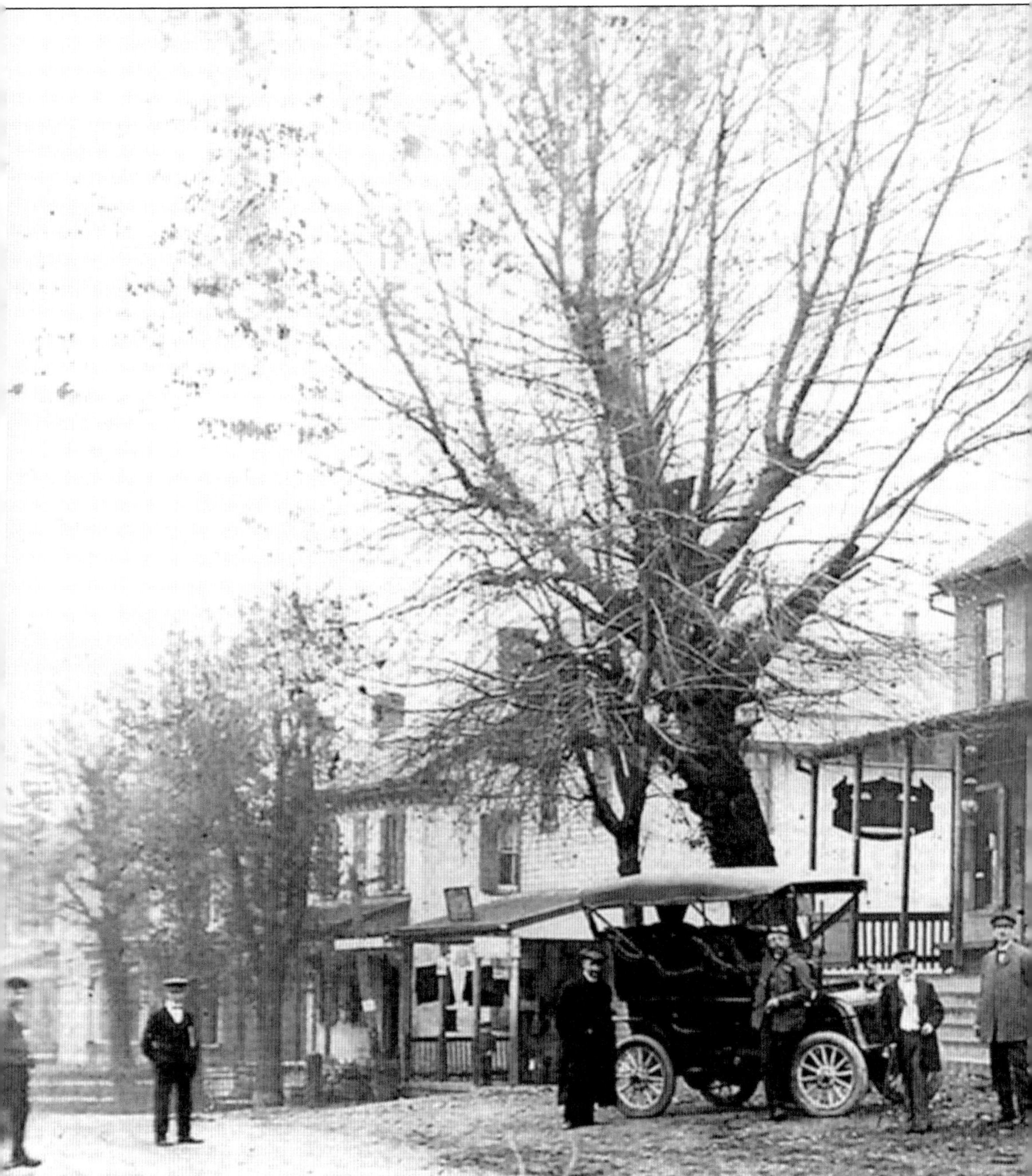

The Bally union house was located at the intersection of Main Street along Route 100 and Sixth Street. The first meeting of town council for the borough of Bally was held April 3, 1913, at the public house owned by Horace Quigley. The first meeting was attended by, seen here from left

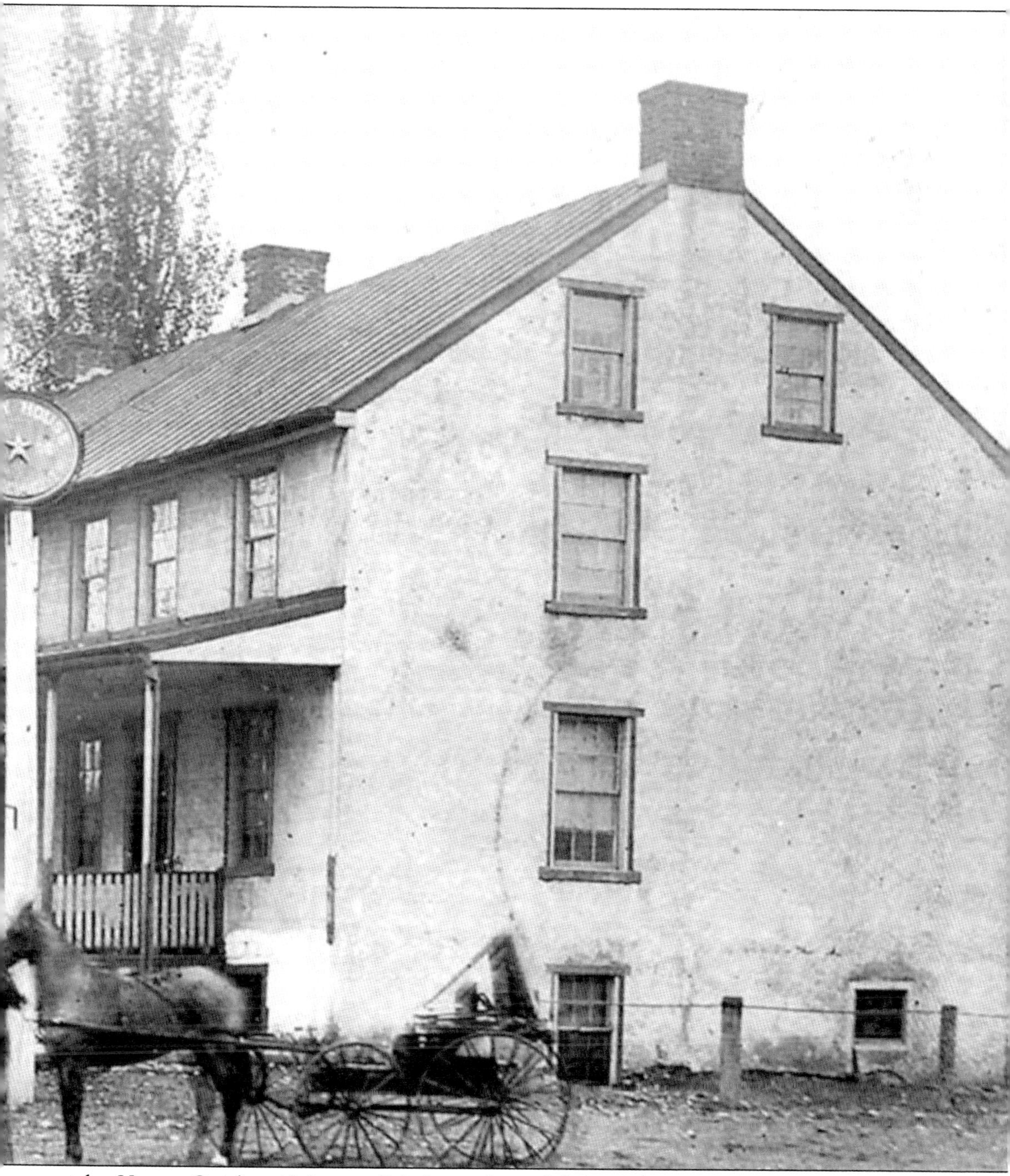

to right, Horace Quigley, Alphonsus Eck, Lewis Stengel, John Gehringer, Edward Shirey, A. B. Pennepacker, and Edward Grim. Henry Eddinger was appointed the chief burgess.

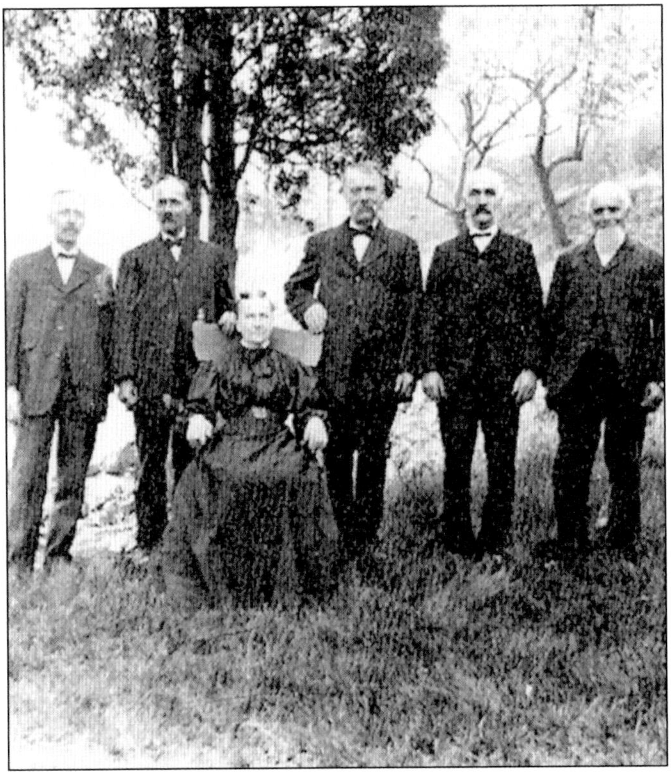

Henry Bauer and his family resided on Crow Hill.

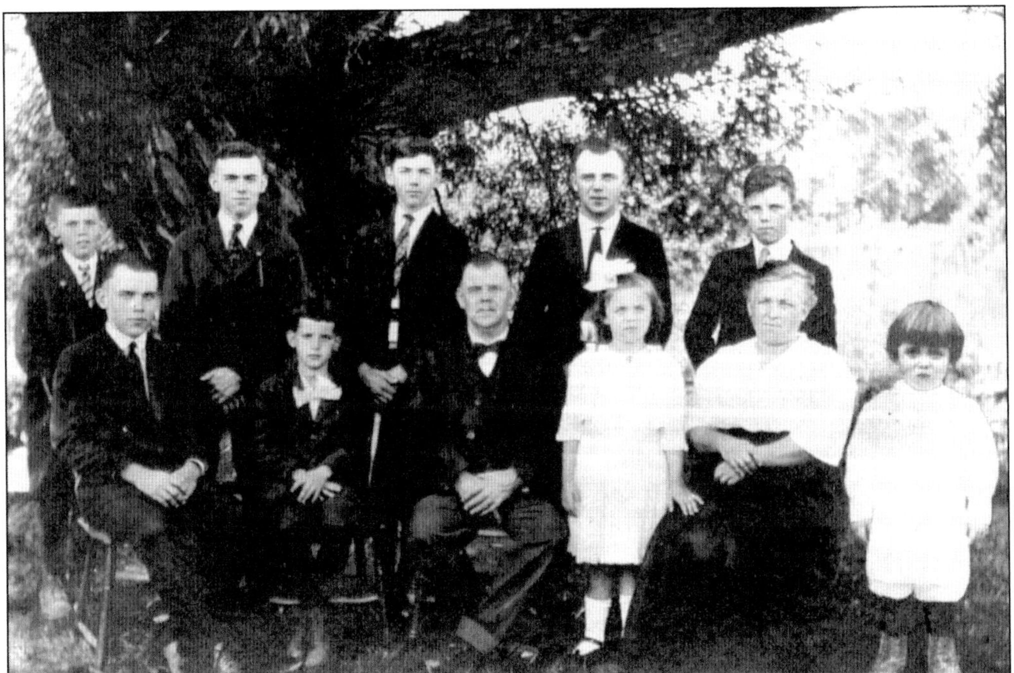

Pictured in this 1914 portrait of the Stahl family are, from left to right, (first row) George, Russell, Isaac, Mabel, Lilly, and Clarence; (second row) Joe, Paul, Francis, Charles, and Gerald.

Gerald "Gib" and Kathryn "Cass" Stahl lived along Barto Road until their deaths, and both spent much of their working careers at Bally Case and Cooler. They never lost a day's work due to inclement weather since they lived only a few steps from the plant. Gib ran the trucking department, and Cass was known for managing the stockroom.

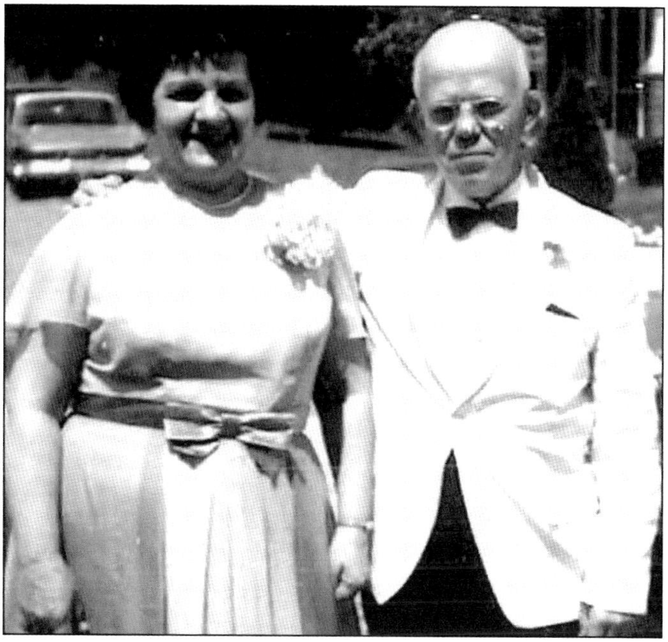

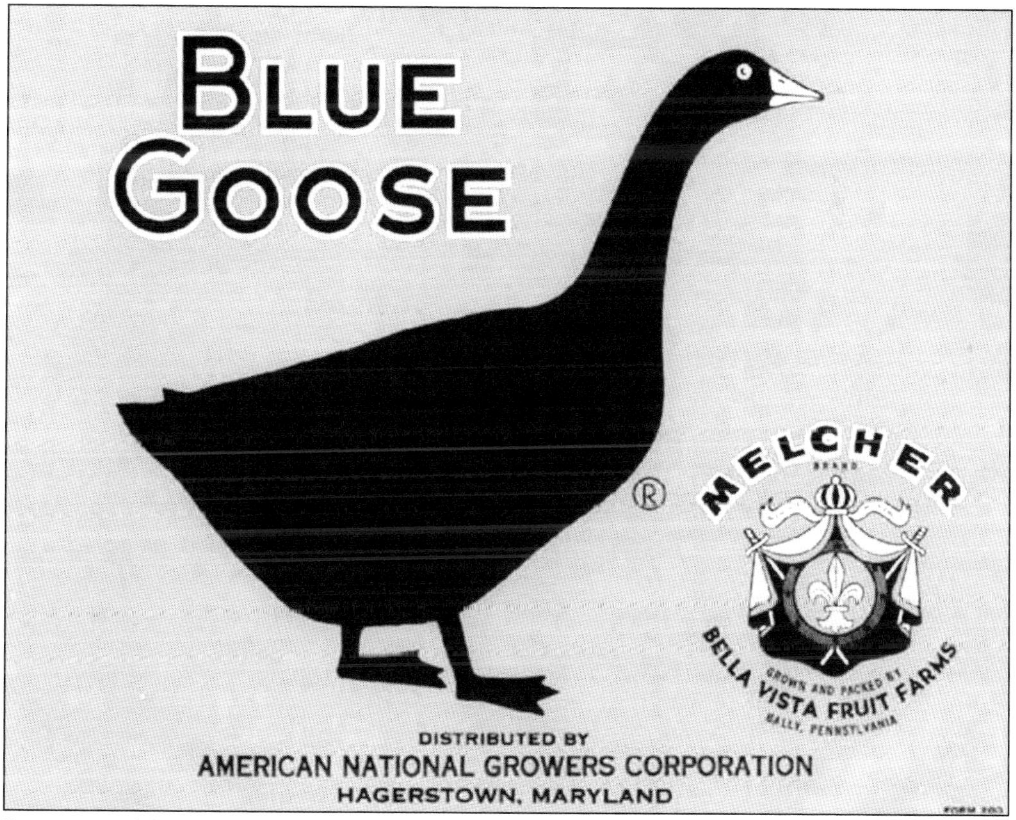

Bennett Melcher of Bally owned and operated a fruit orchard on Crow Hill until his death, at which time his son George continued the operation. This label was the trademark of "Blue Goose" for the company.

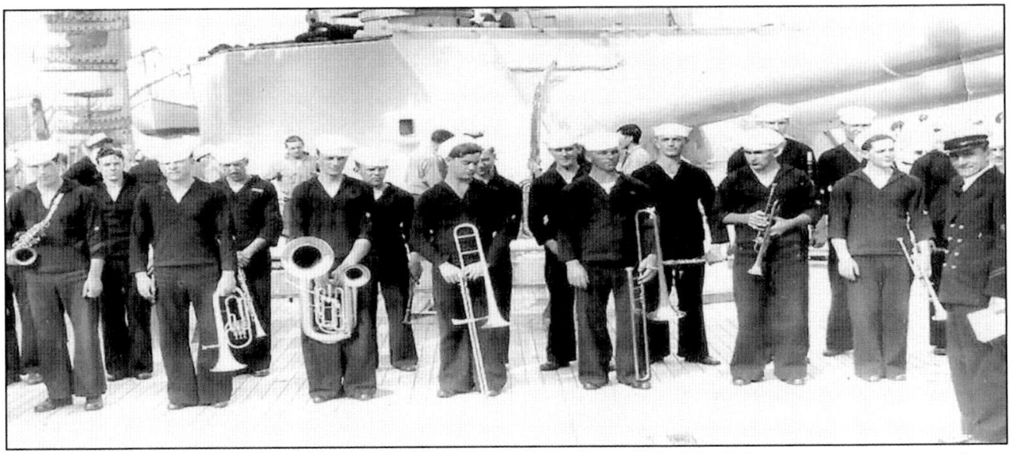

Many did not know that Gib Stahl served in the U.S. Navy on the USS *Arizona* prior to its sinking at Pearl Harbor. Below is the Christmas menu for the USS *Arizona* for December 25, 1930.

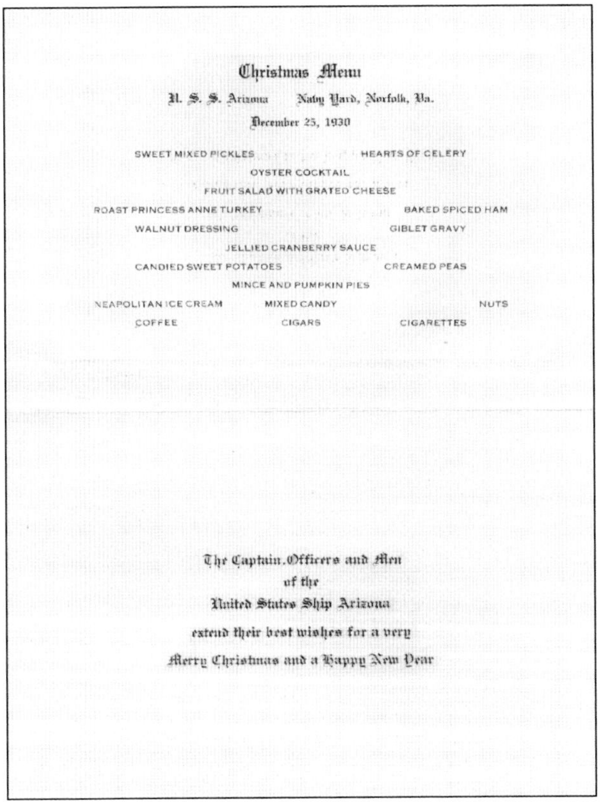

Christmas Menu

U. S. S. Arizona   Navy Yard, Norfolk, Va.

December 25, 1930

SWEET MIXED PICKLES   HEARTS OF CELERY

OYSTER COCKTAIL

FRUIT SALAD WITH GRATED CHEESE

ROAST PRINCESS ANNE TURKEY   BAKED SPICED HAM

WALNUT DRESSING   GIBLET GRAVY

JELLIED CRANBERRY SAUCE

CANDIED SWEET POTATOES   CREAMED PEAS

MINCE AND PUMPKIN PIES

NEAPOLITAN ICE CREAM   MIXED CANDY   NUTS

COFFEE   CIGARS   CIGARETTES

The Captain, Officers and Men
of the
United States Ship Arizona
extend their best wishes for a very
Merry Christmas and a Happy New Year

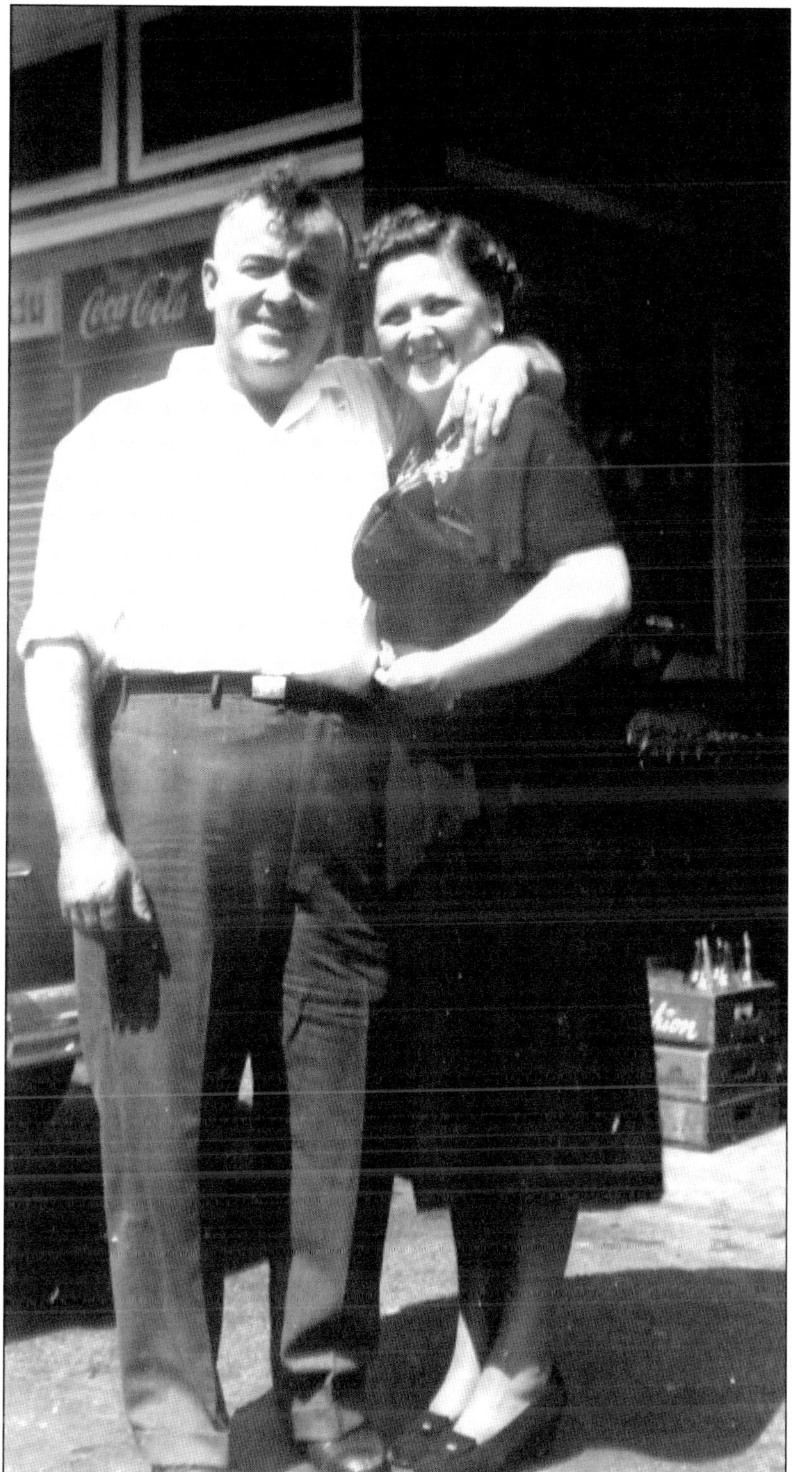

Bally was known for its family-owned grocery stores. Fronheiser's Store, located between Church and Seventh Streets, was operated by husband and wife Charlie and Lizzie Fronheiser.

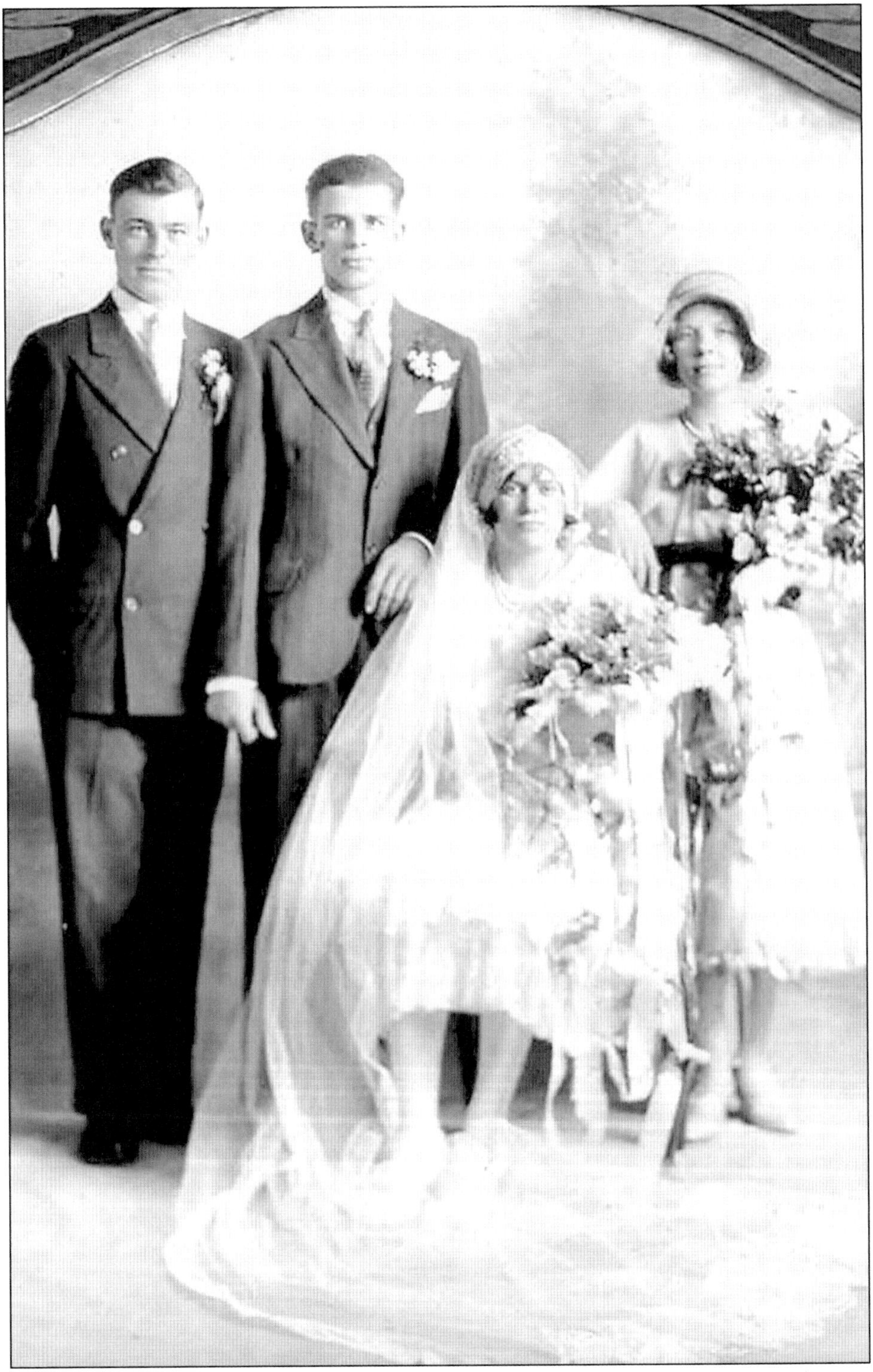

John and Victoria Benfield's wedding photograph is shown here. John was known for his gas and automobile repair station in Schultzville. John's sister Emma Campbell (née Benfield) was maid of honor and the best man, Baltzer Eline, was Victoria's brother.

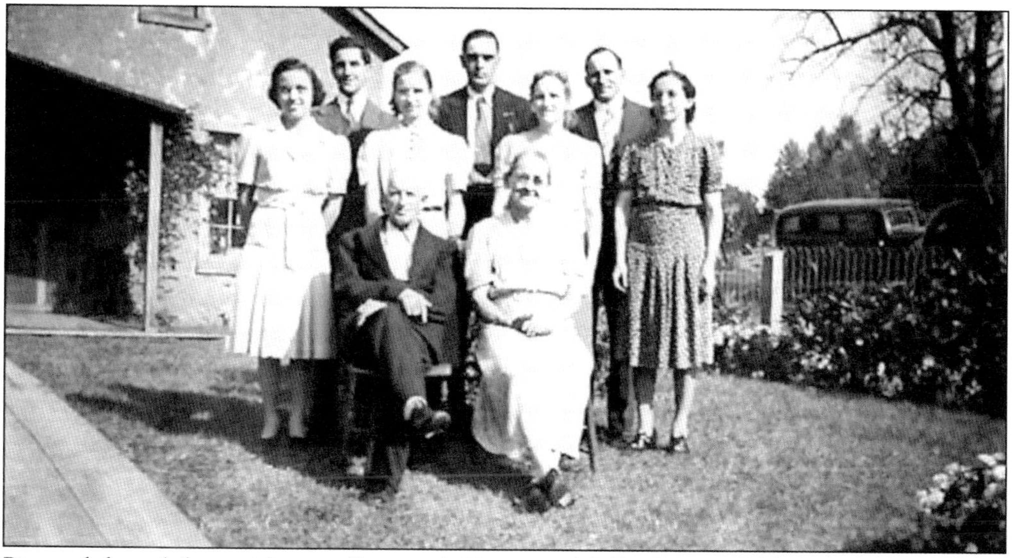

Pictured from left to right are (first row) Henry and Lillie R. Benfield; (second row) Helen Drumheller, Eva Kleinsmith (grandmother of Richard Hoffman), Ida Fronheiser (mother of Kenneth Fronheiser), and Mary Herbert; (third row) Russell Benfield, Harvey Benfield of Crow Hill, and Lloyd Benfield. The family photograph was taken at the Benfield farm at Lenape and Benfield Roads. Benfield Road is now Deer Run Road.

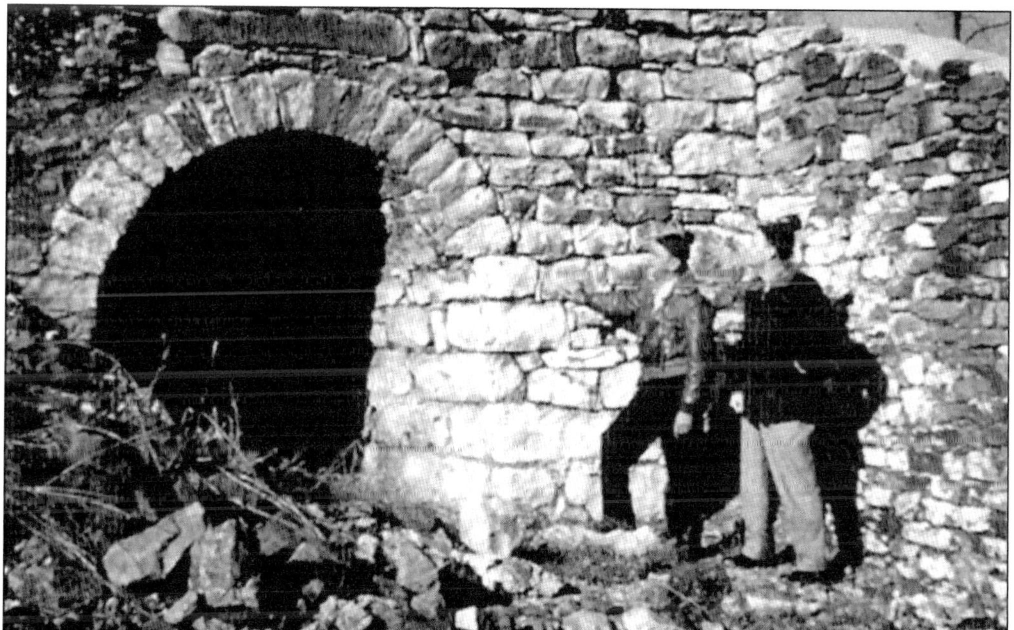

Ed Kulp (left) of Bally is seen here exploring remains of lime kiln in area. Kulp was known for his dedication to the town, his love of photography, and his years of service at the Bally Block Company.

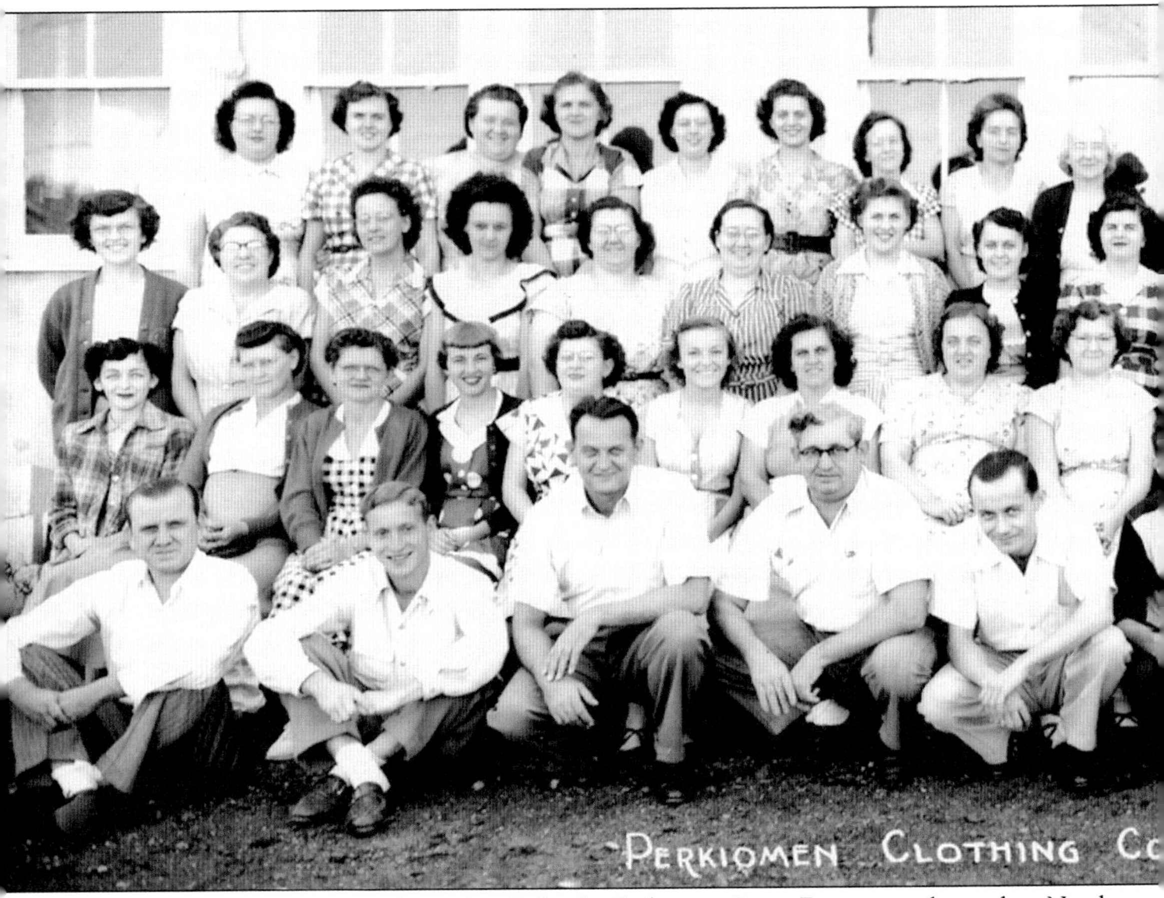

Along with many factories located in Bally, the Perkiomen Pants Factory was located on North Seventh Street across from Bally Ribbon Mill. Industry was booming in Bally in the mid-1940s and 1950s. Almost everyone who lived in Bally and the surrounding villages was employed by one of the diversified industries, ranging from refrigeration equipment, men's hose, butcher block tables, ribbon and silk products, and pantaloons (as pants were known). Today only two survive out of approximately six companies. The August 31, 1903, edition of *Town & Country* newspaper

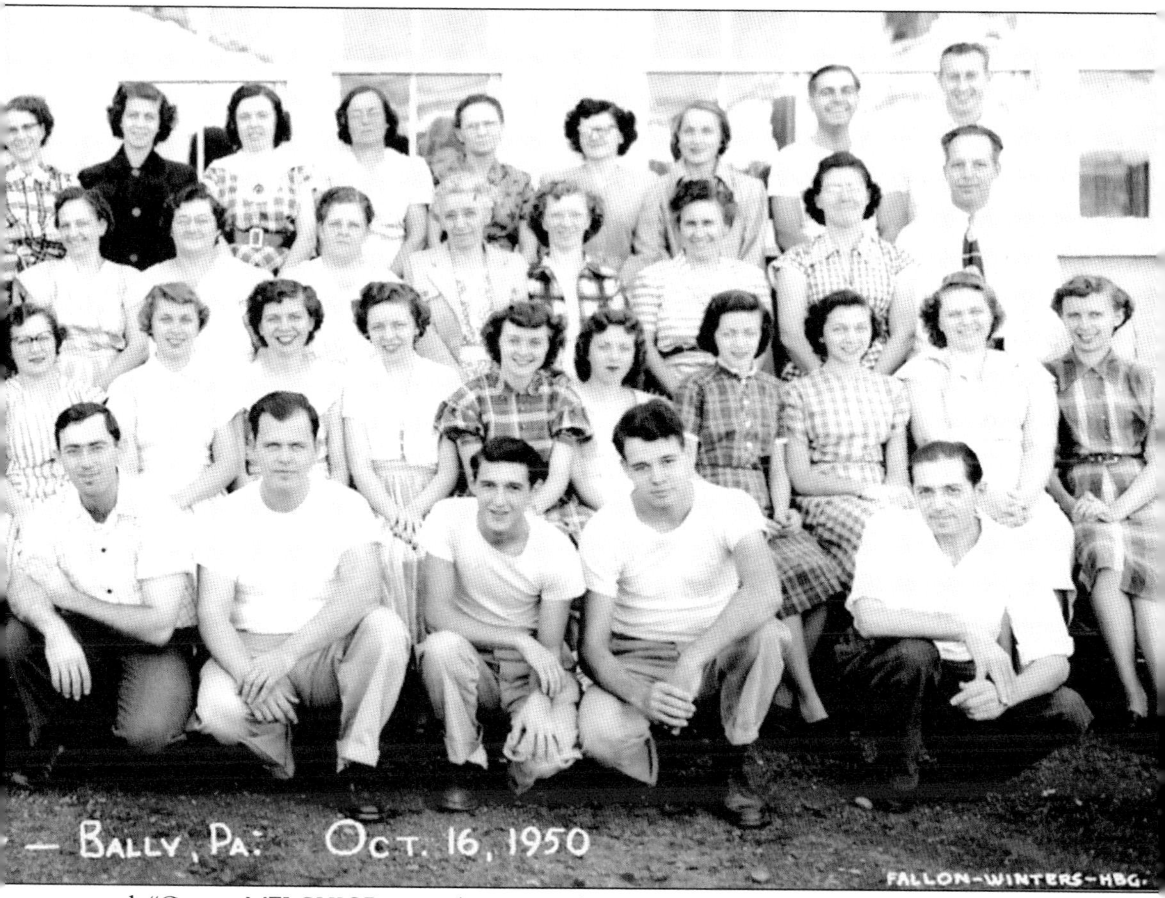

reported, "George MELCHIOR, pantaloon manufacturer of Bally, has broken ground to build an addition to his factory. The business has so increased that he must have more room and more help. Mr. MELCHIOR started the business about two years ago, with fifteen hands. At present he employs about sixty and expects to employ some more as soon as he has sufficient room. At the same time he will erect a steam engine to take place of the present gasoline engine. He will also fit the factory with steam pipes for heating purposes."

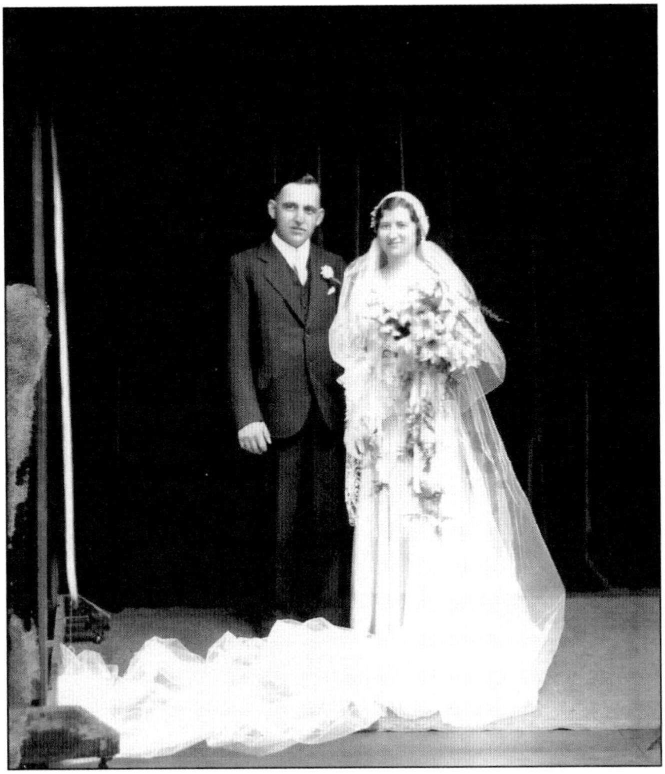

This is the wedding of William Quigley to Anna Stompf. William was known for his Irish wit and also as original owner with brother Joe in the garage and dealership on Main Street (next to Fronheiser Grocery Store). Anna was brought to Bally by the Catholic priest of Most Blessed Sacrament Church from St. Vincent's Orphanage in Tacony. Anna was the sister of the author's father, Alex, who also came to the Bally area when Anna was established in the area. William and Anna had three children, William Jr., Michael, and a daughter deceased at an early age.

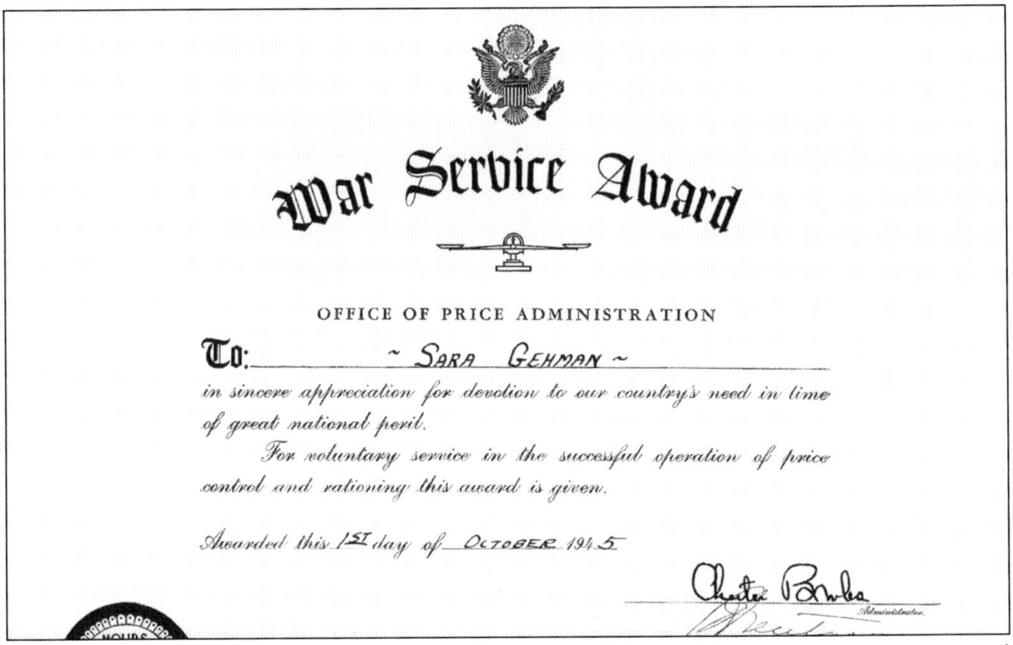

War Service Award

OFFICE OF PRICE ADMINISTRATION

To: ~ SARA GEHMAN ~

in sincere appreciation for devotion to our country's need in time of great national peril.

For voluntary service in the successful operation of price control and rationing this award is given.

Awarded this 1ST day of OCTOBER 1945

Chester Bowles
Administrator.

In December 1945, Sarah Gehman received a service award for her assistance in price control during World War II.

Two

BARTO AND SCHULTZVILLE REVISITED

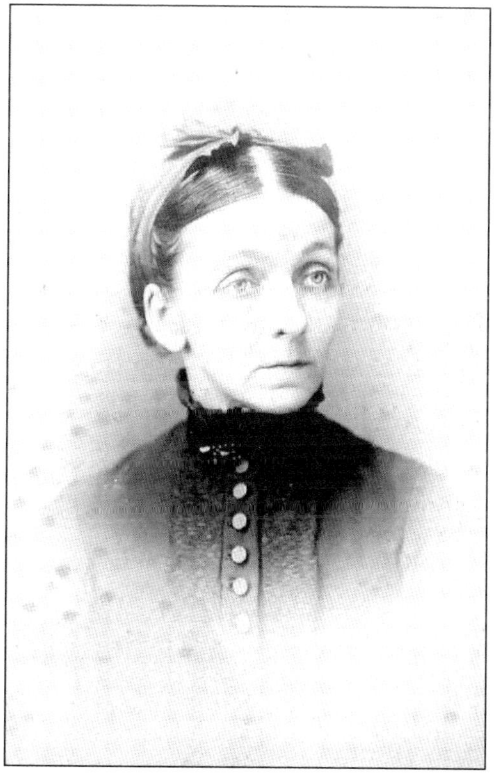

Anna Hoffman (née Yeakel) (1843–1890) is pictured here. She was a Schwenkfelder and the leader of one of the Schwenkfelder movements. She was a descendant of Christian Yeakel, leader of one of the Schwenkfelder movements. Hoffman died only one year after the purchase of the County Line Farm.

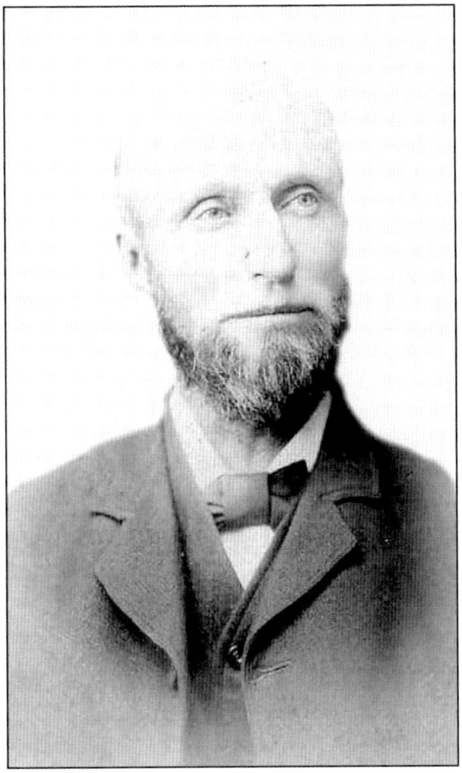

Jacob Hoffman was born in 1833 and died in 1914. He was the first Hoffman to live at the County Line Road farm in Barto. It was purchased by him in 1889. Jacob was married to Anna Yeakel. They are buried in a little cemetery along Kutztown Road east of Clayton. Jacob continued to live with son Horace after Anna died.

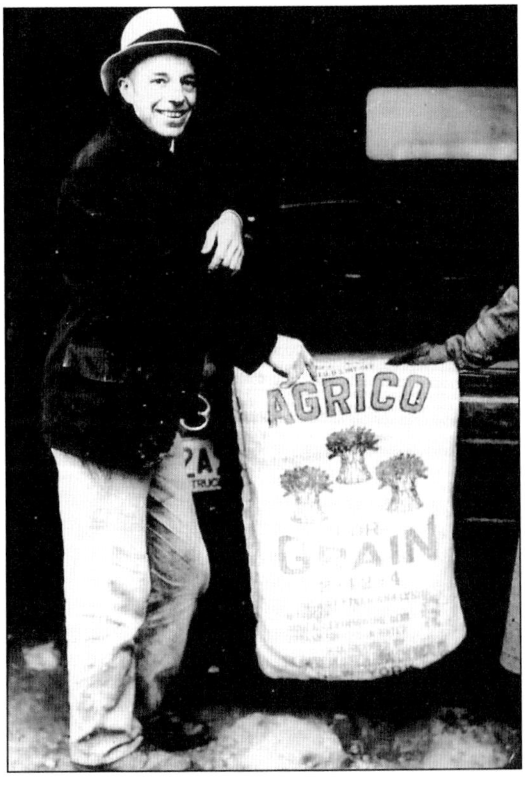

Chester Hoffman, grandfather of Richard Hoffman of Barto, was born in 1900 and died at age 89 in 1989.

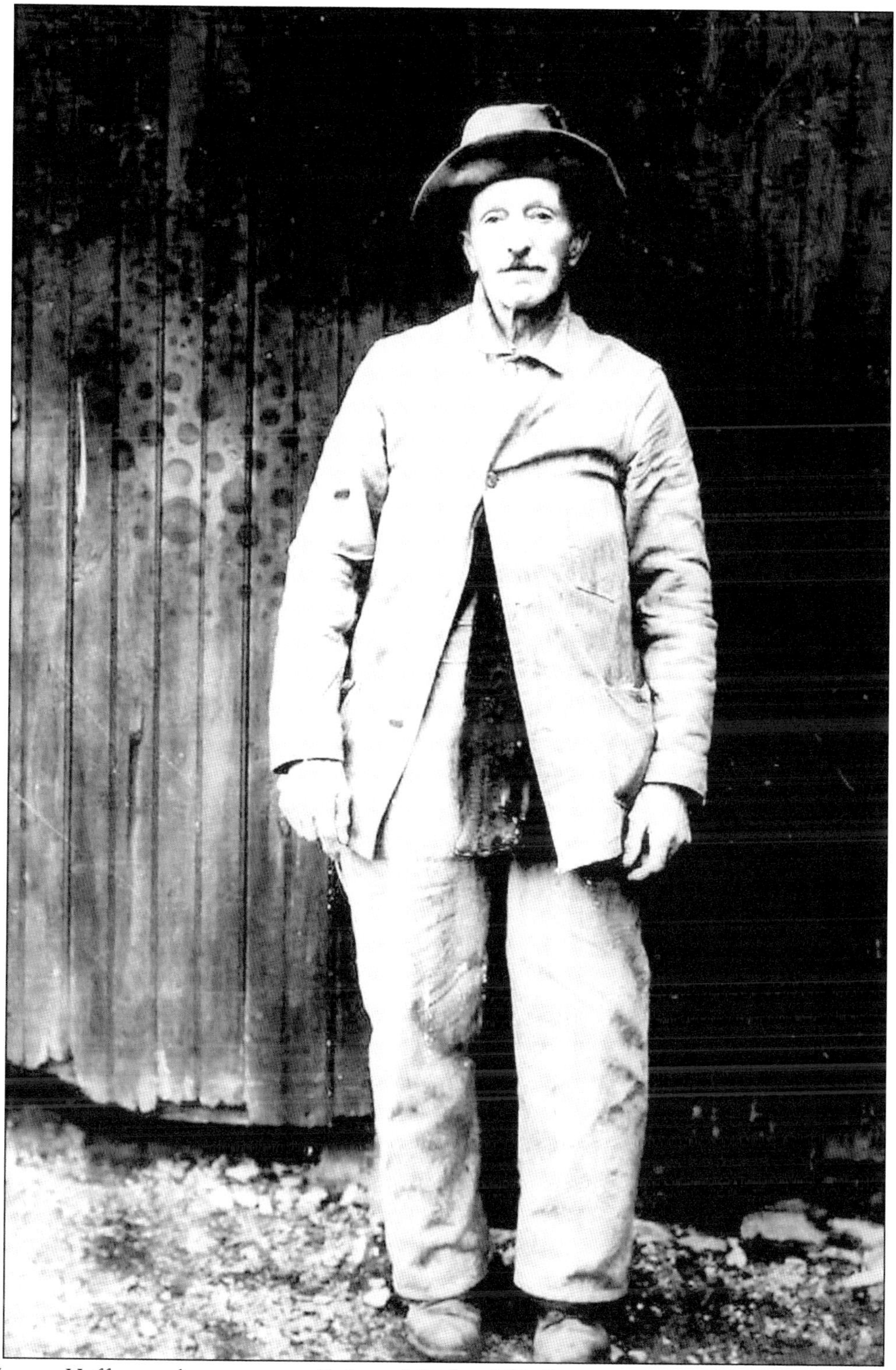

Horace Hoffman, the great-grandfather of Richard Hoffman, is pictured here. He died on December 25, 1957.

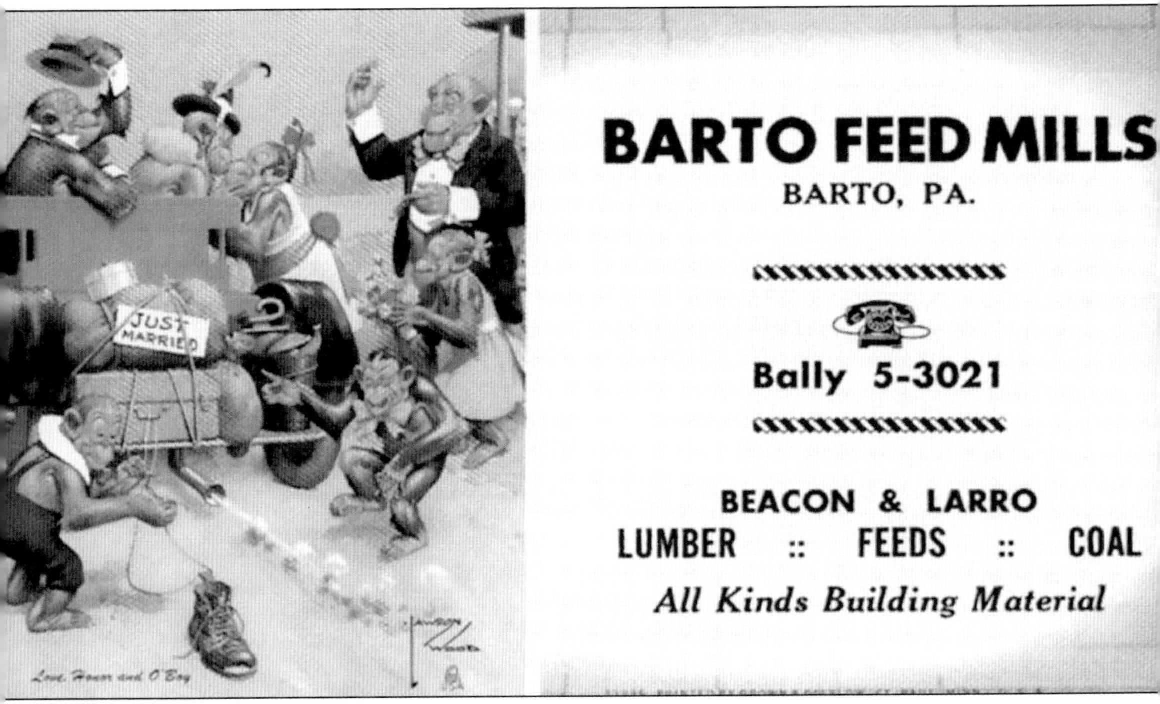

This is an original advertisement from the Barto Feed Mills.

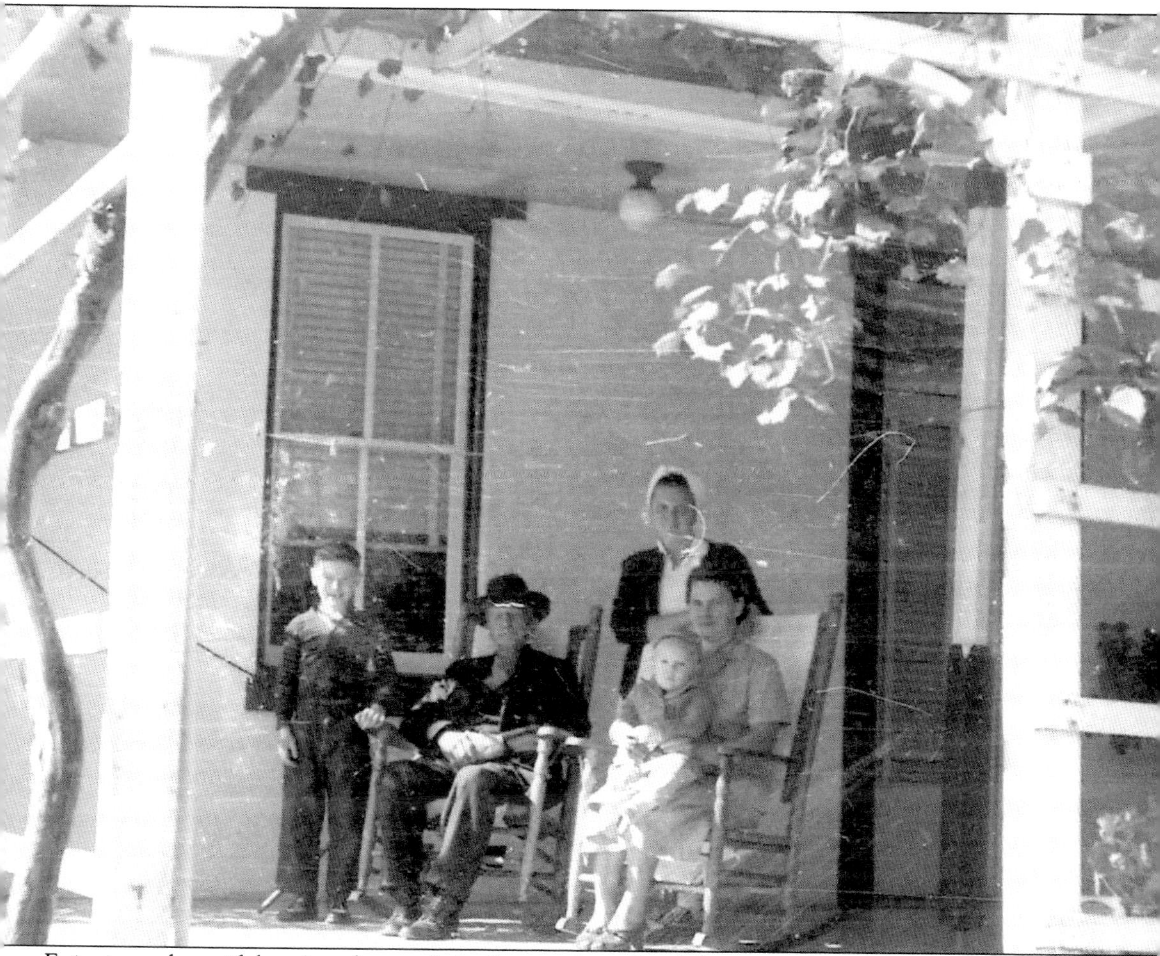

Enjoying a beautiful spring day at their County Line Road farm are, from left to right, Roy, Horace, Richard, Lillian, and Ella Mae Hoffman.

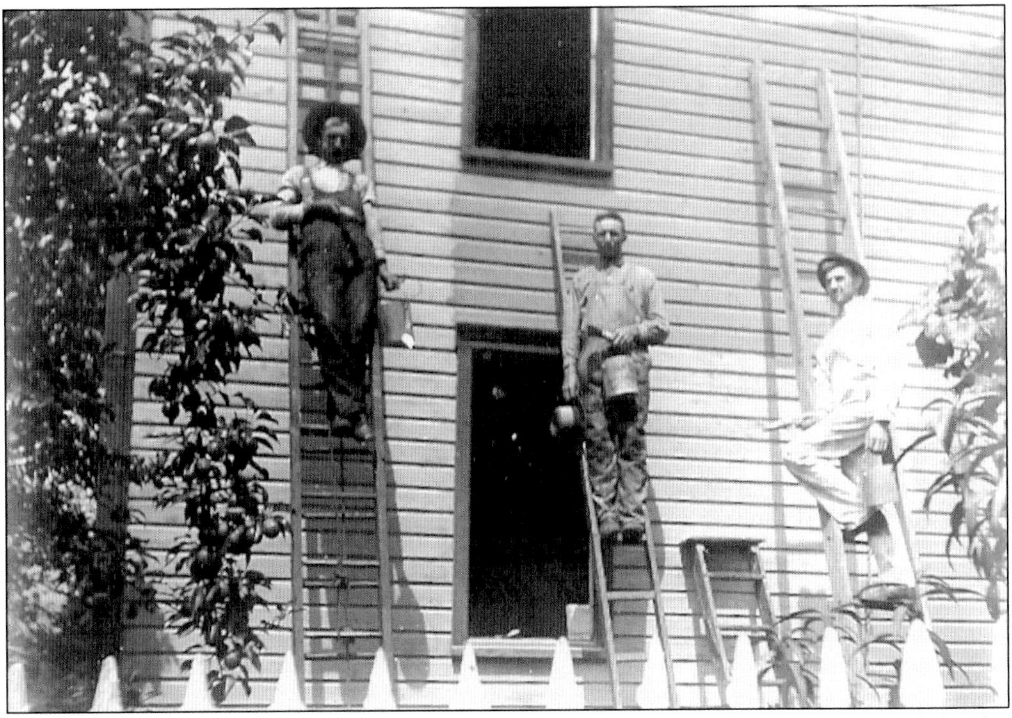

Seen here, from left to right, Charles Reppert, John Reitnauer, and Charles Fox spend the day painting a local Schultzville farmhouse.

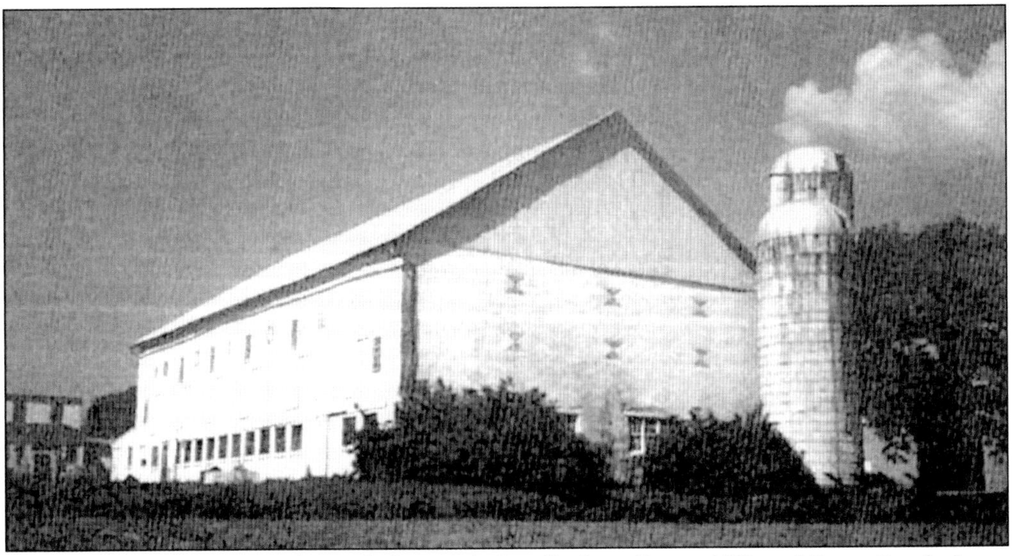

The Barto family farm was located along Schultzville (now Route 100) and Barto Roads. Later this farm was taken over and farmed by Leonard Gehringer. The Gehringer farmland has now become the home of the National Centre for Padre Pio. Years back, it was part of the Abram Barto farmland, which the town was named after.

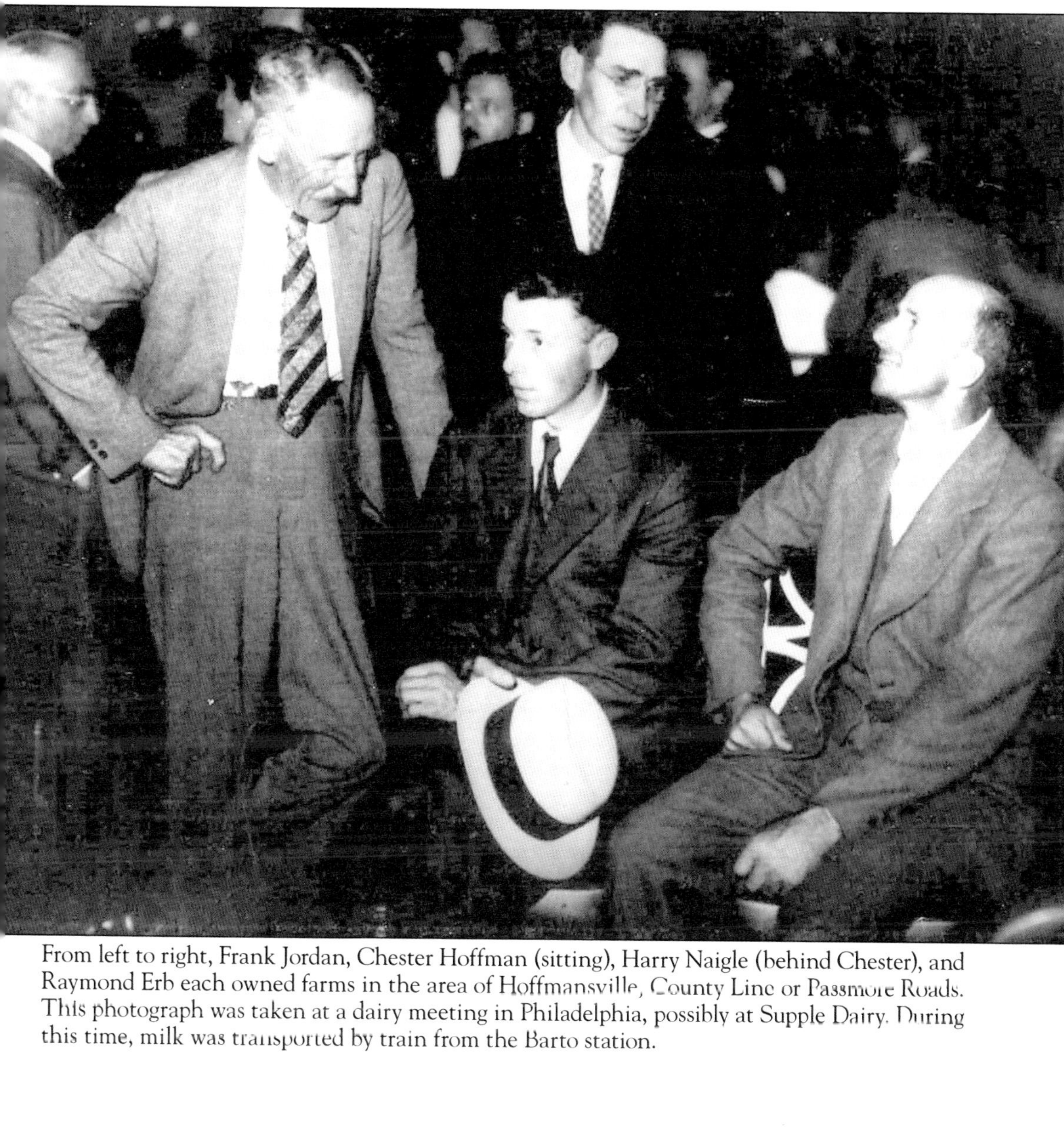

From left to right, Frank Jordan, Chester Hoffman (sitting), Harry Naigle (behind Chester), and Raymond Erb each owned farms in the area of Hoffmansville, County Line or Passmore Roads. This photograph was taken at a dairy meeting in Philadelphia, possibly at Supple Dairy. During this time, milk was transported by train from the Barto station.

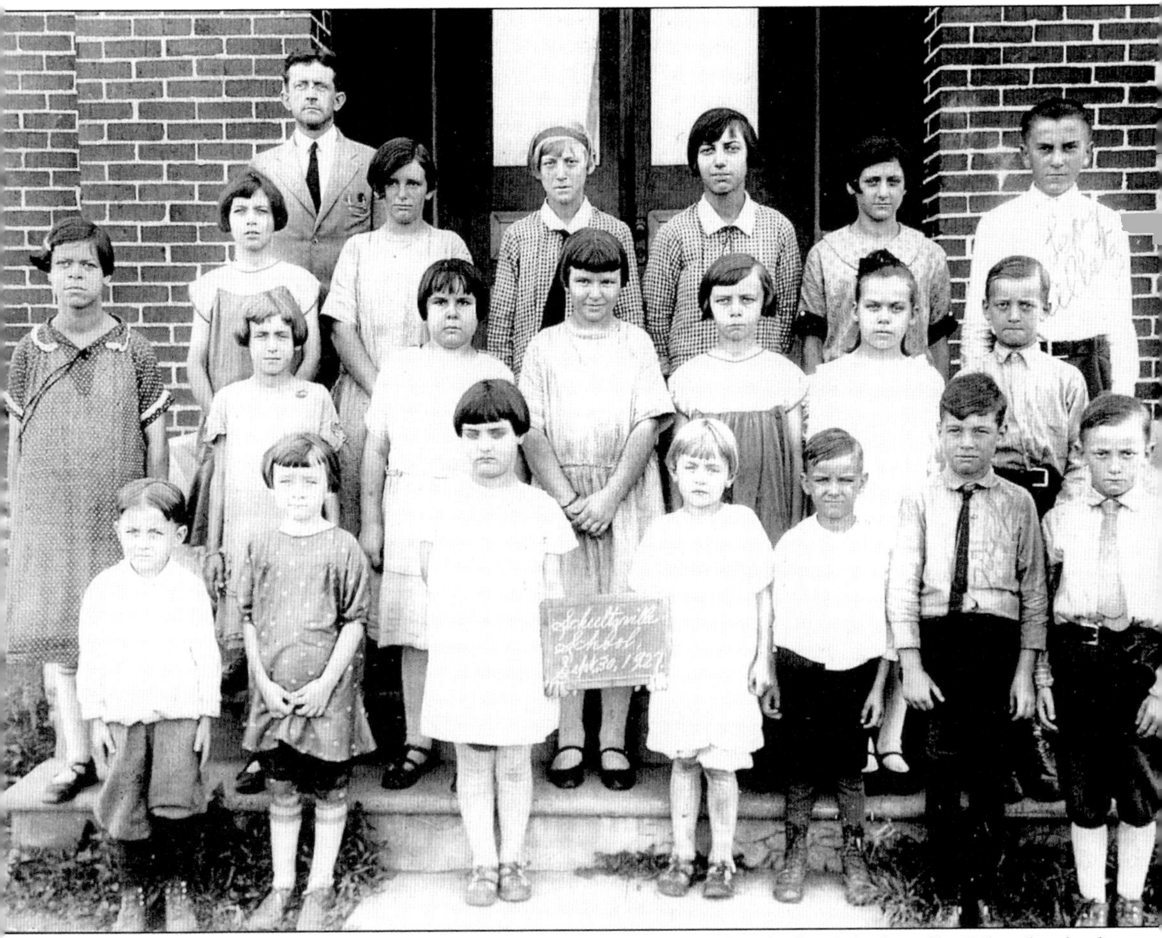

This class poses for a school photograph outside of their school, the Schultzville School, which was located along Schultzville Road (now Route 100).

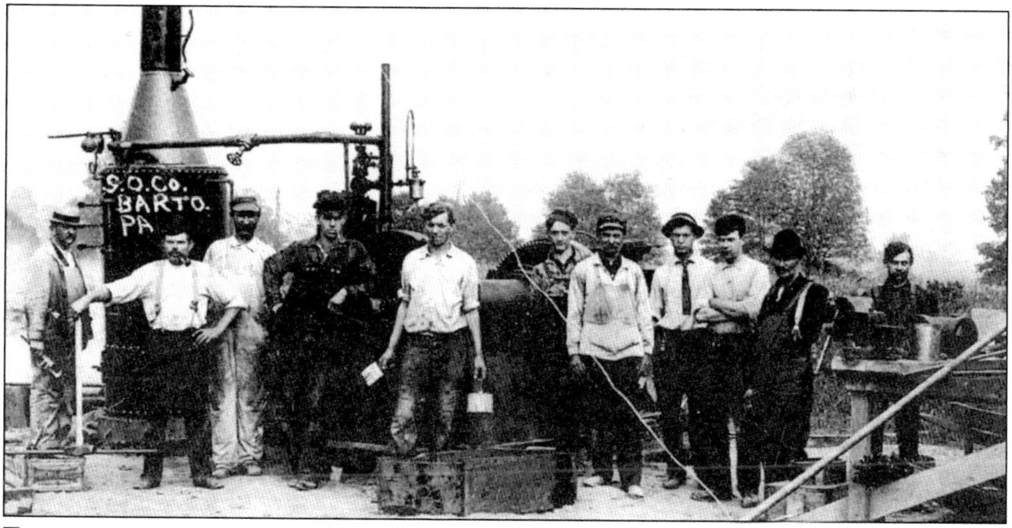

Tuscarora pumping station workmen are seen here in Barto.

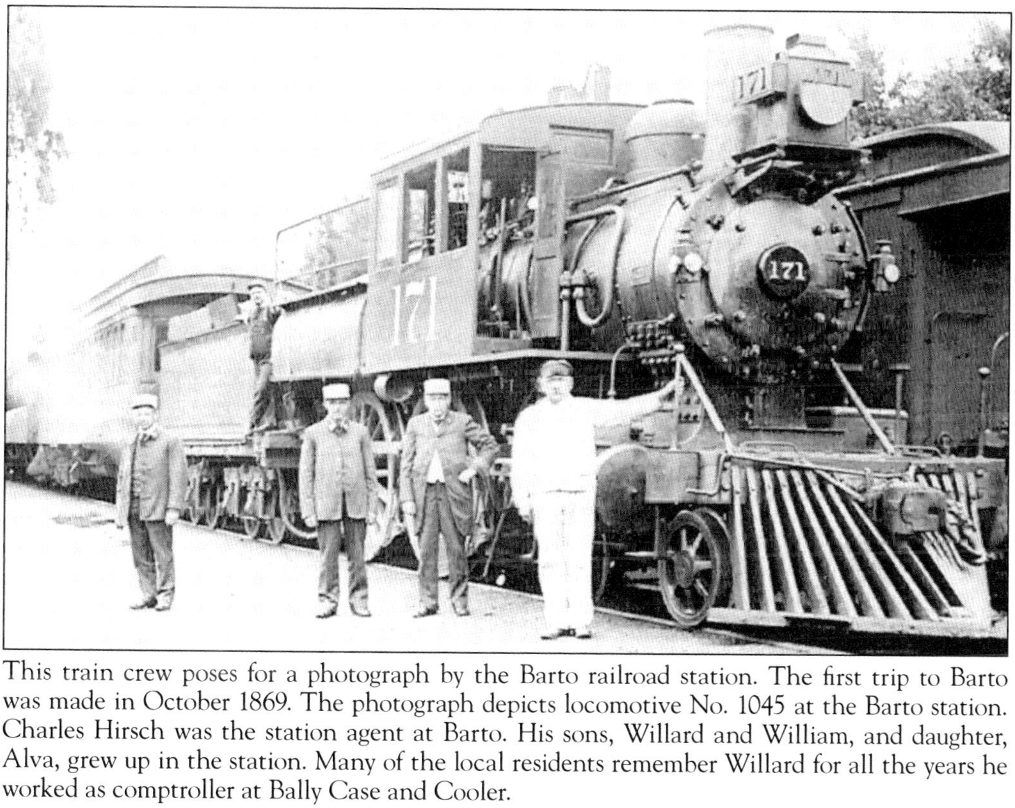

This train crew poses for a photograph by the Barto railroad station. The first trip to Barto was made in October 1869. The photograph depicts locomotive No. 1045 at the Barto station. Charles Hirsch was the station agent at Barto. His sons, Willard and William, and daughter, Alva, grew up in the station. Many of the local residents remember Willard for all the years he worked as comptroller at Bally Case and Cooler.

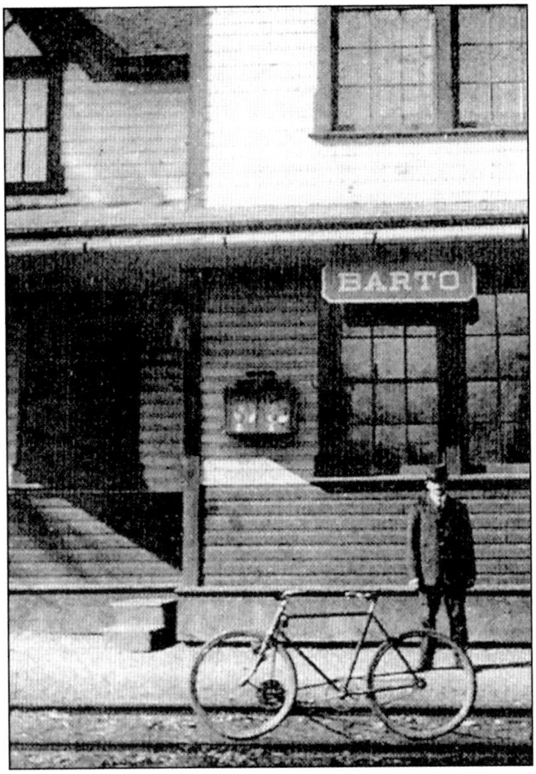

People are familiar with all types of bicycles, but there was a special bicycle that was used to ride the rails. This photograph shows how it looks similar to the standard bicycle with an exception—the rims are fashioned to fit over the rails. Today this would be quite a collectible.

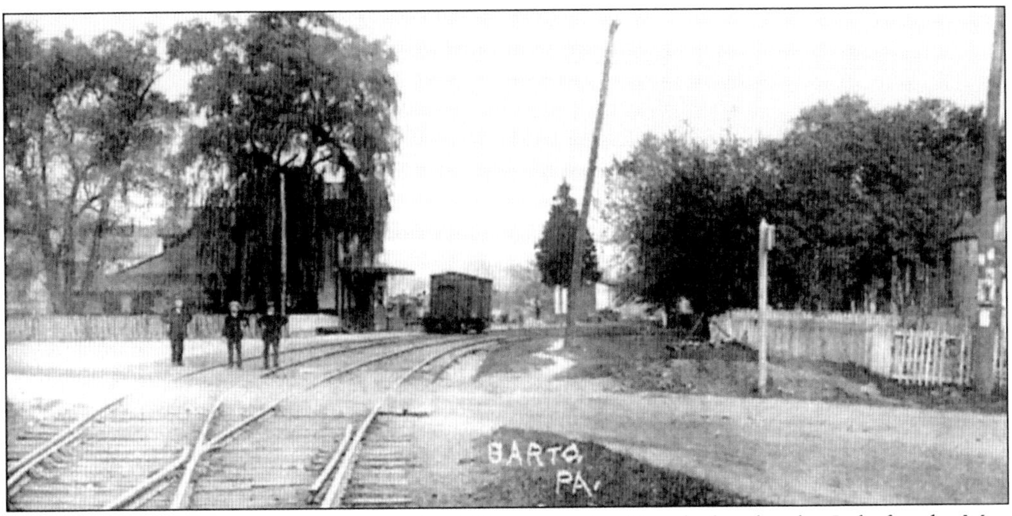

Frequent riders of the Barto train in the 1930s were the Hirsch family, the Leh family, Mae Latshaw, who rode the train to high school in Boyertown, and Mary Heins, who taught at the high school.

The area has been well known for underground springs, but the Barto Spring continued to supply good quantities and great-tasting water, which helped during dry years when local wells were very low. Many times, lines of people waited to fill their containers. The spring is located by the bridge at Barto along the old Route 100.

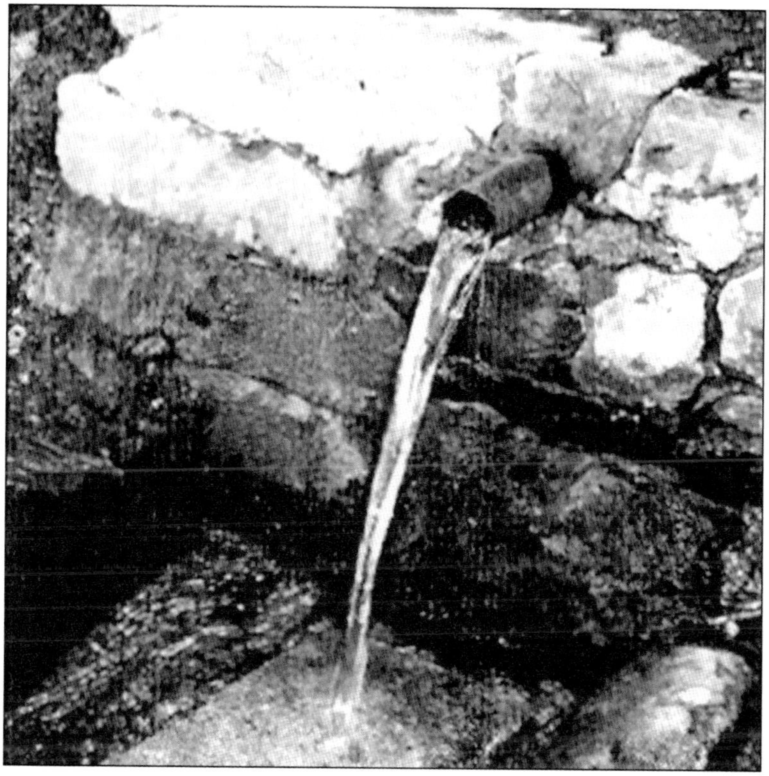

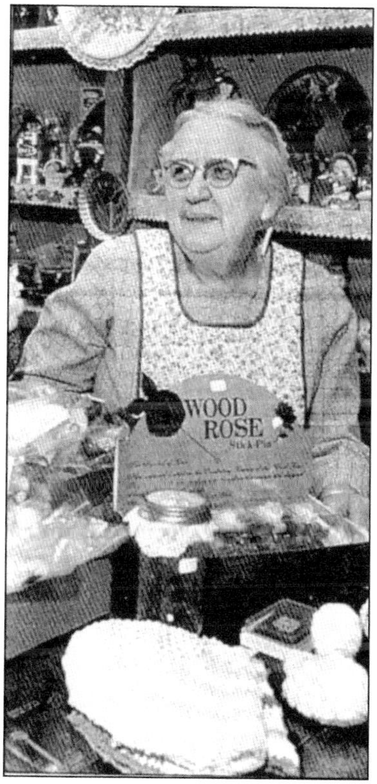

Sarah Gehman was known by everyone as always smiling and ready to help everyone who entered Gehman's Store. She always wrote the price on a little piece of paper and did not want to overcharge anyone. When people lost the screw out of their eyeglasses, they would just stop by to see Sarah. She saved many a child by fixing their glasses—many times early in the morning prior to going to school.

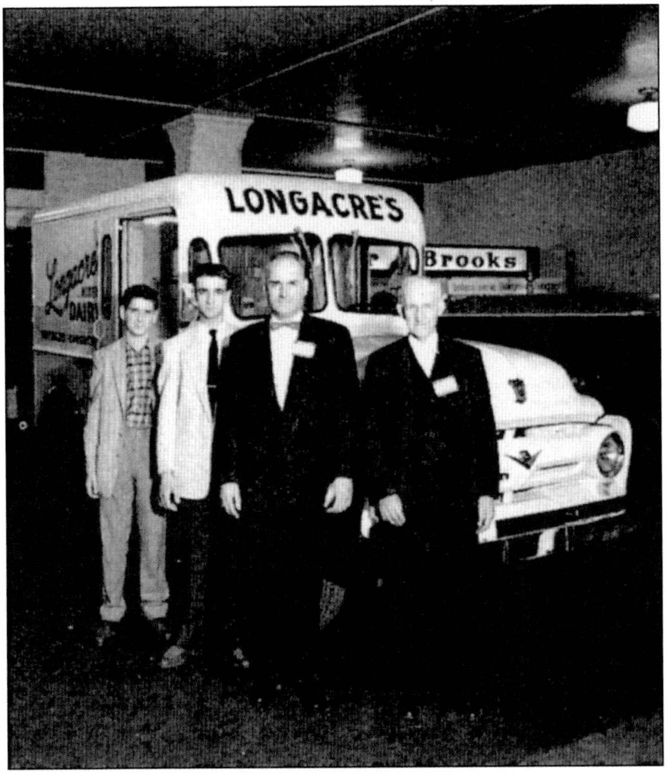

The men of the original Longacre family from the early days of Longacre's Dairy include John S. Longacre, son Daniel, and grandsons Daniel Jr. and Newton. The dairy and its dairy store, located along Route 100, is a famous stop along the highway and brings travelers from miles away just to savor Longacre's wonderful homemade flavors.

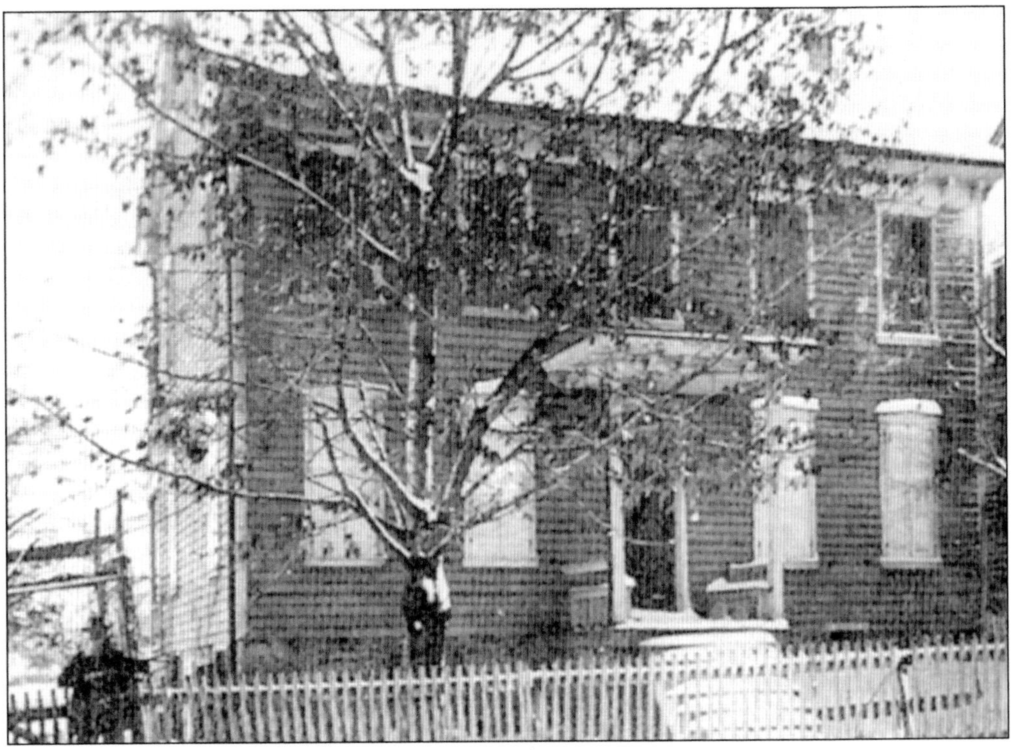

The old Schwartz home, located in Barto, is seen here.

Three

Bechtelsville Revisited

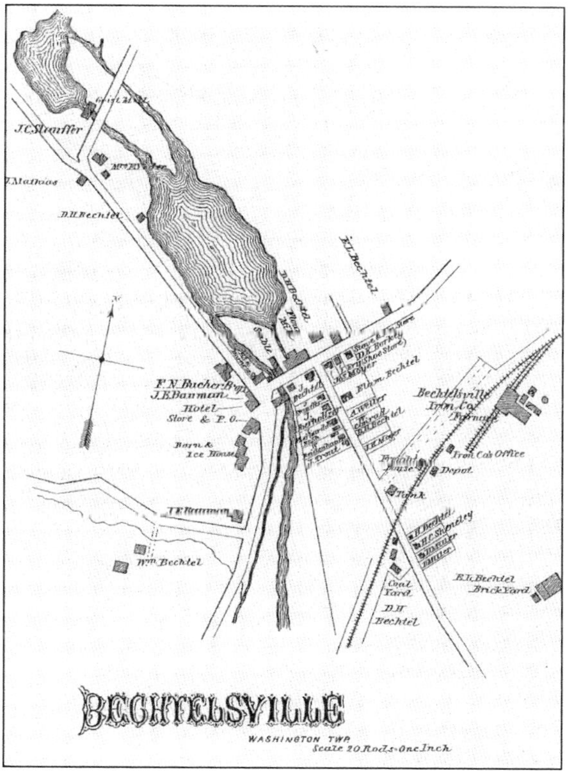

This map of Bechtelsville dates back to 1876 and details where many of the small businesses were located along with the railroad depot and freight house.

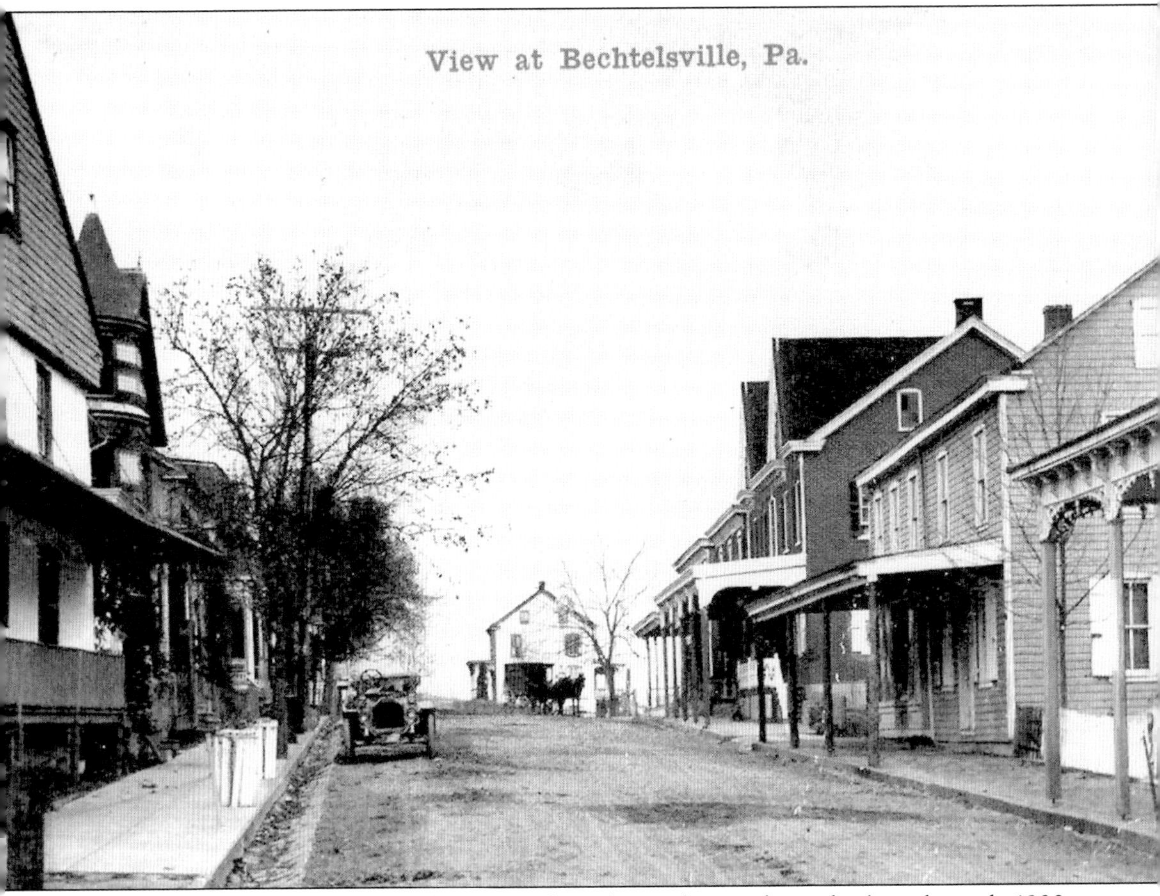

The postcard of Bechtelsville that is seen here depicts homes dating back to the early 1900s.

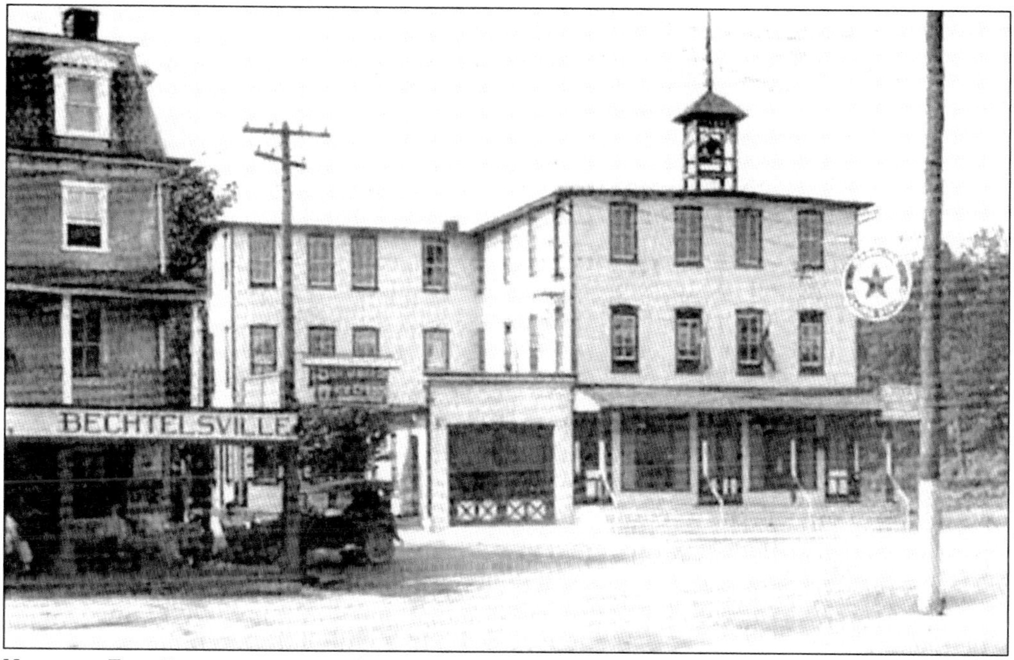

Keystone Fire Company No. 1 of Bechtelsville, organized on April 10, 1916, was housed in a three-story frame building at Main and Race Streets. An engine house was built onto the Race Street side of the building. In the rear of the engine house, Bechtelsville Borough Council maintained a jail until 1922, when the town hall was built.

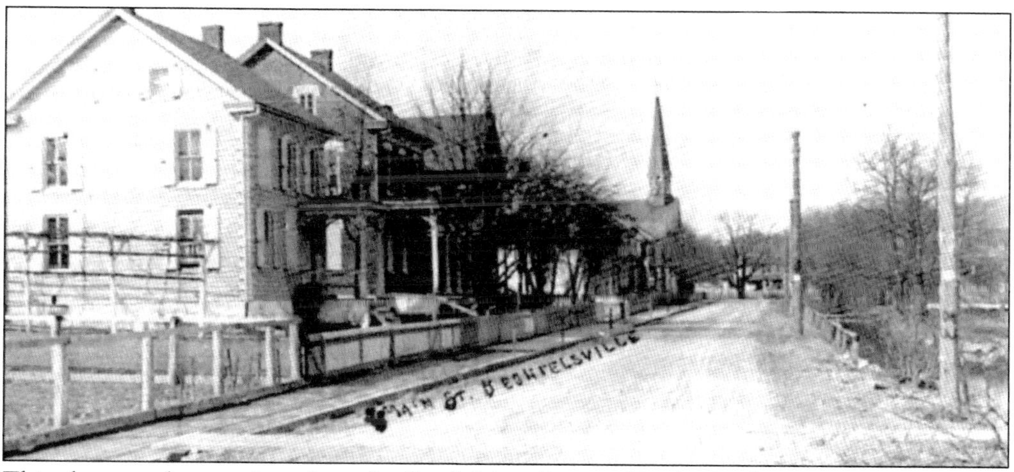

This photograph was taken along the South Main Street of Bechtelsville, entering the town. In the distance one can see the original church steeple and the stream on the right, which is now the home of Bechtelsville Community Park.

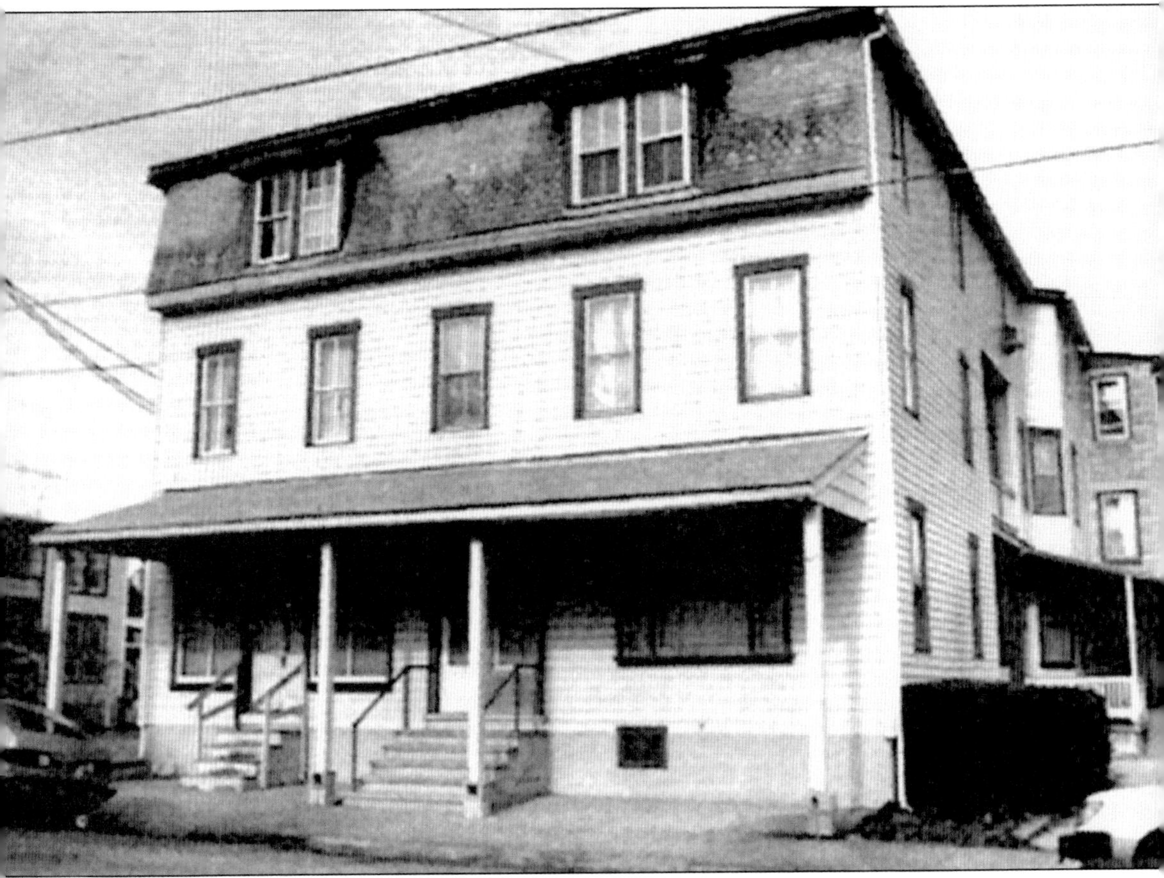

William Conrad and Son owned and operated a funeral home, which dates back to the early 1900s, in Bechtelsville. Clayton Moyer took over the business in 1920 and continued until his retirement. Melvin Kuser, who owned the building later, turned it into a furniture store. It also was his residence. As a youngster, the author remembers Melvin Kuser's was the local store to buy any furniture needs. The store pales in comparison to the large furniture warehouses today—it was only a few rooms.

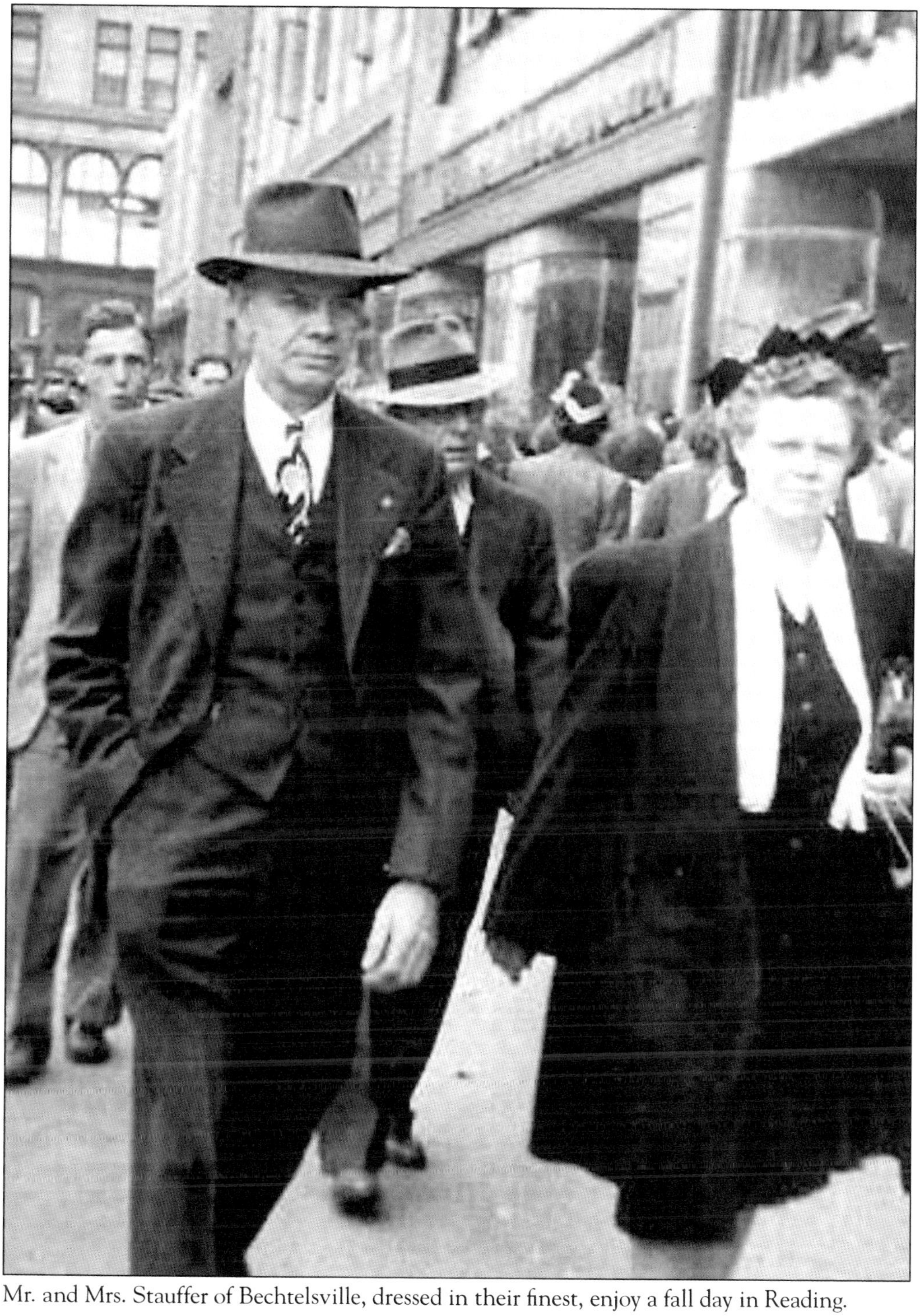

Mr. and Mrs. Stauffer of Bechtelsville, dressed in their finest, enjoy a fall day in Reading.

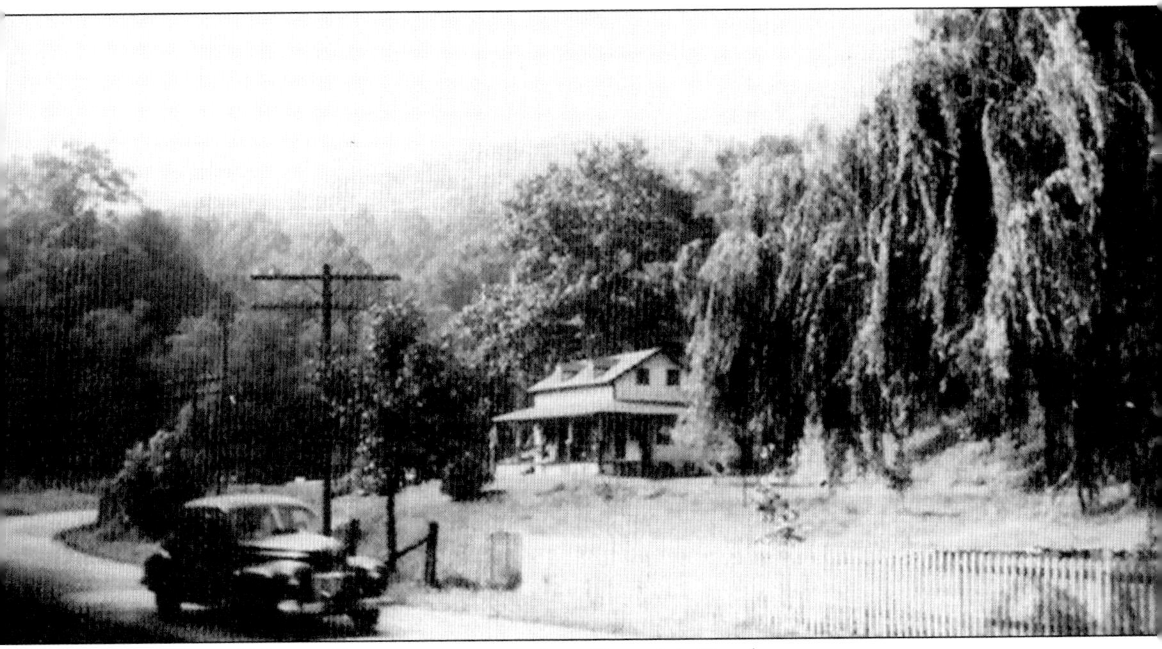

The home of Harvey Kemp was located along Forgedale Road.

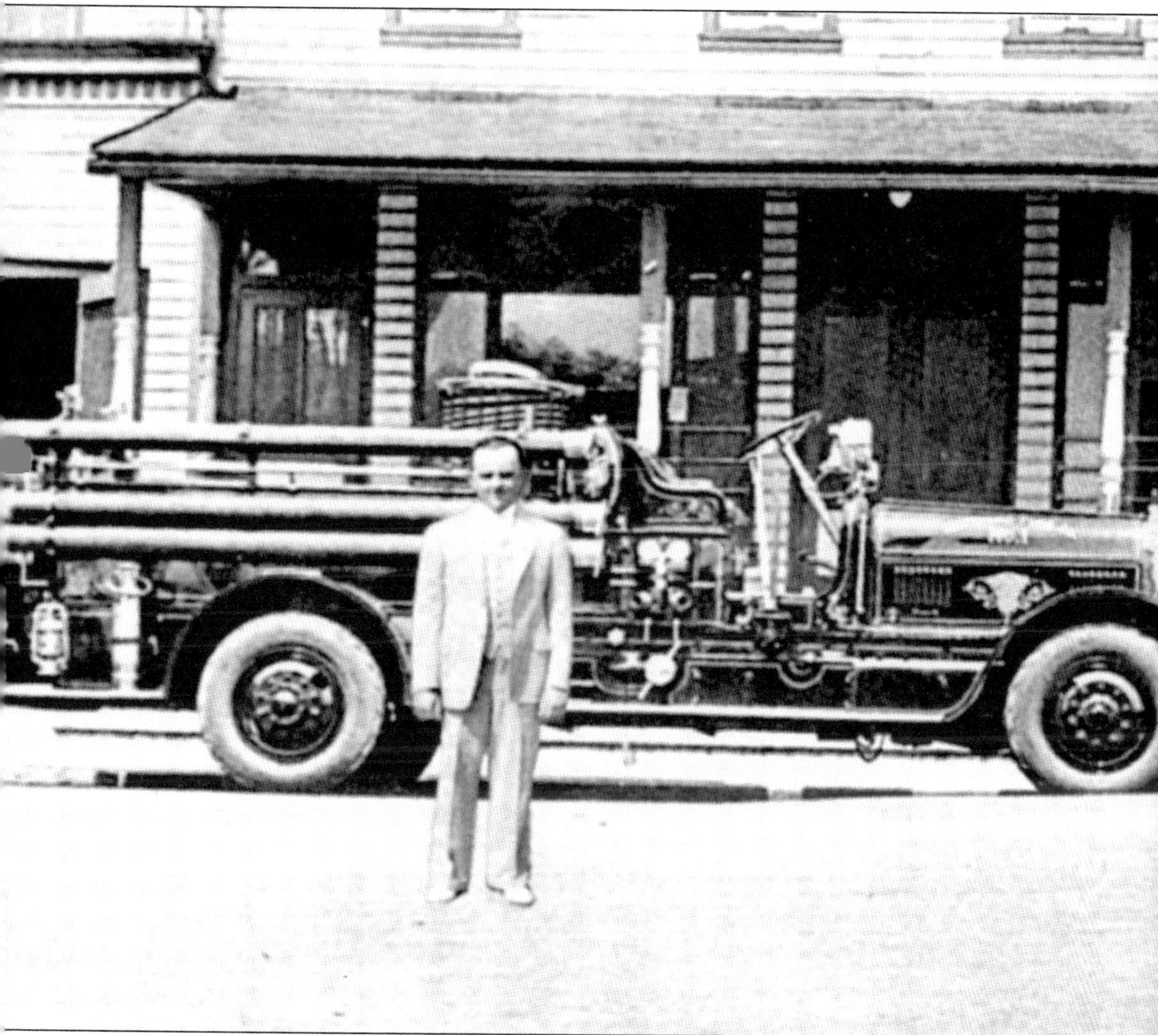

Melvin S. Herb, son of Mr. and Mrs. William M. Herb of Bechtelsville, is seen here. On the night of July 11, 1938, Melvin accompanied the crew of the Keystone Fire Company to a barn fire at the residence of Harry Nagle, where a bolt of lightning had struck the barn. As fire apparatus passed by the gable end of the barn while searching for a source of water, a heavy beam dropped and struck Melvin on the head. Melvin, at the age of 23, died the next day at St. Joseph's Hospital in Reading.

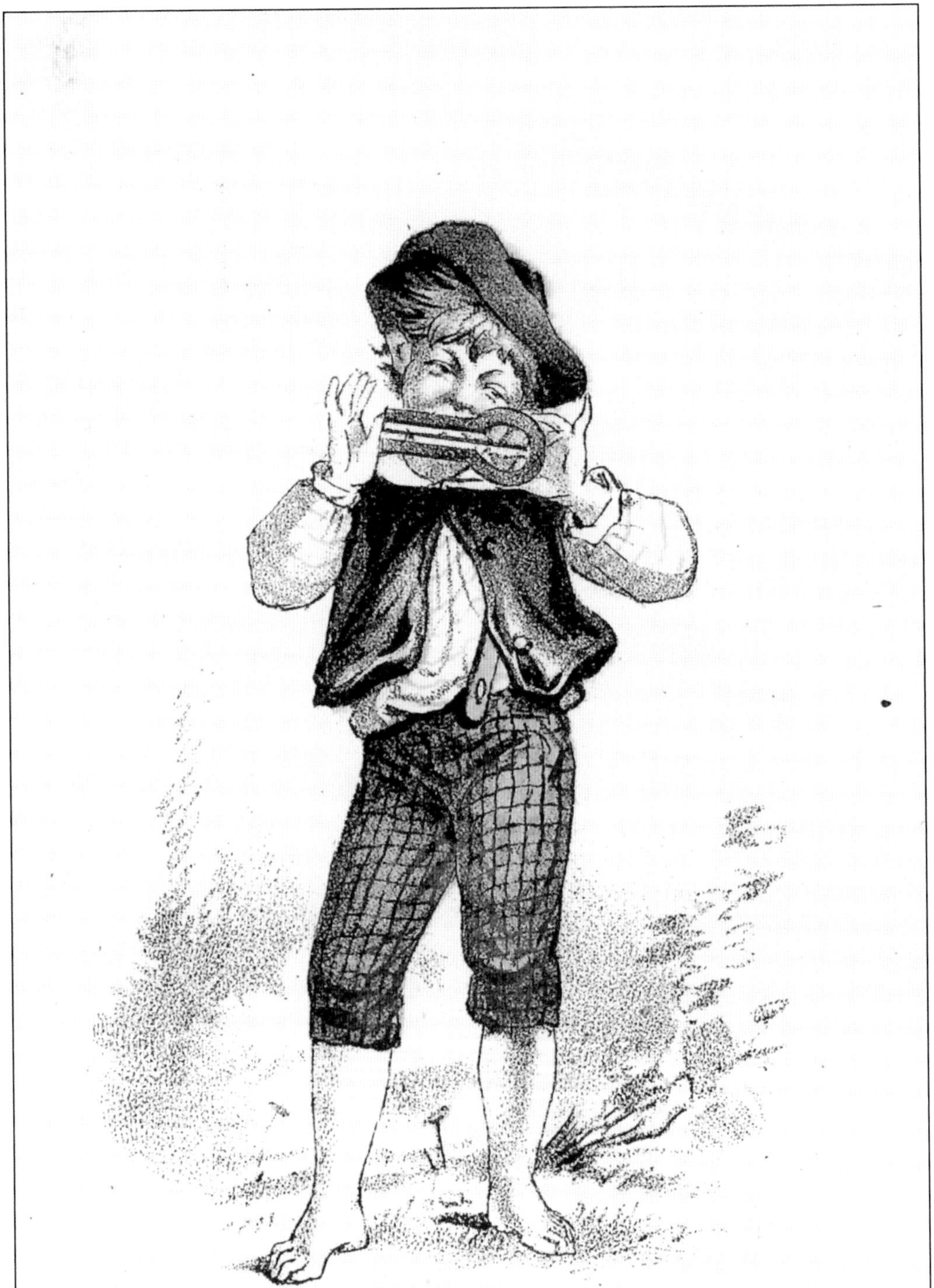

Business cards not only are used today but were widely utilized in early history. This photograph depicts a business card for Spangler's in Bechtelsville.

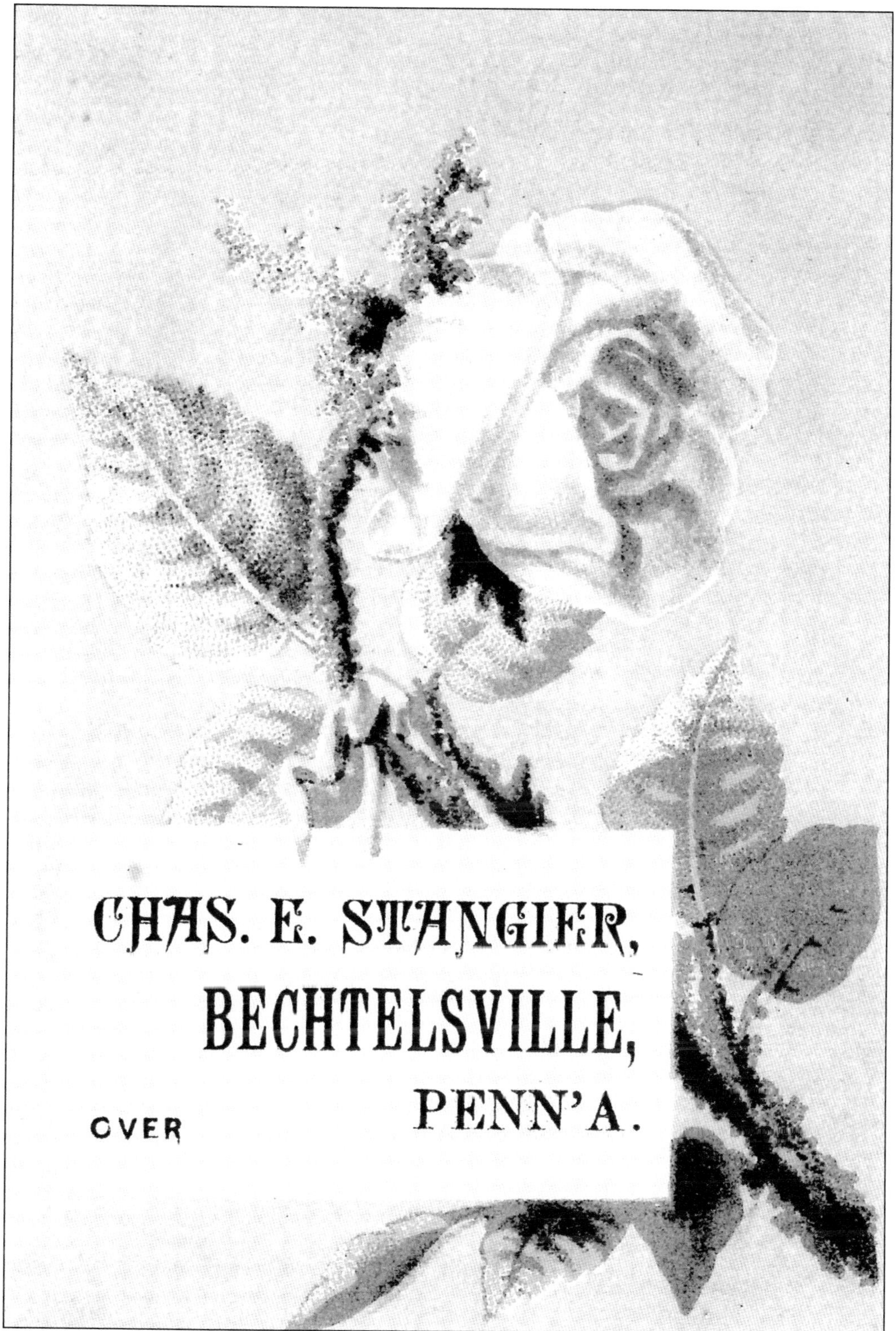

Seen here is another business card that was used by Spangler's.

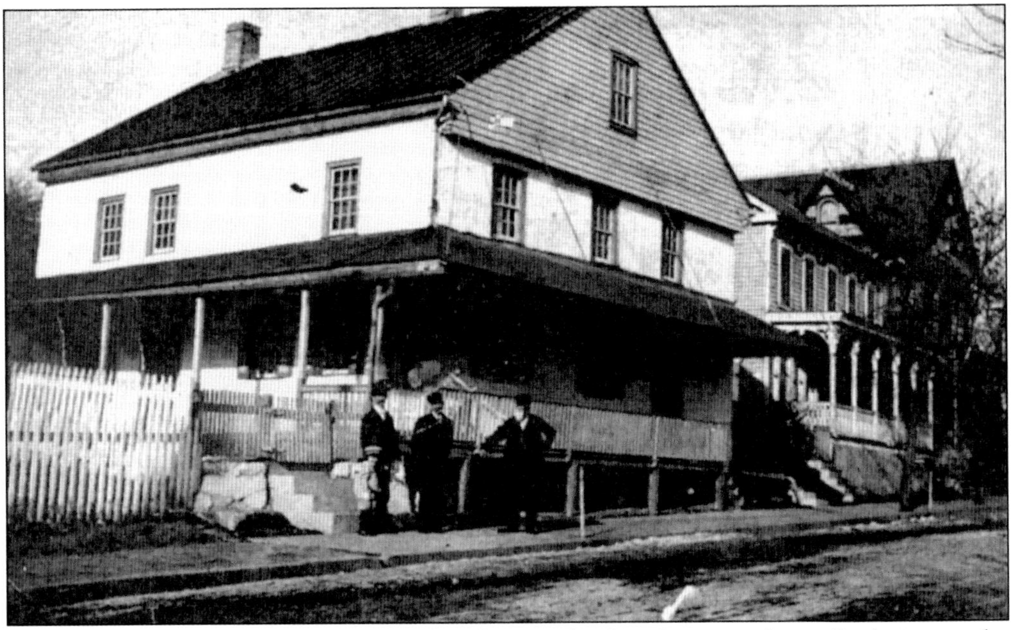

The first house in Bechtelsville was referred to as the "revolutionary house," relating to the American Revolution. It was located along North Main Street. Part of the home was an actual log cabin.

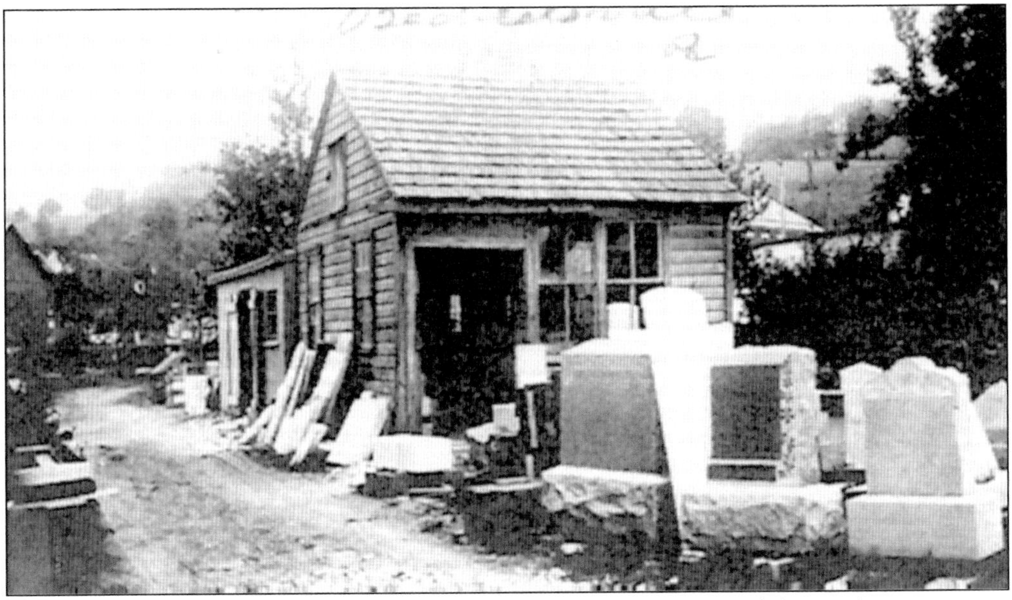

At one time, Oliver Hoffman and his son William owned and operated the tombstone cutting operation. Later it was relocated to the last house on North Main Street and operated by Oliver's other son, John Hoffman.

The cost of funerals today is approximately $5,000 or higher. This receipt from March 24, 1928, details the costs from the vault, casket, flowers, singers, slippers, and stockings, which total $236.71. The receipt is from C. H. Moyer of Bechtelsville, who manufactured furniture in addition to the items needed for his undertaking business. Take note of the grave digging price, which is only $20.

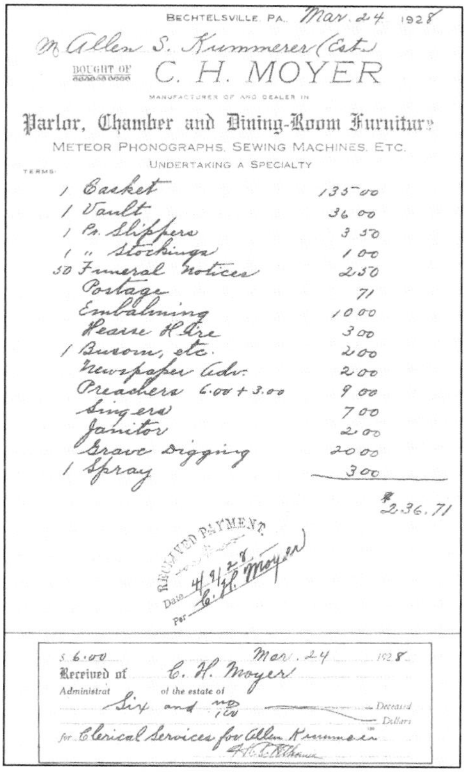

Bechtelsville, Pa. Mar. 24 1928

M Allen S. Kummerer (Est)

Bought of C. H. MOYER

Manufacturer of and Dealer in

Parlor, Chamber and Dining-Room Furniture

Meteor Phonographs, Sewing Machines, Etc.

Undertaking a Specialty

Terms:

1 Casket	135 00
1 Vault	36 00
1 Pr. Slippers	3 50
1 " Stockings	1 00
50 Funeral notices	2 50
Postage	71
Embalming	10 00
Hearse Hire	3 00
1 Buroom, etc.	2 00
Newspaper Adv.	2 00
Preachers 6.00 + 3.00	9 00
Singers	7 00
Janitor	2 00
Grave digging	20 00
1 Spray	3 00
	$236.71

Received Payment. Date 4/9/28 Per C. H. Moyer

$ 6.00 Mar. 24 1928

Received of C. H. Moyer

Administrat of the estate of Deceased

Six and 00/100 Dollars

for Clerical Services for Allen Kummerer

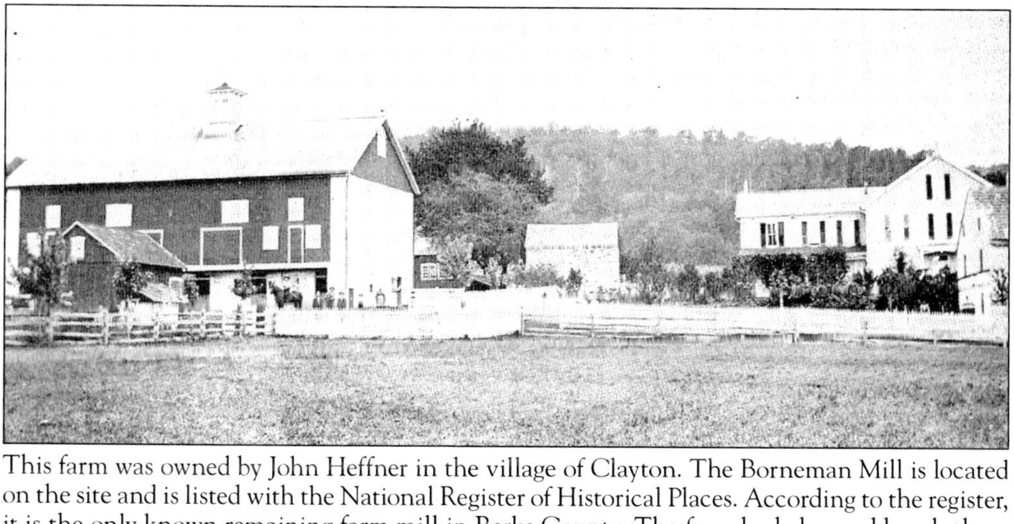

This farm was owned by John Heffner in the village of Clayton. The Borneman Mill is located on the site and is listed with the National Register of Historical Places. According to the register, it is the only known remaining farm mill in Berks County. The farm had changed hands three times in the year 1901, ending up with Sidney Borneman. The Heffners purchased the farm in 1969. The house was built in 1812 and an addition added around 1850.

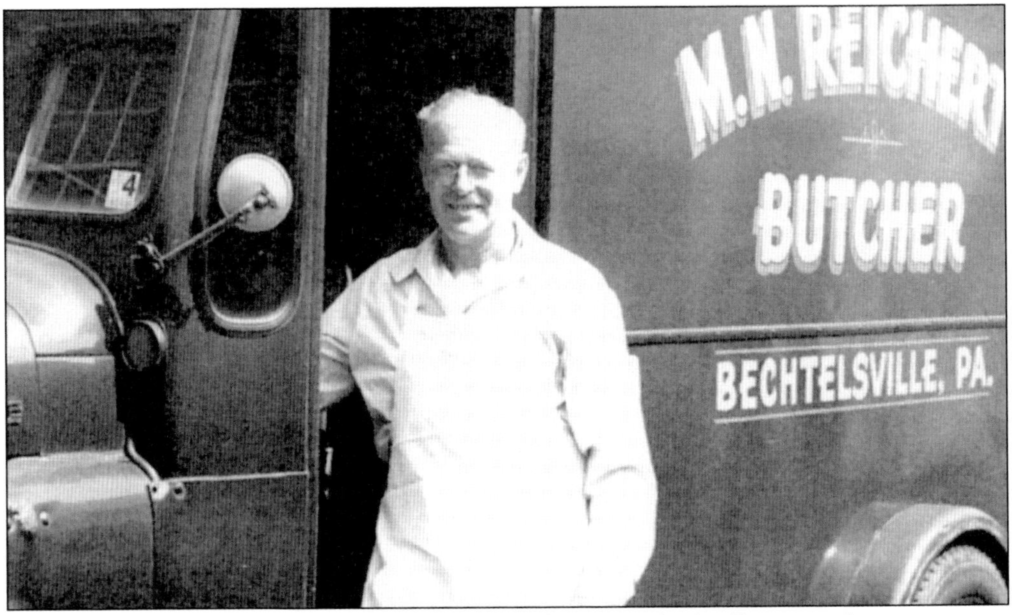

Melvin Reichert, the owner of Reichert's Butcher Shop in Bechtelsville, is seen here.

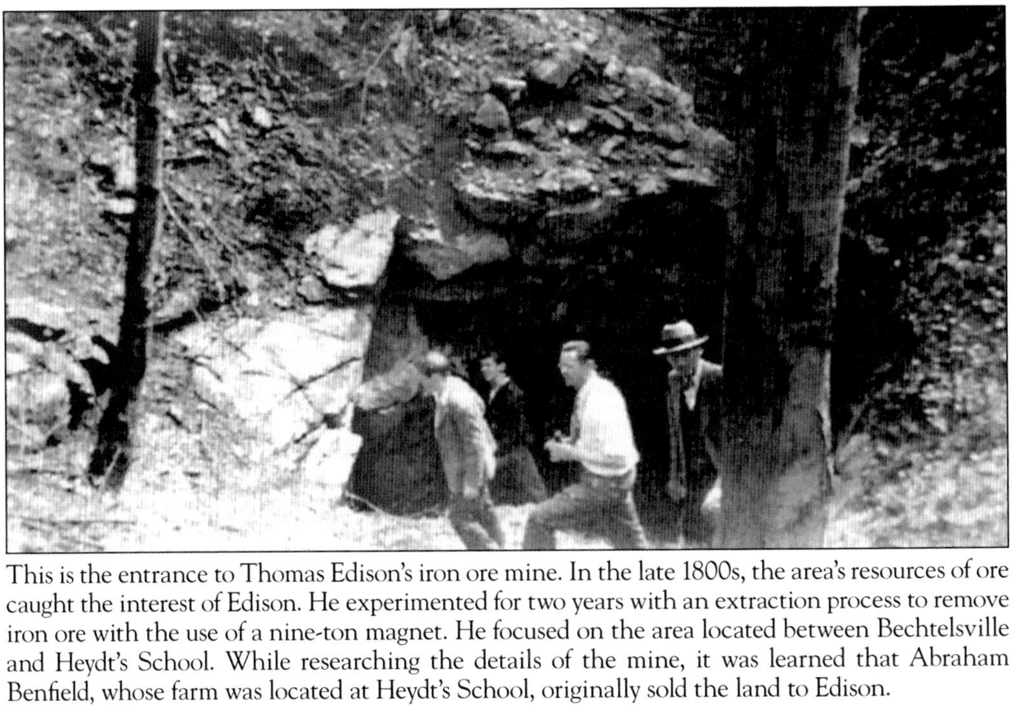

This is the entrance to Thomas Edison's iron ore mine. In the late 1800s, the area's resources of ore caught the interest of Edison. He experimented for two years with an extraction process to remove iron ore with the use of a nine-ton magnet. He focused on the area located between Bechtelsville and Heydt's School. While researching the details of the mine, it was learned that Abraham Benfield, whose farm was located at Heydt's School, originally sold the land to Edison.

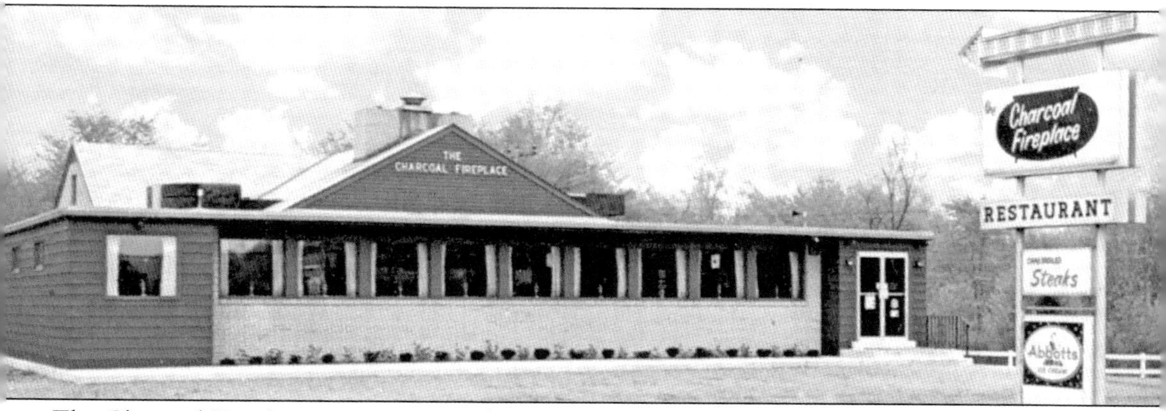

The Charcoal Fireplace restaurant was first opened by Francis and Gloria Stahl along Route 100 between Bechtelsville and New Berlinville. Since that time, it has gone through a number of owners.

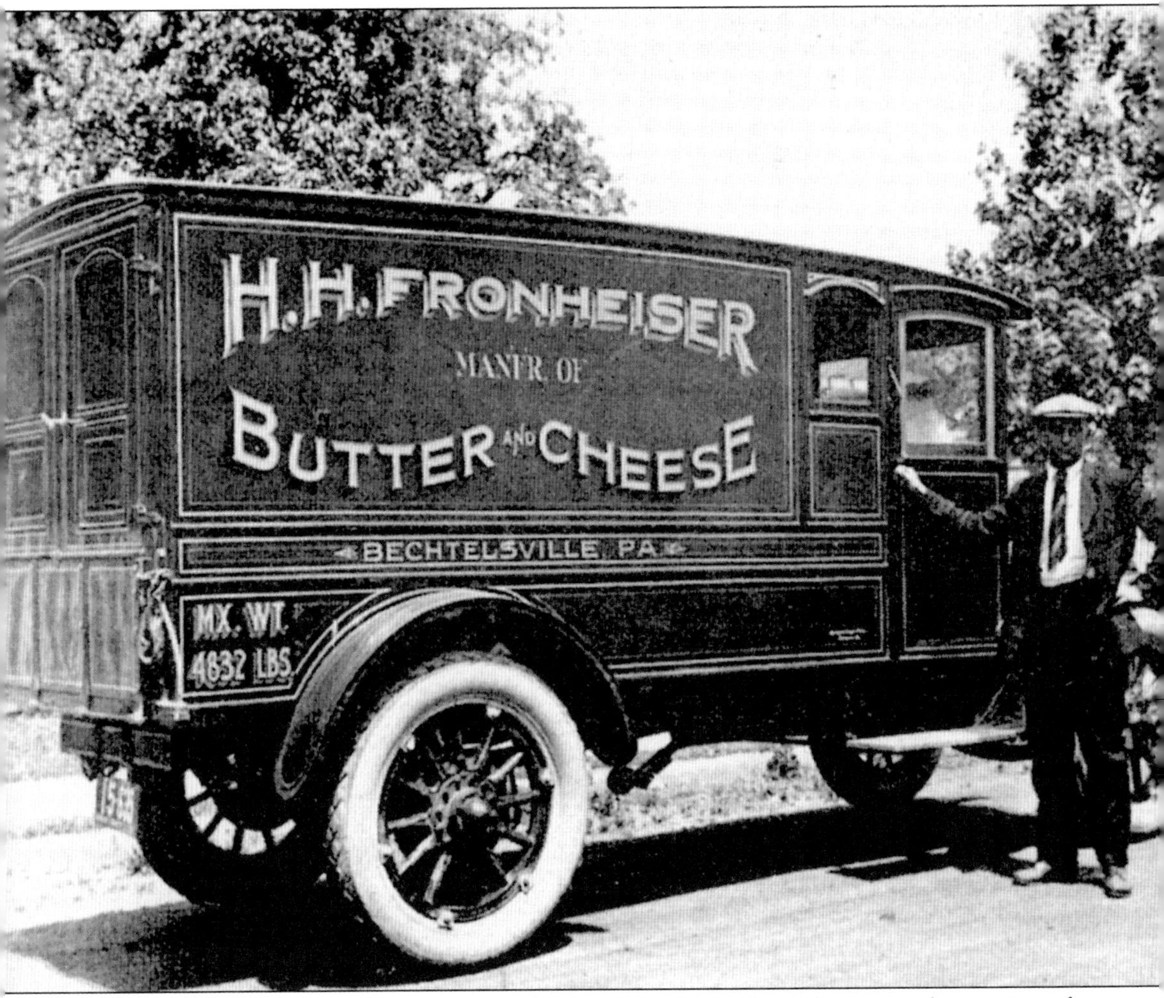

Henry Young started a creamery around 1885 in Bechtelsville and continued operations for a number of years, after which H. H. Stauffer ran it for approximately another 15 years. Another owner by the name of Herbert Fronheiser continued the business until the early 1940s. The main products were butter and cheese.

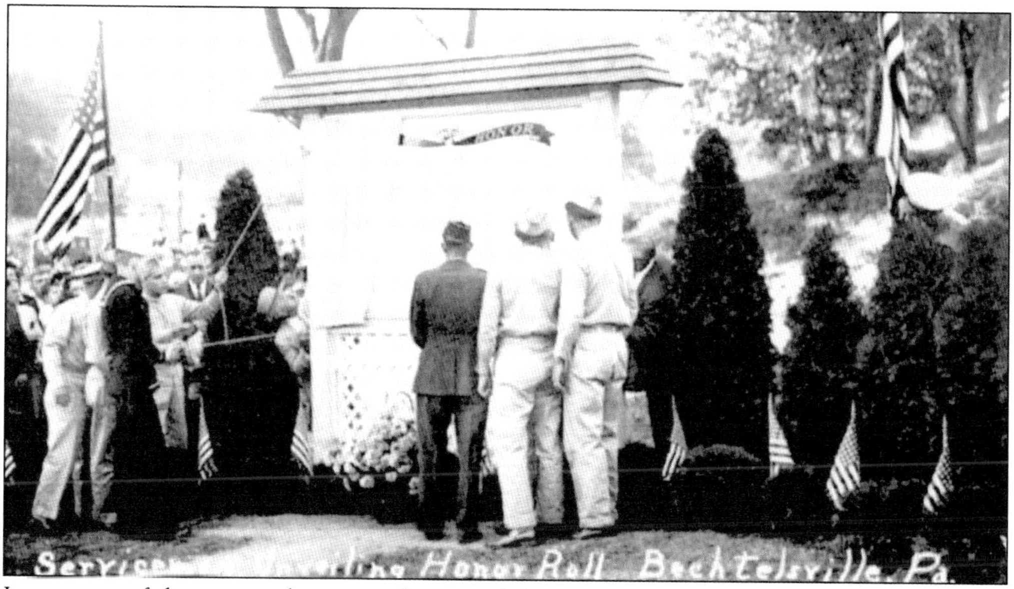

In memory of the men and women who served during World War II, the servicemen unveiled the "Roll of Honor," which took place on September 12, 1943, before the end of the war. Approximately 53 men and women's names are inscribed on the monument.

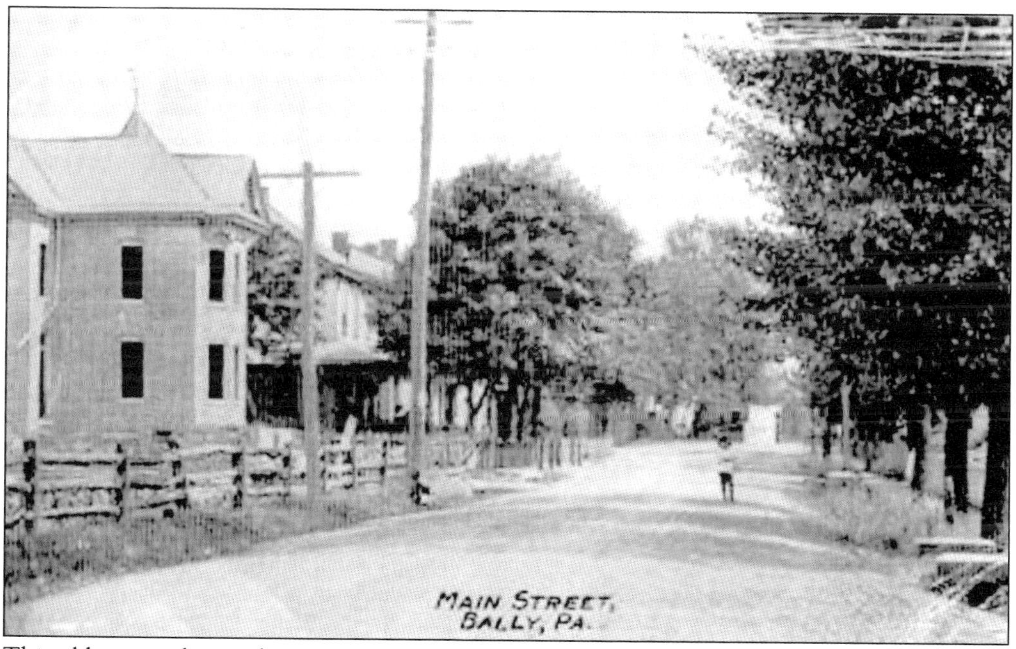

This old postcard view shows Main Street in Bally.

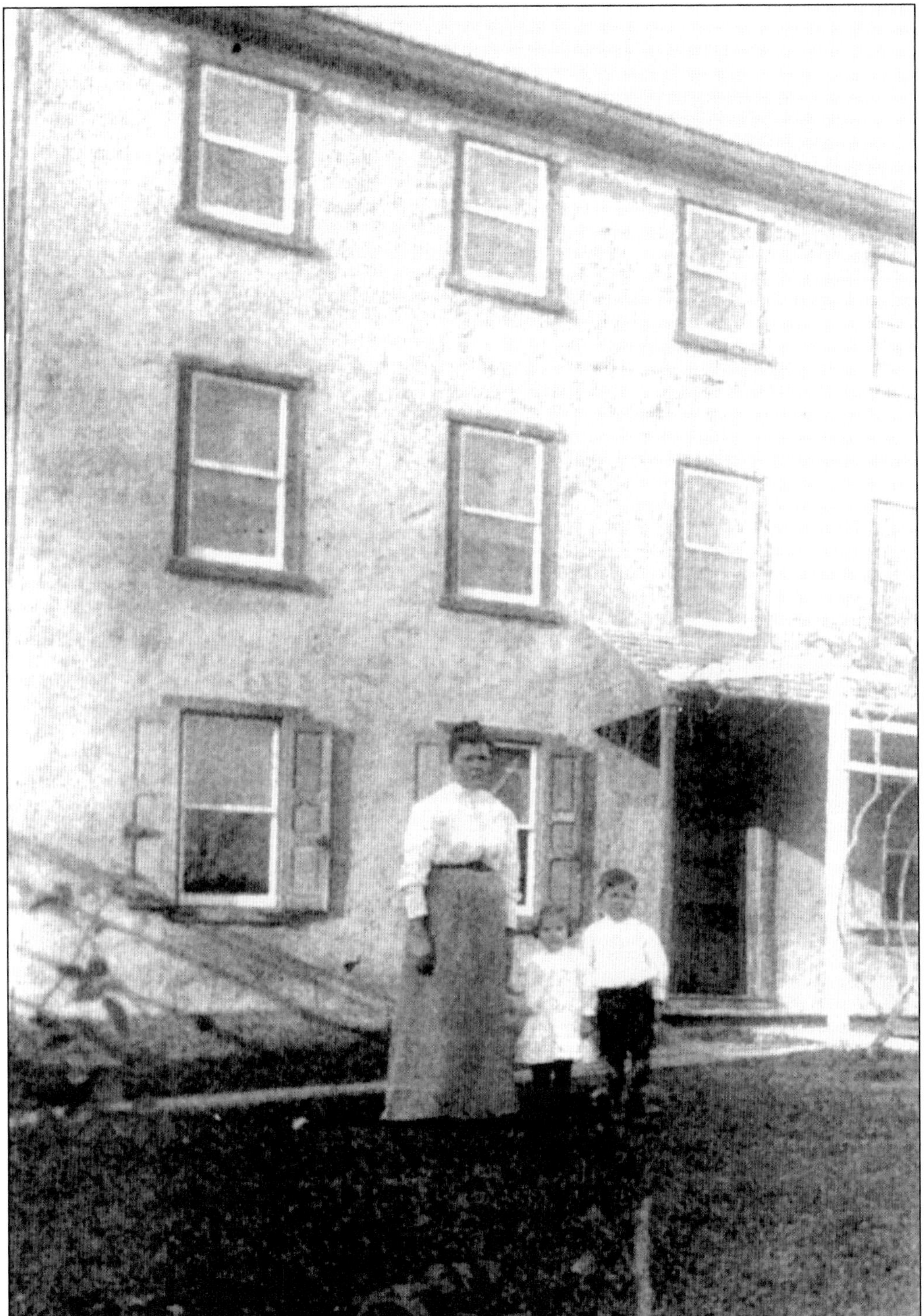

This building was known as the Stone Mill House, which was an 18-room dwelling in Bechtelsville. This house still remains in town and continues to be a residence. Back in 1910, it was purchased by Allen M. Erb from Jacob Oberholtzer.

Four

Around Boyertown

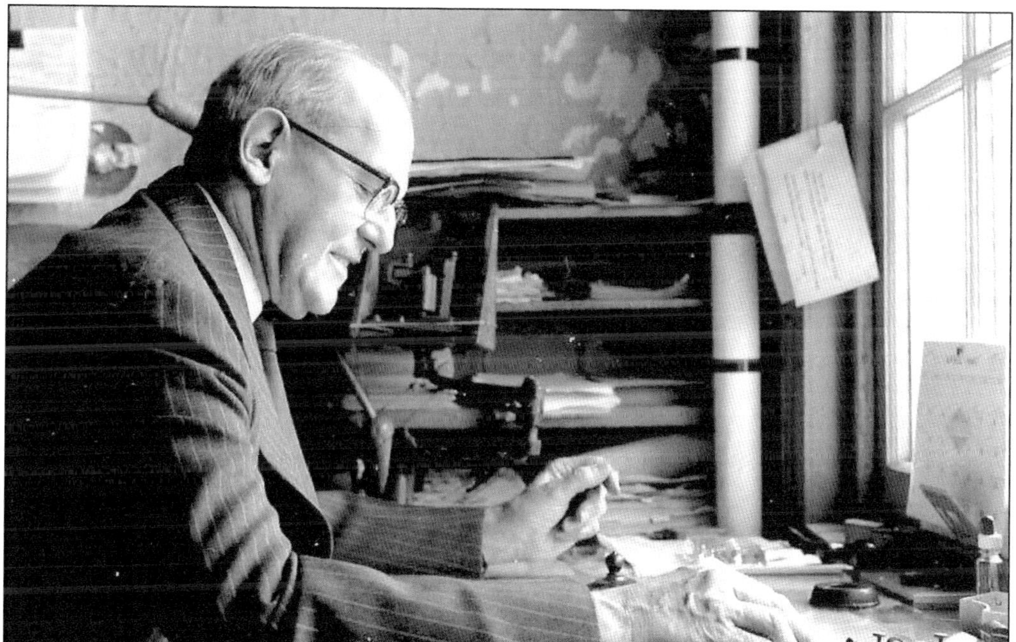

Claude Croll ran the telegraph at the Boyertown railroad station. His desk is displayed at the historical society. December 20, 1955, marked the last day of the telegraph service at Boyertown.

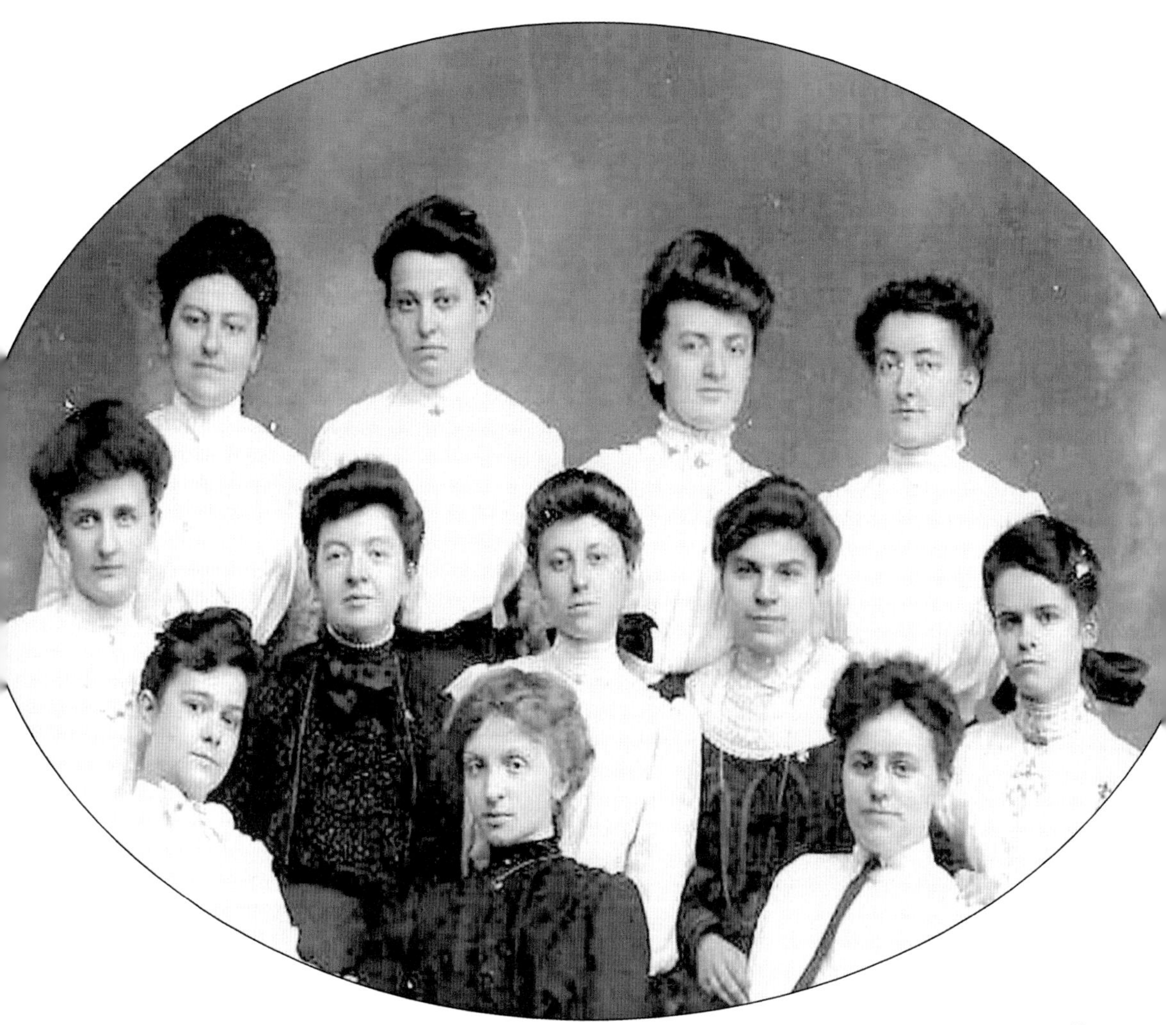

Young ladies from Boyertown are pictured here. The women, from left to right, are as follows: (first row) Miss Lieb, Nora Ruth, and Stella Tabor; (second row) Eva Brunner, Mary Hain, Gertrude Stoudt, Carrie Lorah, and Annie Eberly; (third row) Alice Moyer, Laura Leidy, Minerva Leiss, and Laura Althouse.

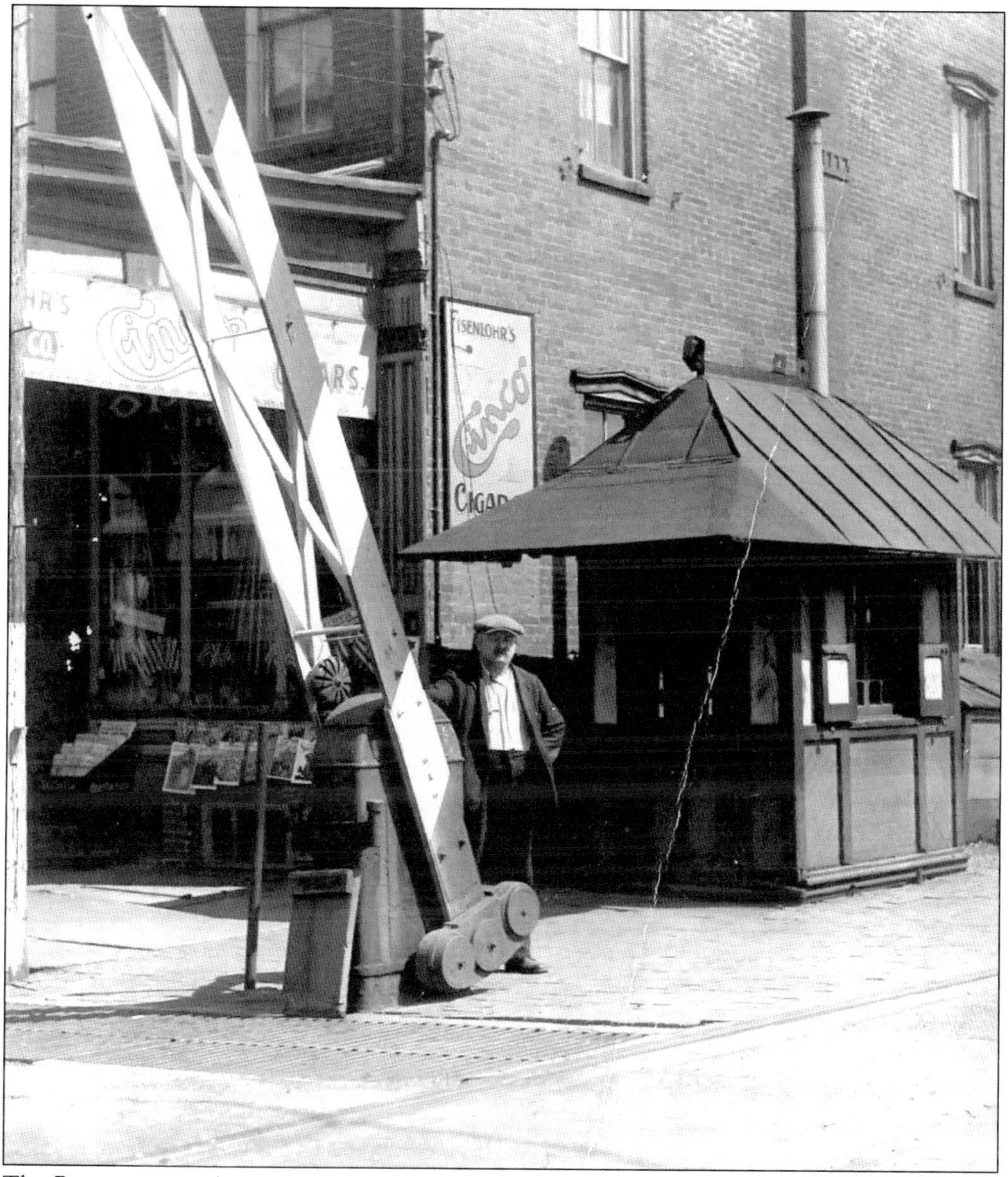

The Boyertown grade crossing is shown here. Jacob Keely served 41 years at this crossing. The gates were abandoned and dismantled by Reading Company in May 1932.

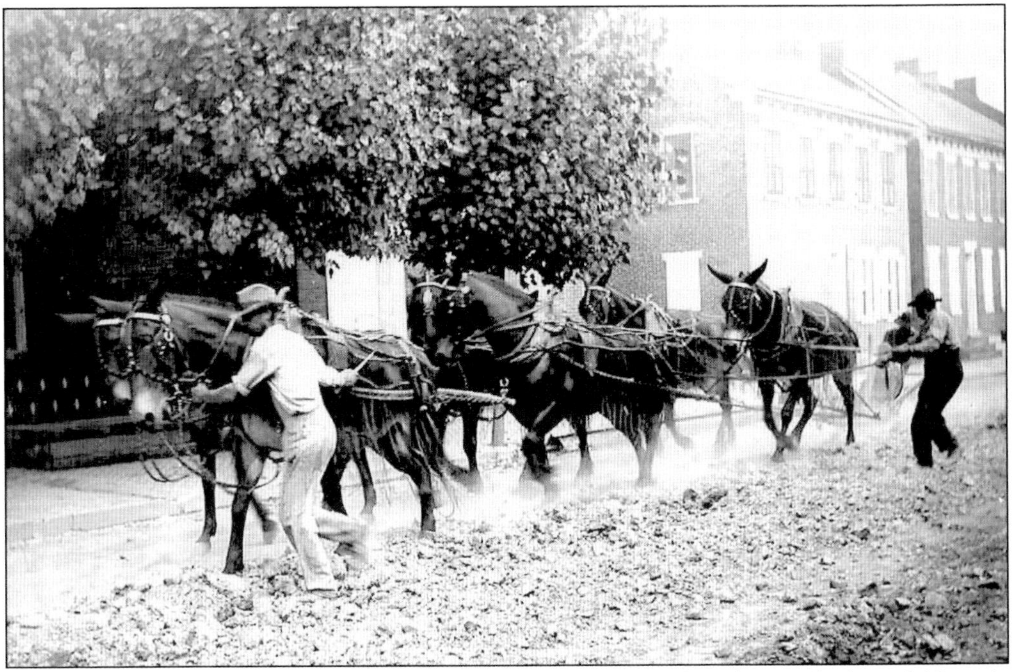

Modern equipment would have made this job faster and easier, but this era had available only manpower and mules to dig up the Boyertown streets to install the trolley tracks.

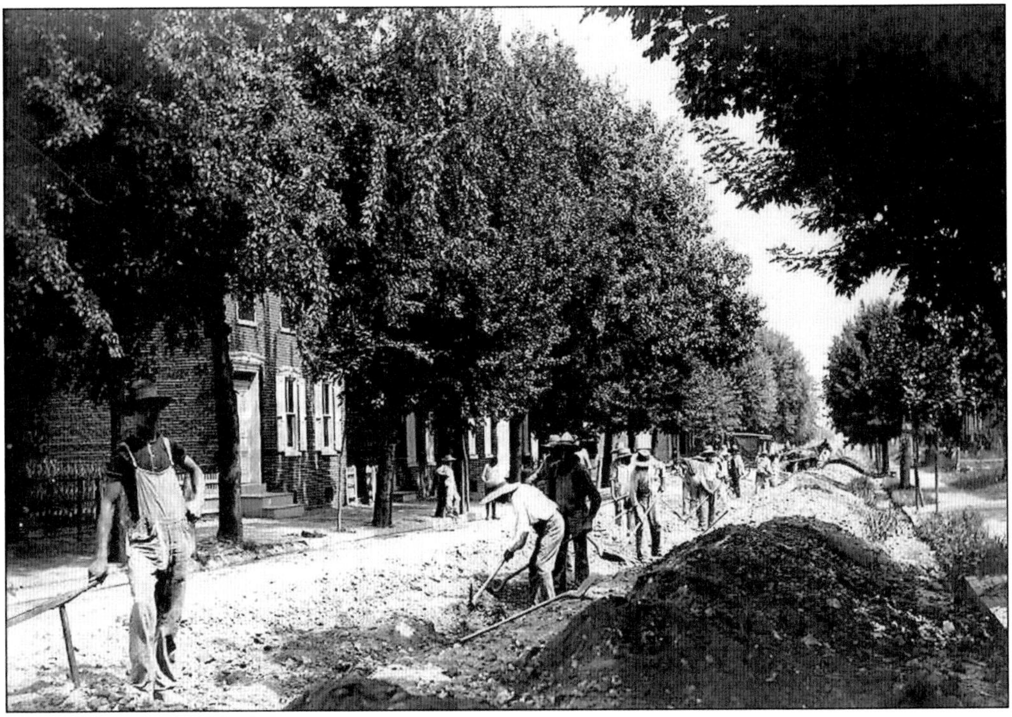

By the end of the day, these men have put in a tough day of manual labor, helping to build the new lines on Philadelphia Avenue.

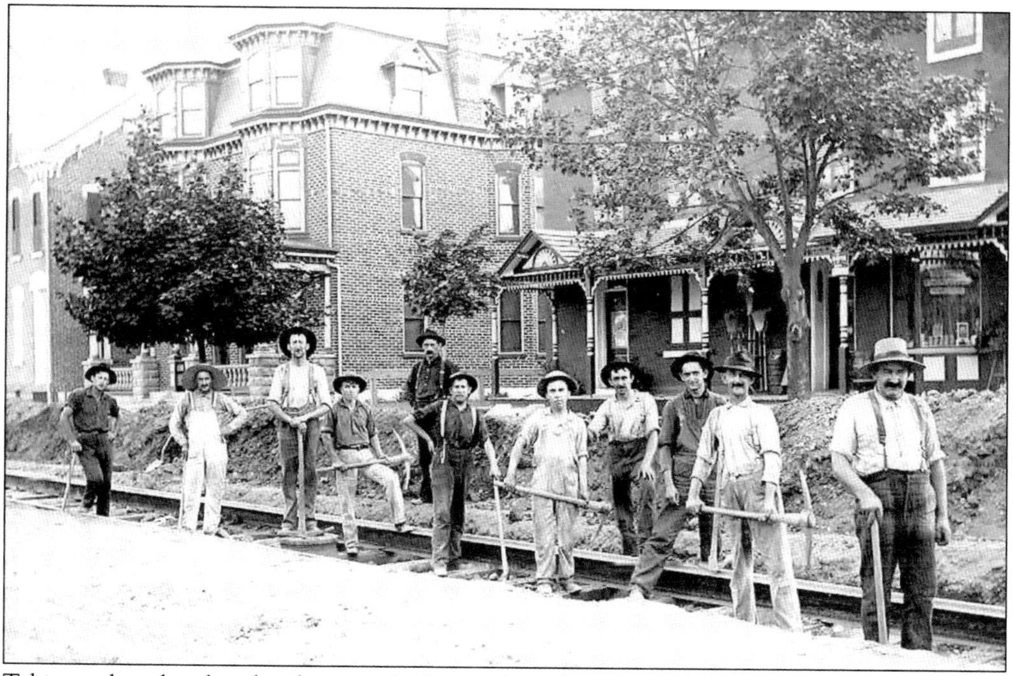

Taking a short break to be photographed, men from the area work long and hard to prepare and lay the tracks.

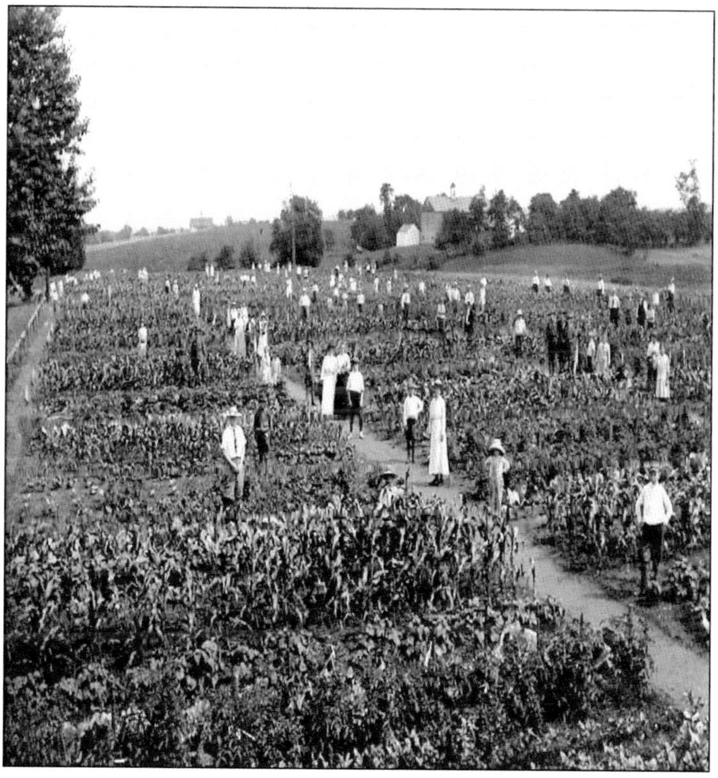

A large community garden helped provide food supplies during the war times in 1917.

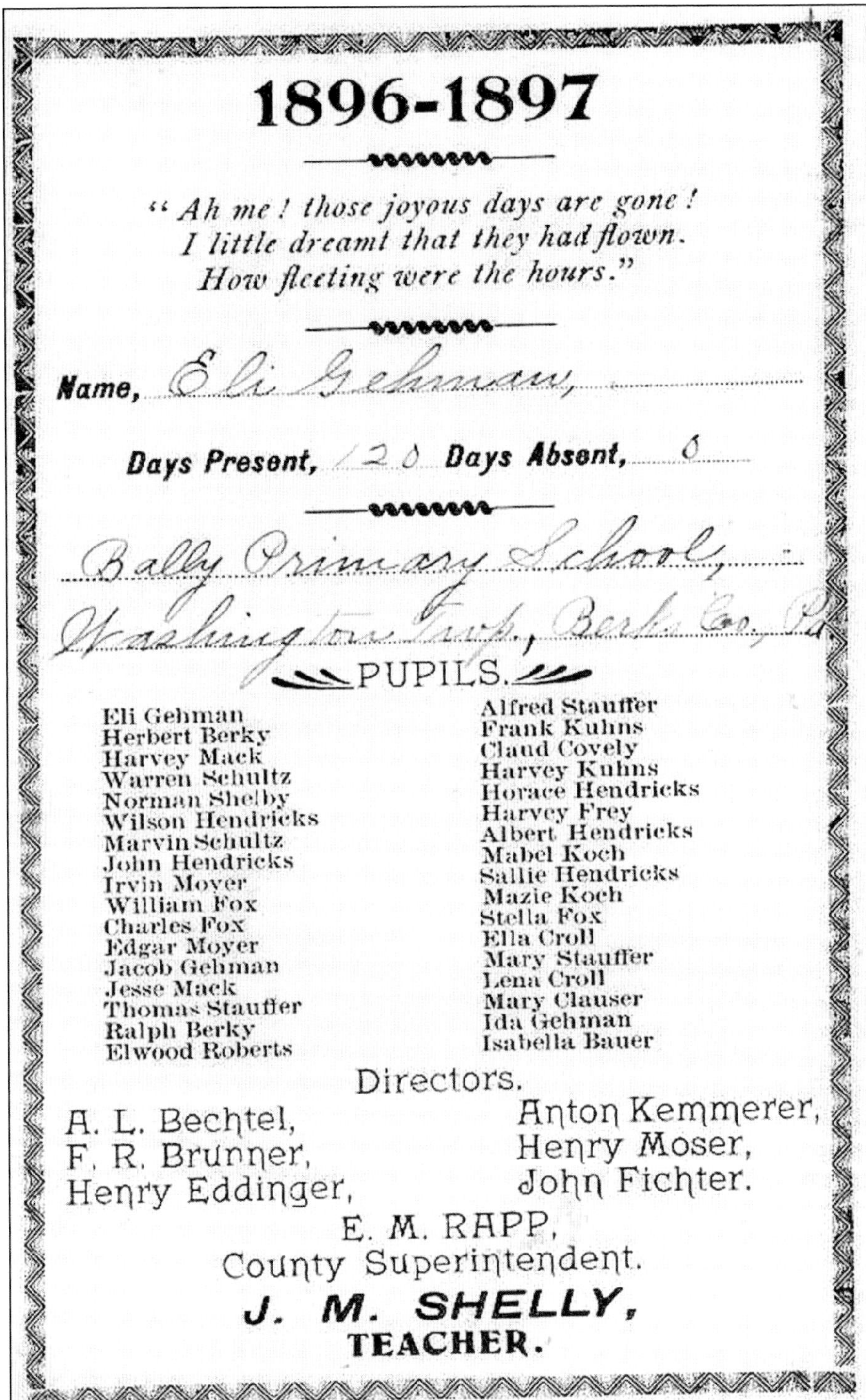

1896-1897

"Ah me! those joyous days are gone!
I little dreamt that they had flown.
How fleeting were the hours."

Name, Eli Gehman,

Days Present, 120 **Days Absent,** 0

Bally Primary School,
Washington Twp., Berks Co., Pa

PUPILS.

Eli Gehman
Herbert Berky
Harvey Mack
Warren Schultz
Norman Shelby
Wilson Hendricks
Marvin Schultz
John Hendricks
Irvin Moyer
William Fox
Charles Fox
Edgar Moyer
Jacob Gehman
Jesse Mack
Thomas Stauffer
Ralph Berky
Elwood Roberts
Alfred Stauffer
Frank Kuhns
Claud Covely
Harvey Kuhns
Horace Hendricks
Harvey Frey
Albert Hendricks
Mabel Koch
Sallie Hendricks
Mazie Koch
Stella Fox
Ella Croll
Mary Stauffer
Lena Croll
Mary Clauser
Ida Gehman
Isabella Bauer

Directors.

A. L. Bechtel,
F. R. Brunner,
Henry Eddinger,
Anton Kemmerer,
Henry Moser,
John Fichter.

E. M. RAPP,
County Superintendent.

J. M. SHELLY,
TEACHER.

This is a typical report card that was received by students, dating back to 1896–1897. The student on this particular report card was Eli Gehman from the Bally Primary School in Washington Township.

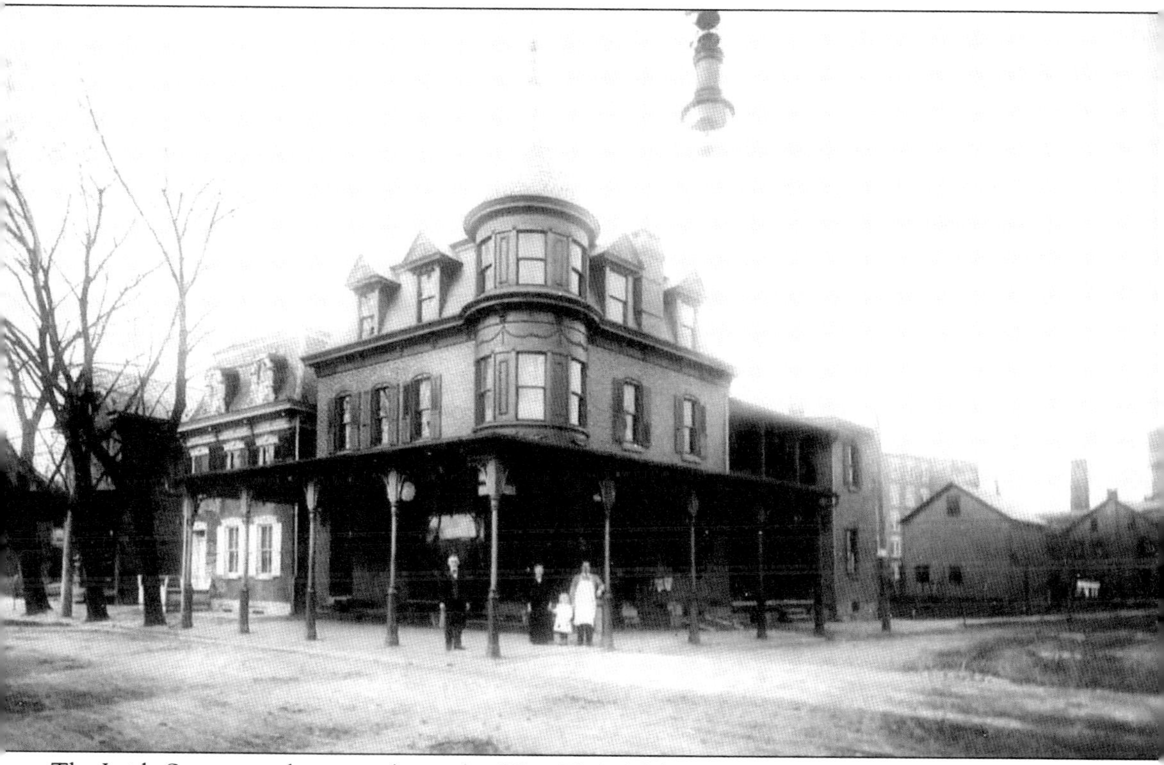

The Leidy Store, seen here, was located at West Philadelphia Avenue and Walnut Street.

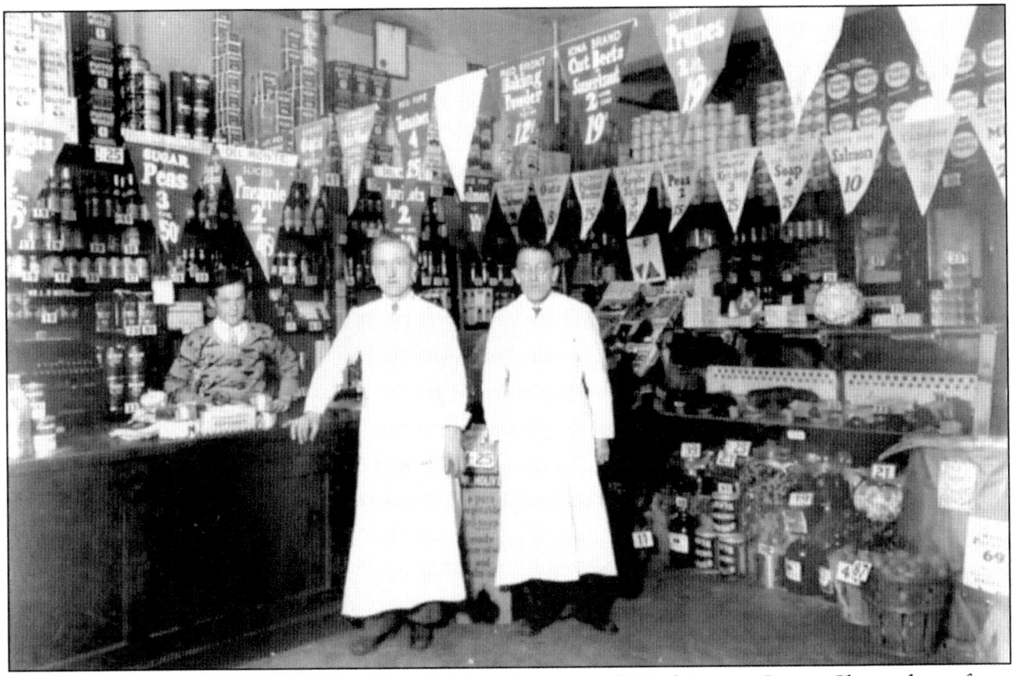

This A&P store was located on East Philadelphia Avenue and Washington Street. Shown here, from left to right, are Lewis Nuss (the boy with the sweater), Leonard Moyer, and George Coleman.

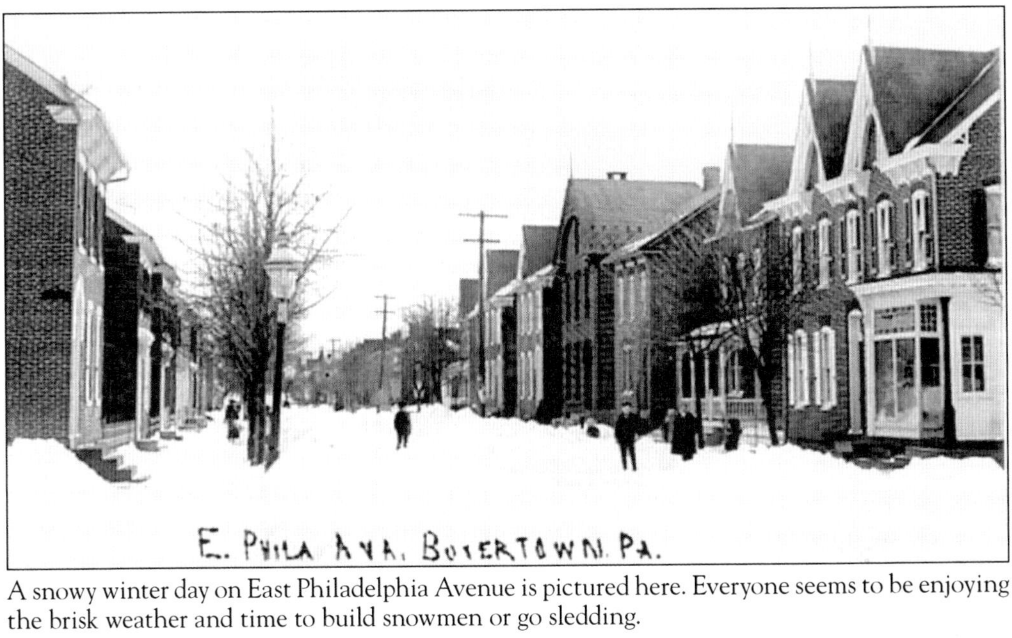

A snowy winter day on East Philadelphia Avenue is pictured here. Everyone seems to be enjoying the brisk weather and time to build snowmen or go sledding.

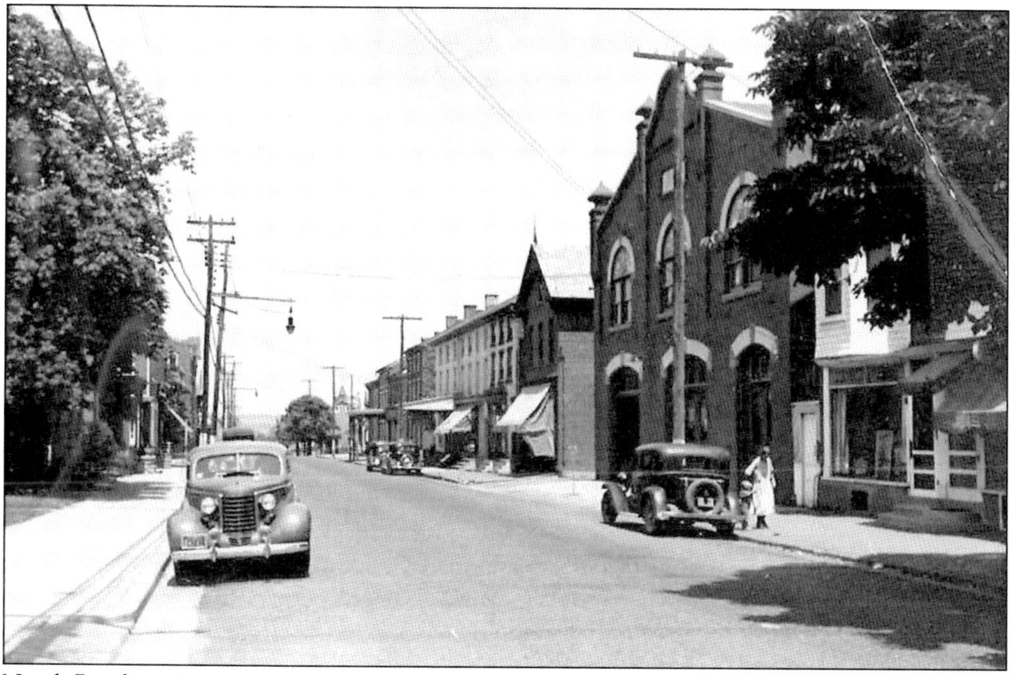

North Reading Avenue in Boyertown is shown here. The fire company was located on the right, and at the end of the block on the left side is the State Theatre.

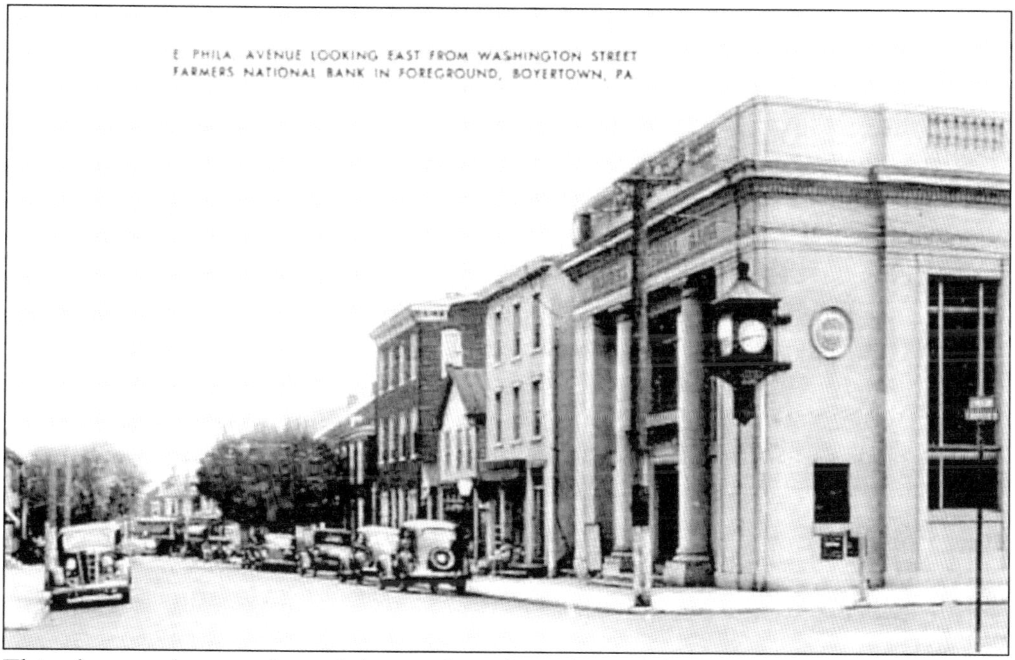

This photograph was taken while traveling down East Philadelphia Avenue. The Farmers National Bank was located on the right corner.

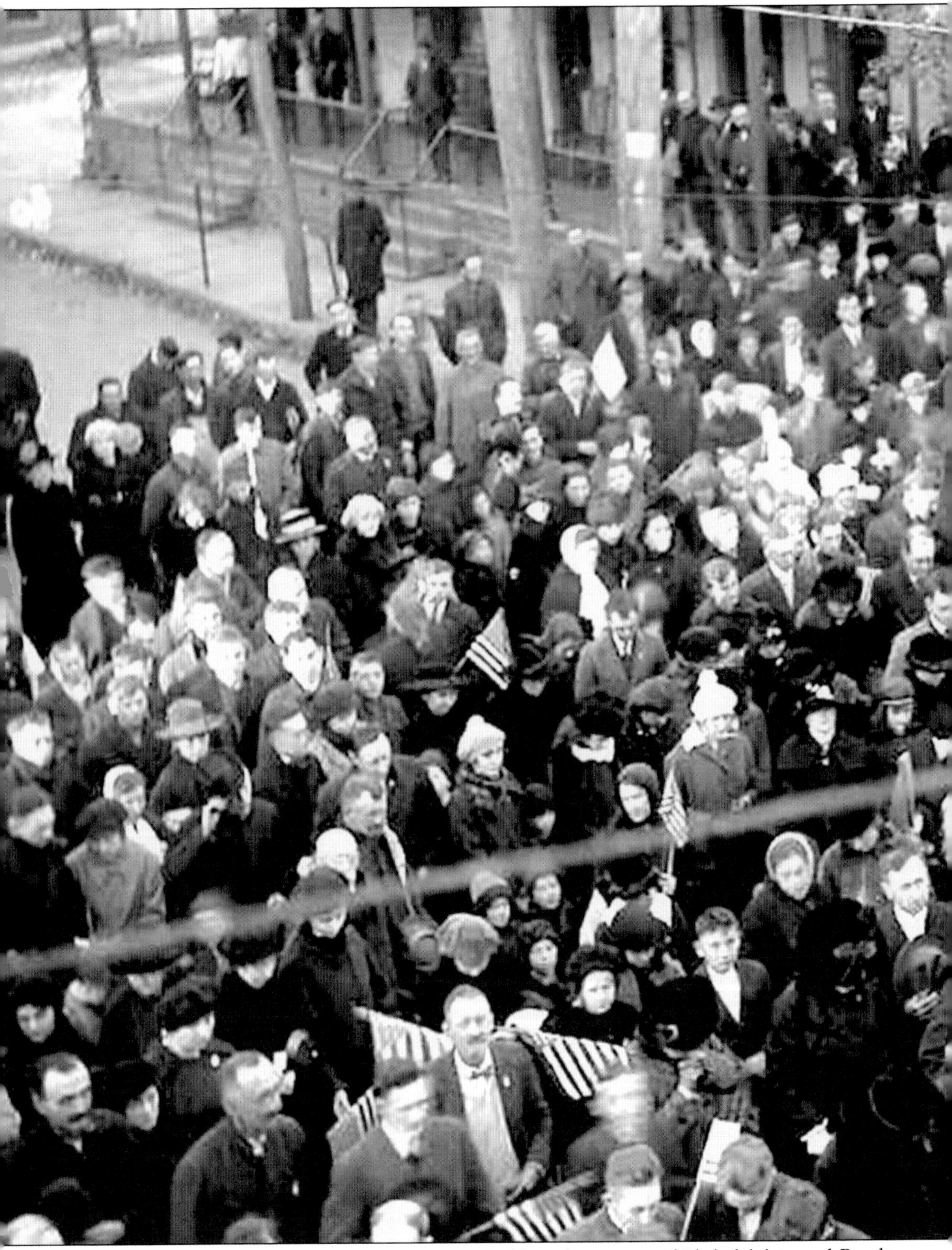

This Armistice Day celebration in 1918 was held at the corner of Philadelphia and Reading

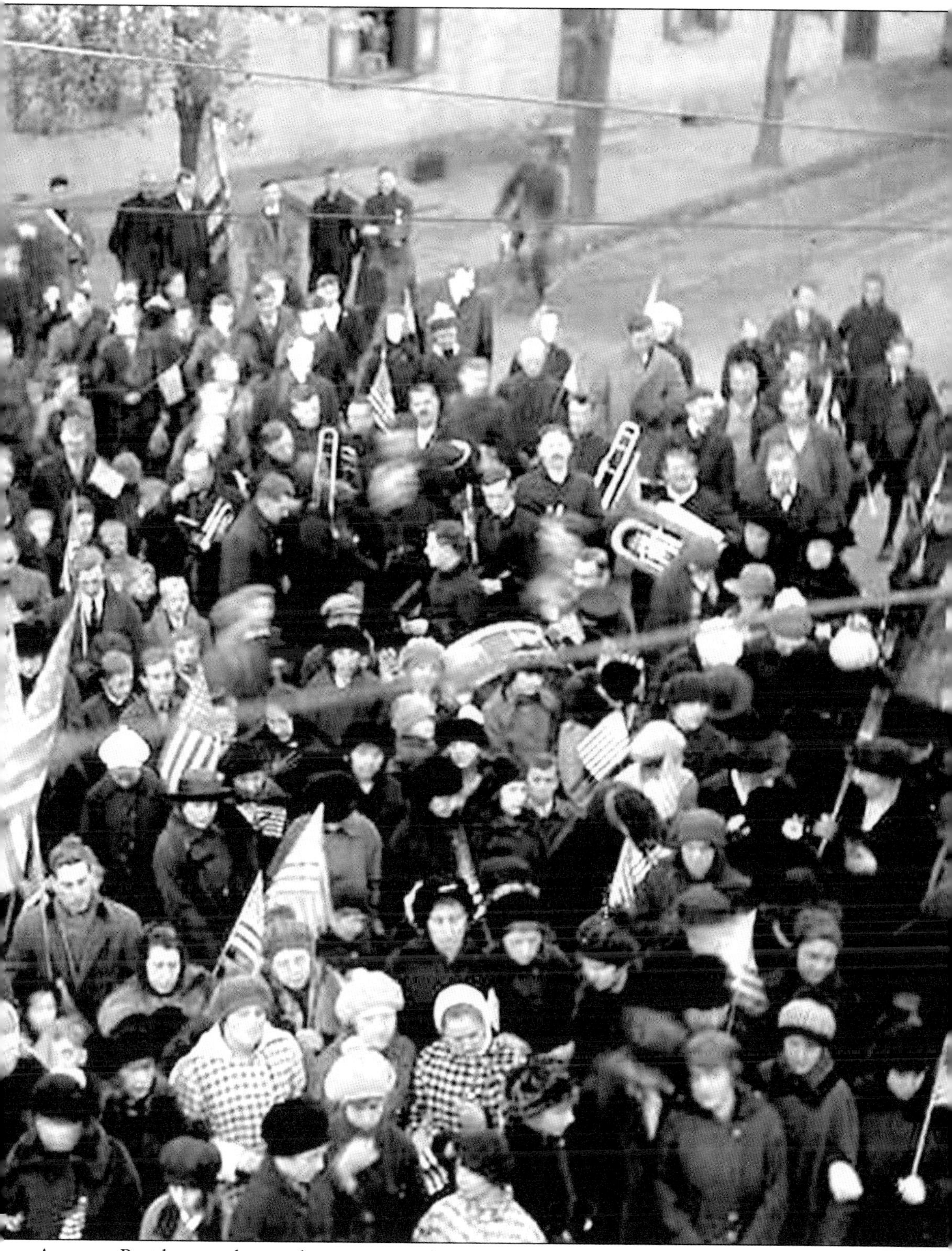

Avenues. Residents gather in the streets to celebrate the end of World War I.

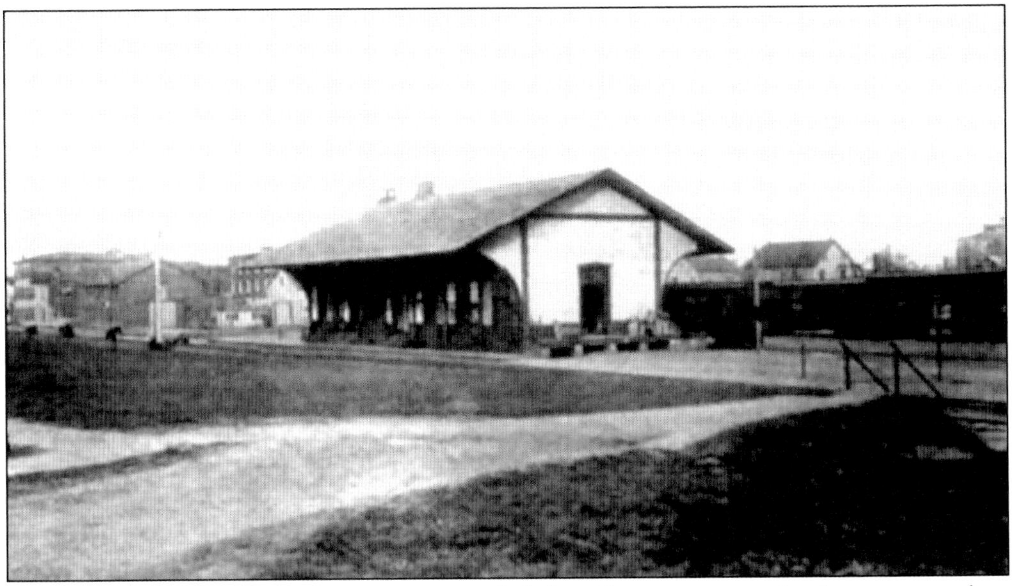

The railroad station in Boyertown was a major hub for railway transportation from areas such as Barto, Pottstown, and Reading. At the time of the opera house fire, funeral directors from as far away as Philadelphia traveled by rail to assist in the mass burials.

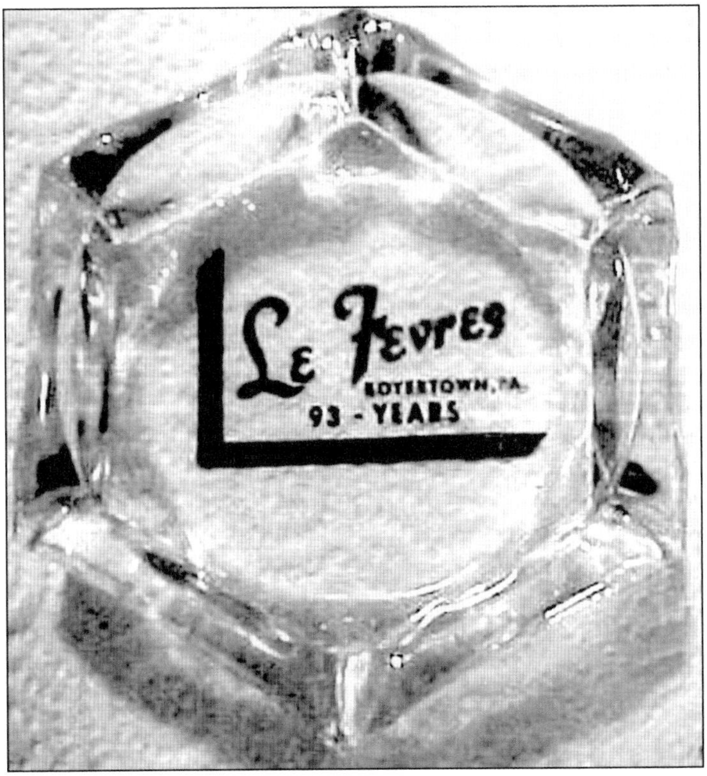

This is a souvenir ashtray from the original LeFevres store, which was the major department store along East Philadelphia Avenue in Boyertown. The store offered all types of goods, including clothes.

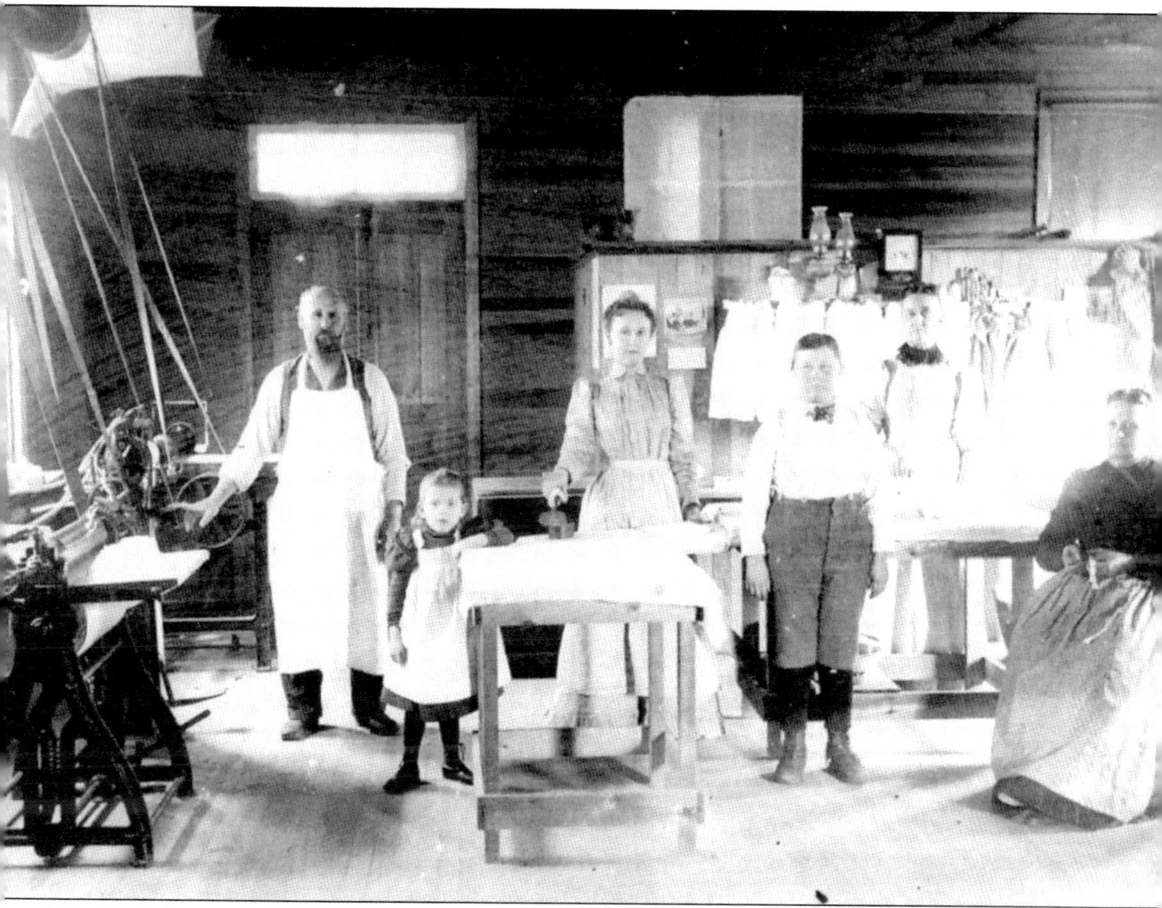

The Buck Steam Laundry was a laundry service that is similar to modern dry cleaners. The actual location of the laundry in Boyertown is not known.

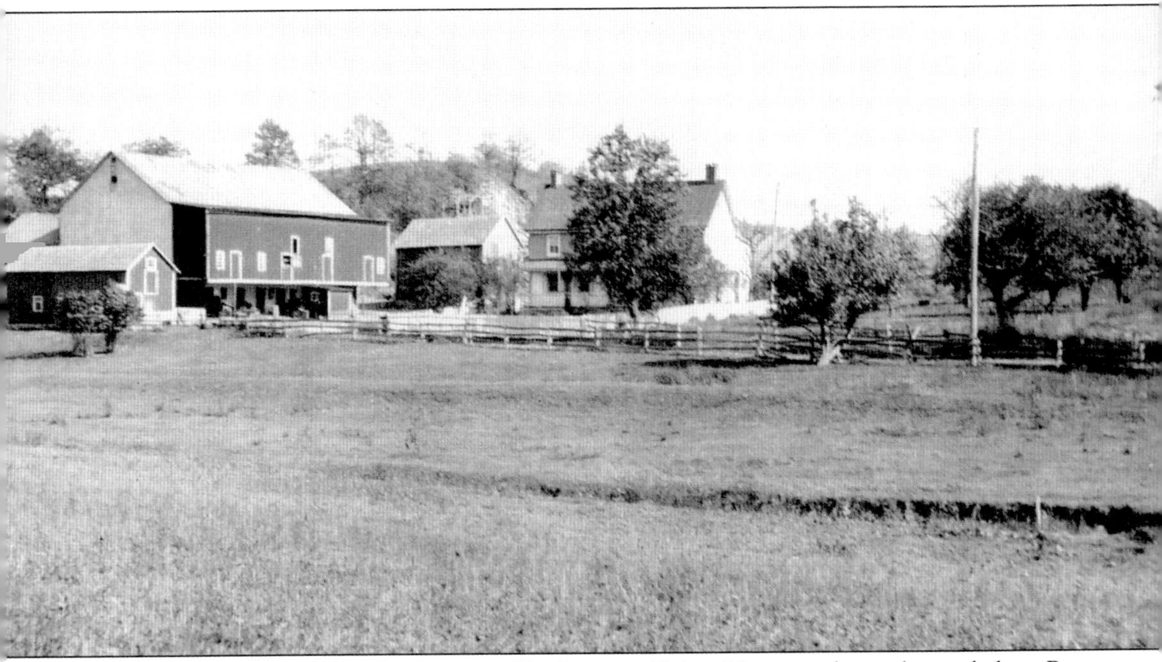

This homestead and quarry were owned by Irvin and Mary Henry and were located along Route 100 in Clayton. Later, Walter Shuhler bought the property after this photograph was taken. Most everyone in the area know this as the Shuhler farm and for home delivery of its fresh eggs. This is common practice even today by son Matthew Shuhler. There is nothing better than fresh eggs direct from the farm.

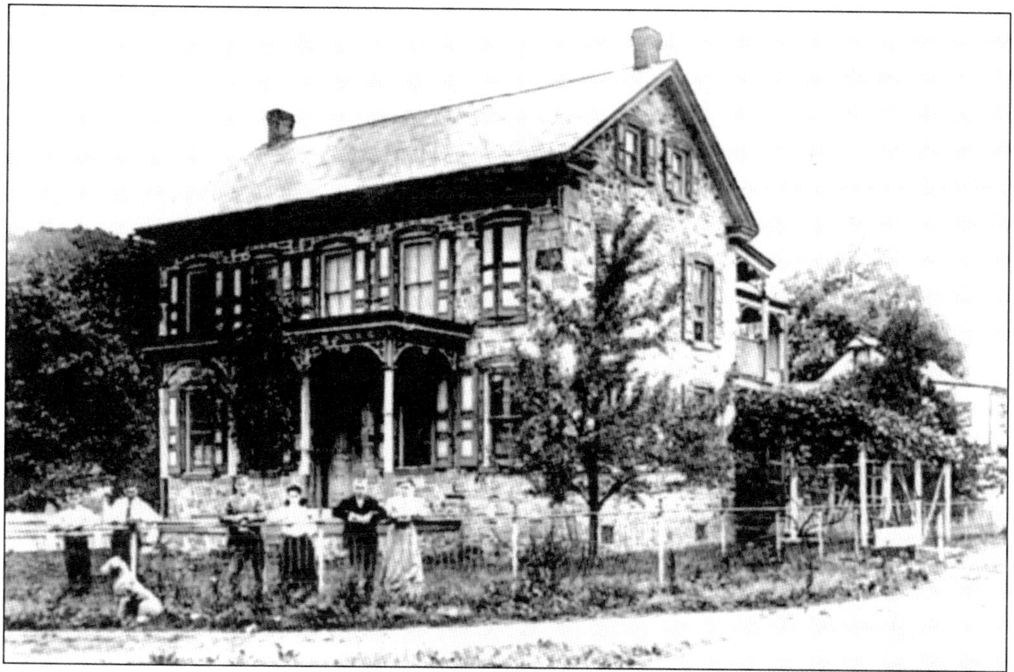

The home of Elmer and Ida Conrad and their family is shown in this 1888 photograph.

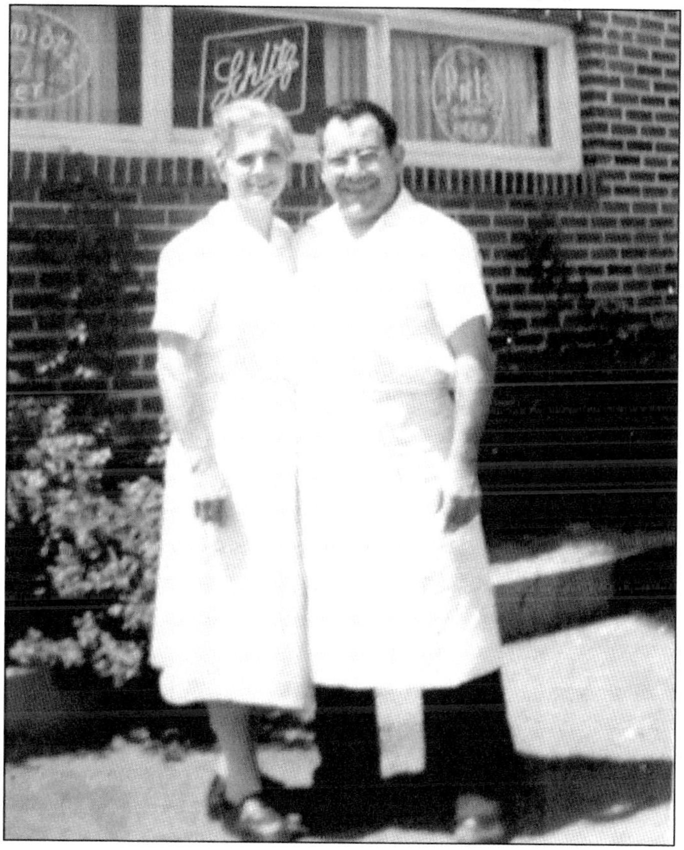

Serafino Talarico, known to all as "Sam," or "Pop" and his wife, Jennie Talarico (née Borelli), opened the original Talarico's Restaurant. At a quick glance, one would think it was Ralph, their son, who has taken over the family business. Ralph is definitely a chip off the old block, as they say. Talarico's has always been known for its high quality, delicious sandwiches, which Ralph attributes to using nothing but the best meats.

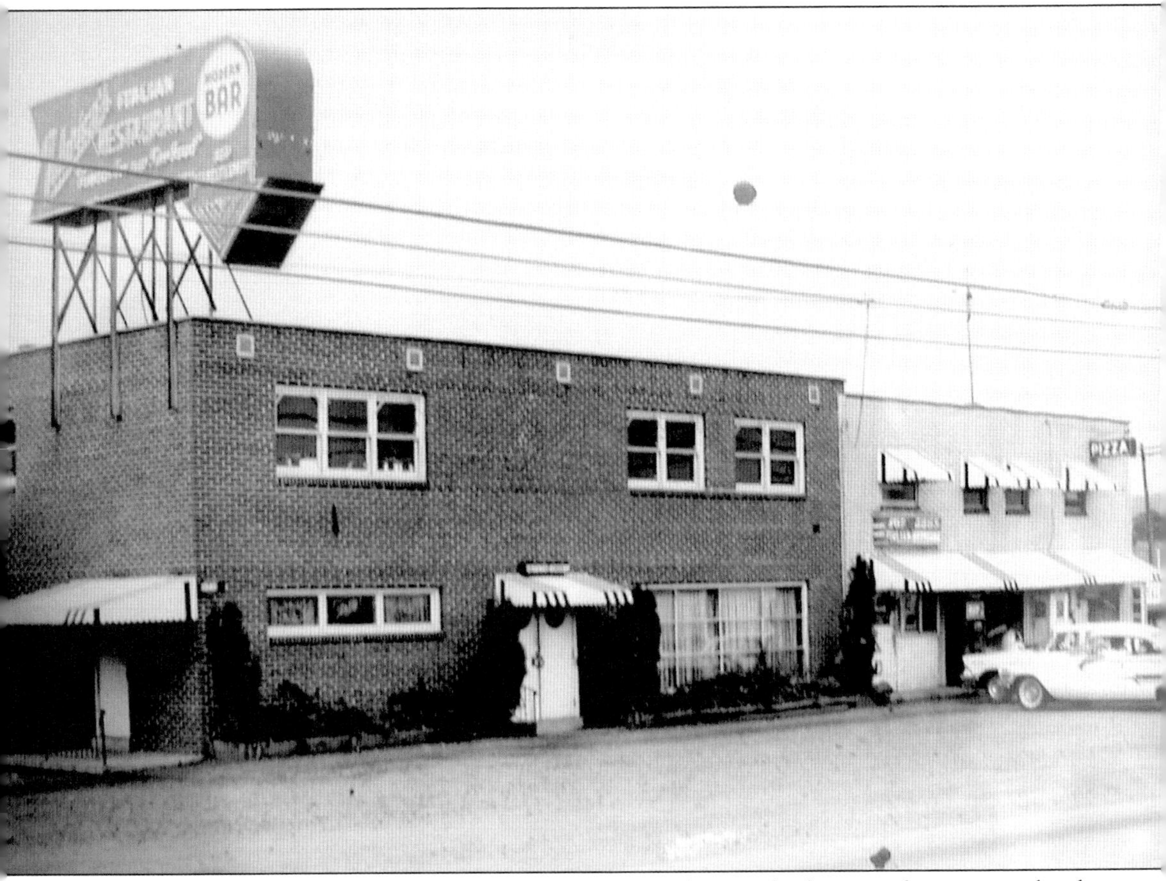

This well-known restaurant, known as Talarico's, was the popular location for great sandwiches and Italian foods. The business was later relocated along East Philadelphia Avenue in Boyertown, and the original building was demolished since it was sitting on the location that is now Route 100. Today the sub shop located along East Philadelphia Avenue continues to be operated by Ralph and has again made the Talarico name synonymous with great food. Hundreds of photographs line the walls of the sandwich shop, featuring visitors from all over the world who return to Boyertown to again savor Talarico's famous hoagies and steak sandwiches.

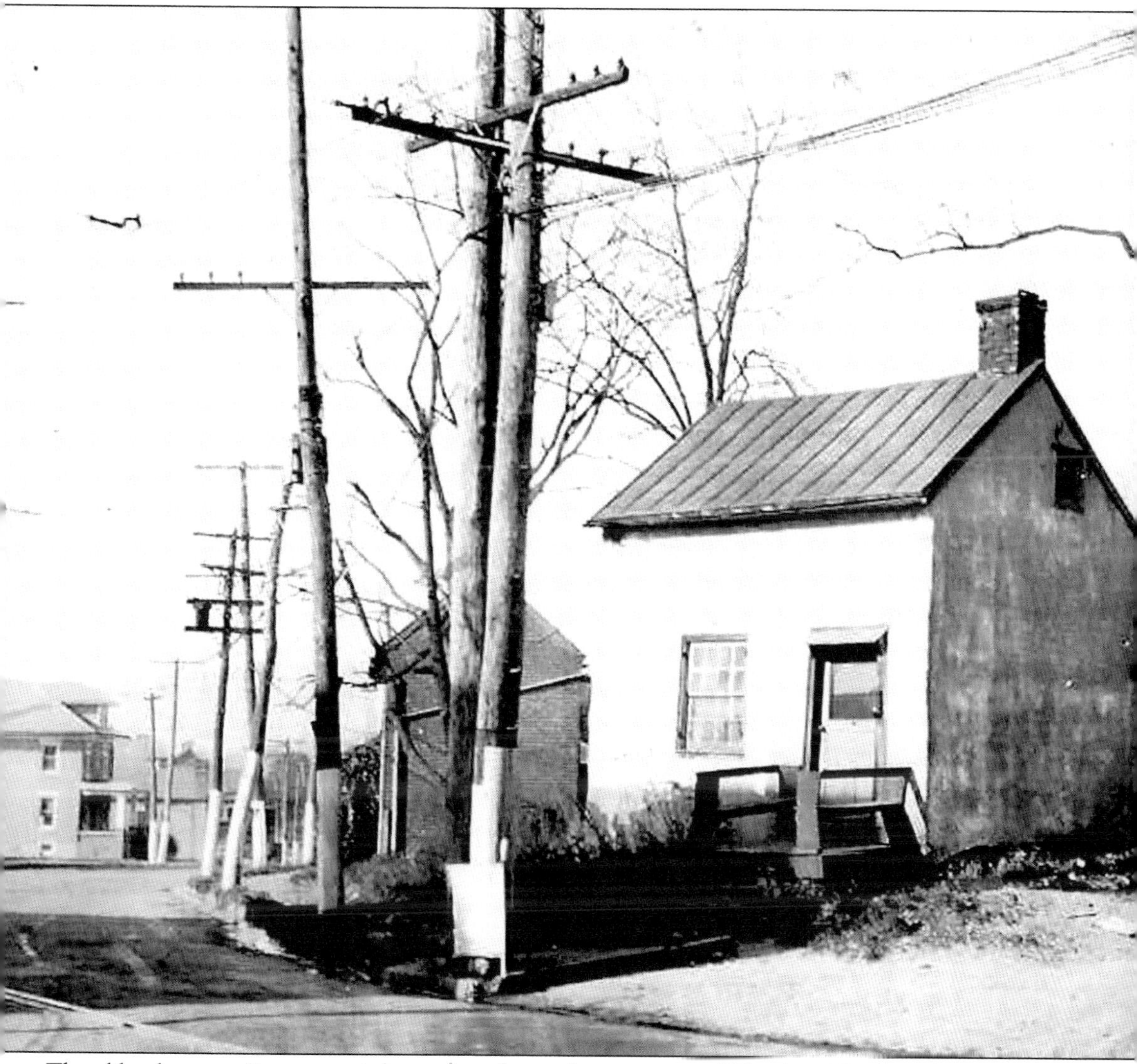
The oldest house in Boyertown is located on the southwest corner of Third and Reading Avenues.

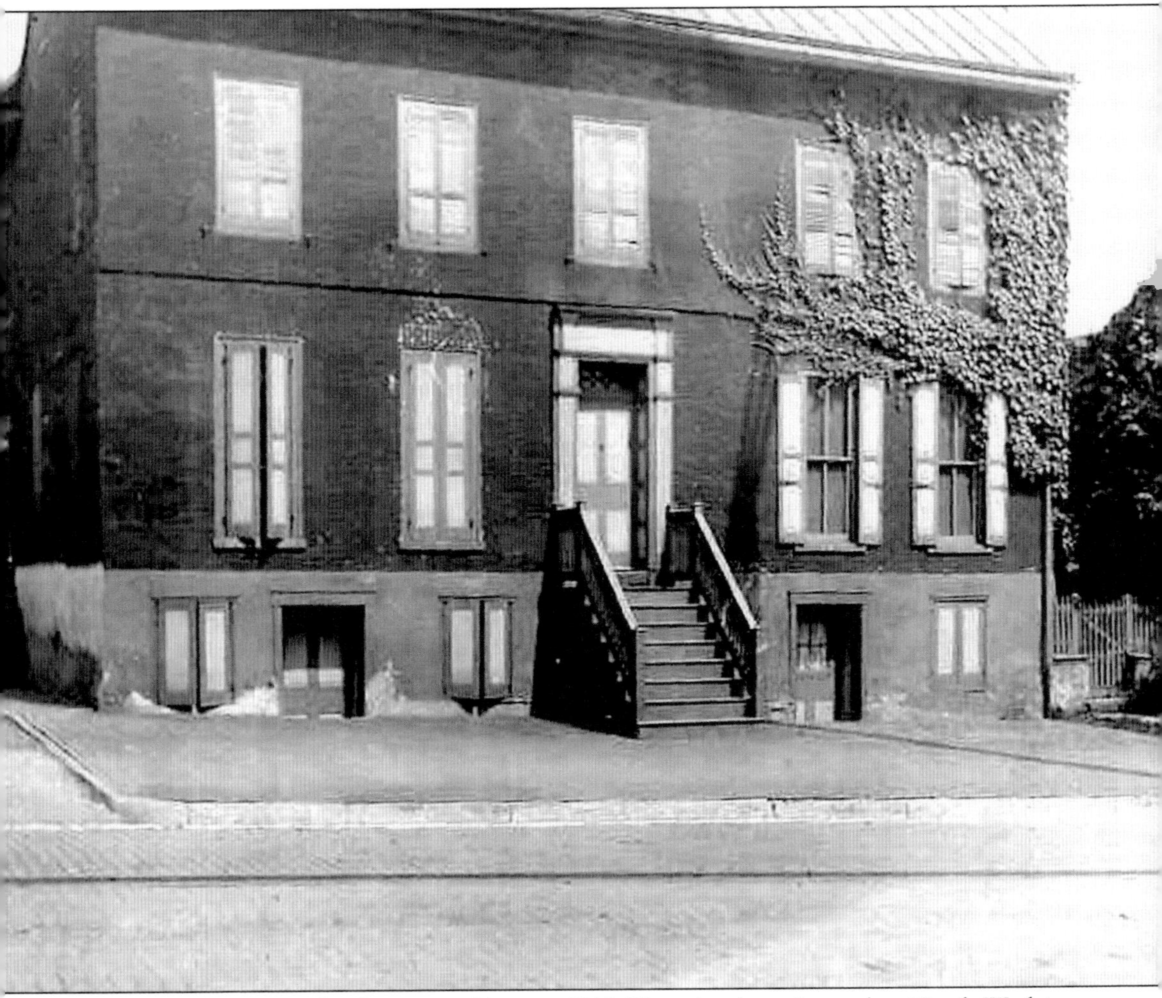

The Washington School is pictured here in 1915. The school was located on North Washington Street in Boyertown.

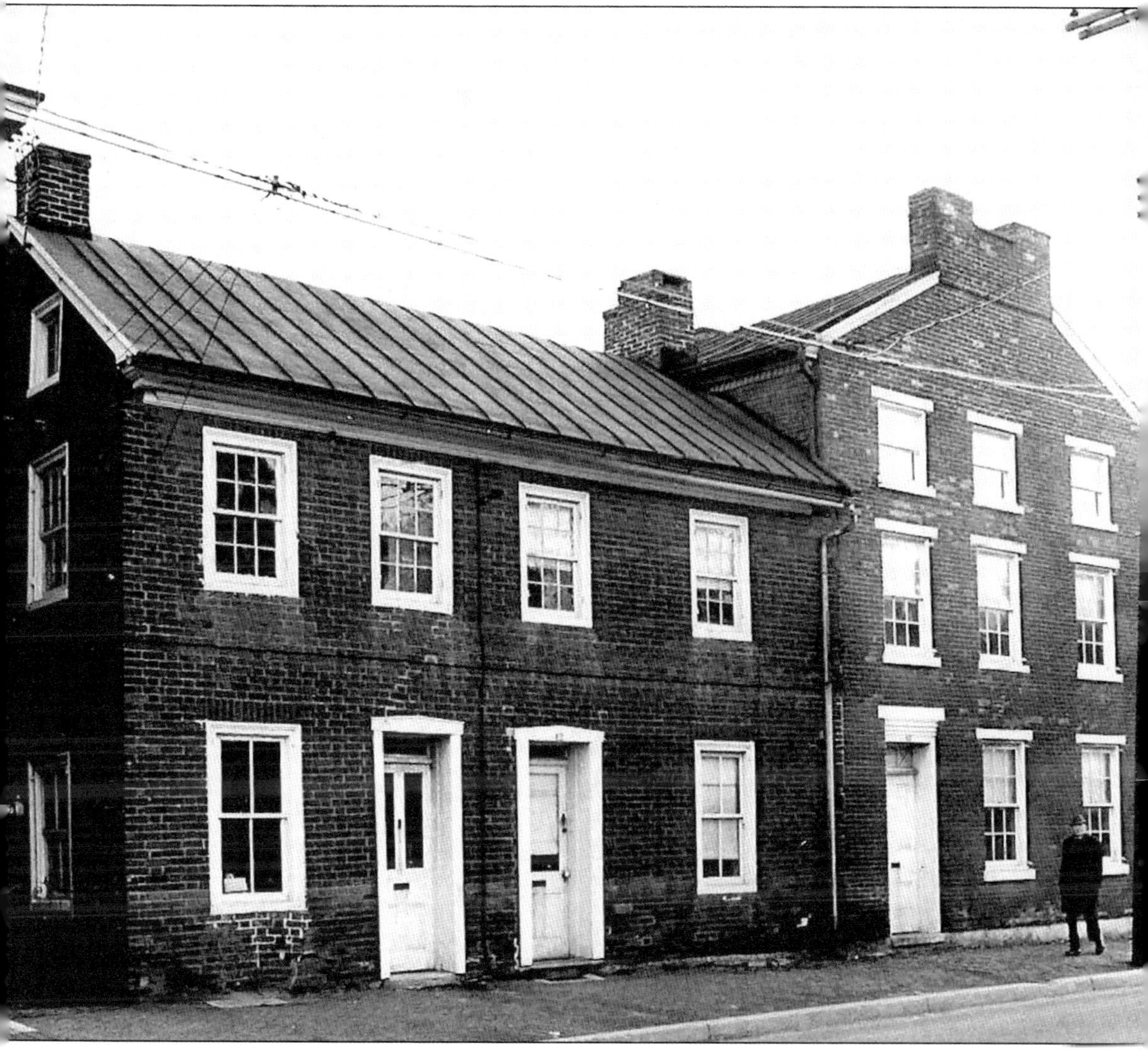

Three connected homes on West Philadelphia Avenue and Walnut Street in Boyertown were where Benjamin and Katherine Reigner lived with their seven children around 1854 to 1865. Here is where Amanda Bower (née Reigner), the seventh child, was born March 14, 1854. Benjamin Reigner was a blacksmith and had his shop on the premises.

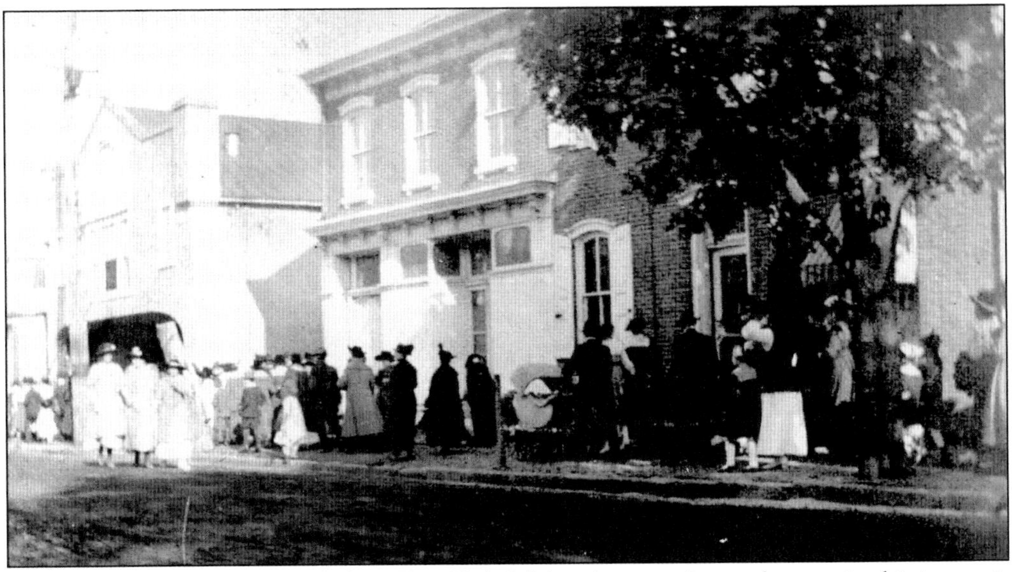

These row houses were located along East Philadelphia Avenue. As can be seen in this image, it is a busy street with many people walking along the main streets.

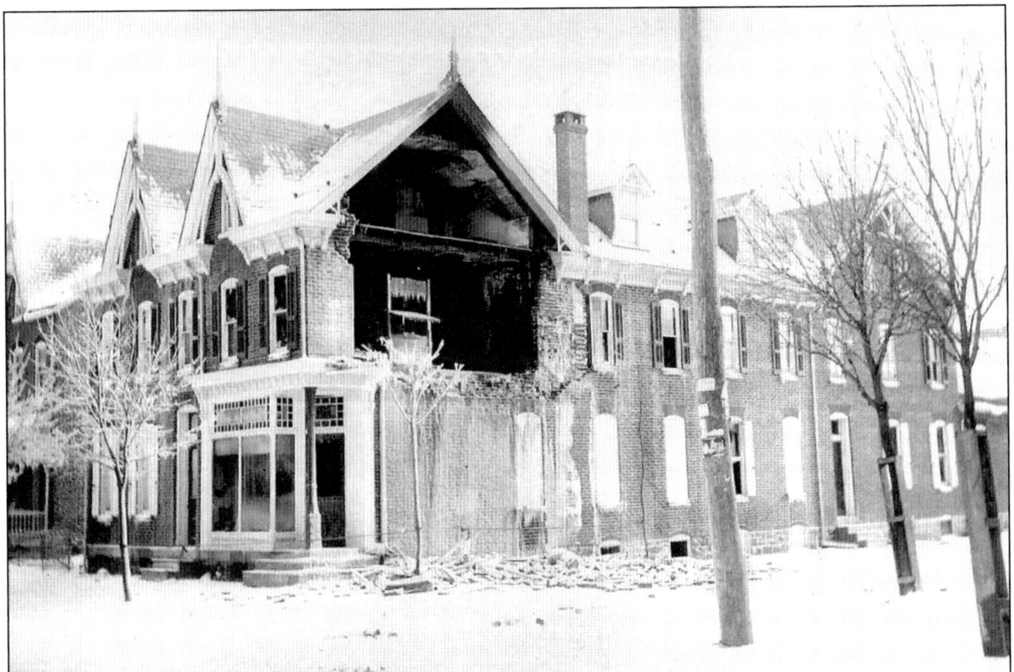

Fire completely destroyed the Carver Bakery facility, seen here.

The Gilbertsville trolley is seen here in 1908. Called the "Queen of the Valley," the trolley operated from 1908 to 1929 between Pottstown and Boyertown, through Gilbertsville. In 1908, the trolley carried persons injured in the Rhodes Opera House fire to the Homeopathic Hospital in Pottstown.

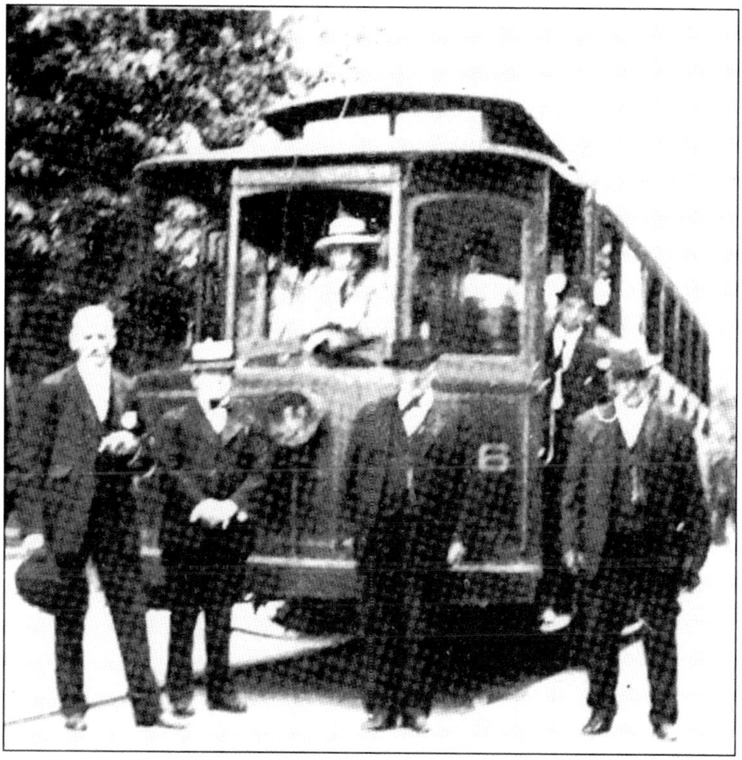

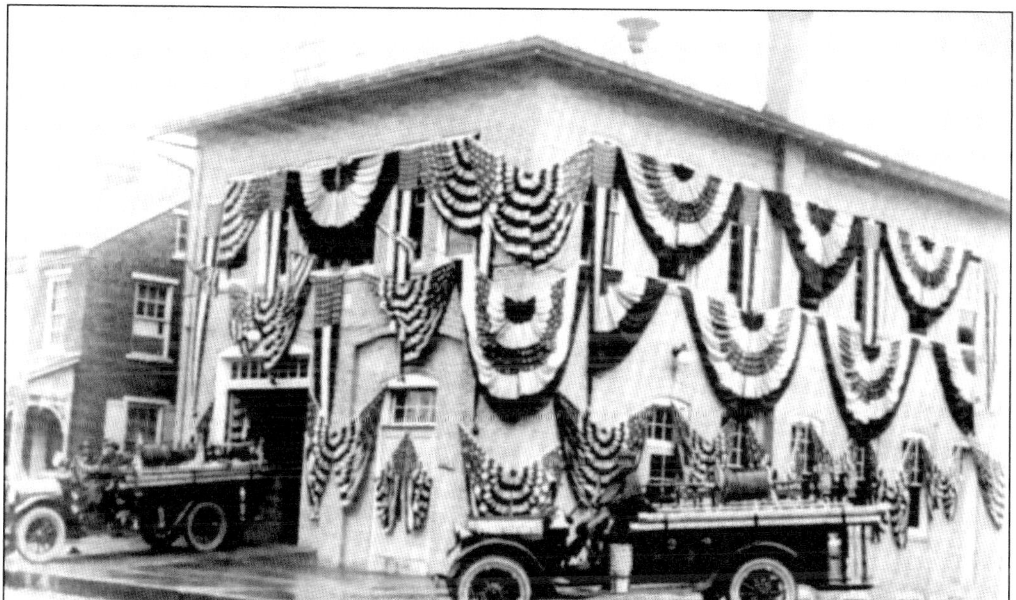

The dedication of the first fire hall of the Gilbertsville Fire Company was held in 1910. The driver of the engine on the right was Harry Steltz. In 1927, an addition was made to the rear of the building, which also underwent extensive alterations in 1940.

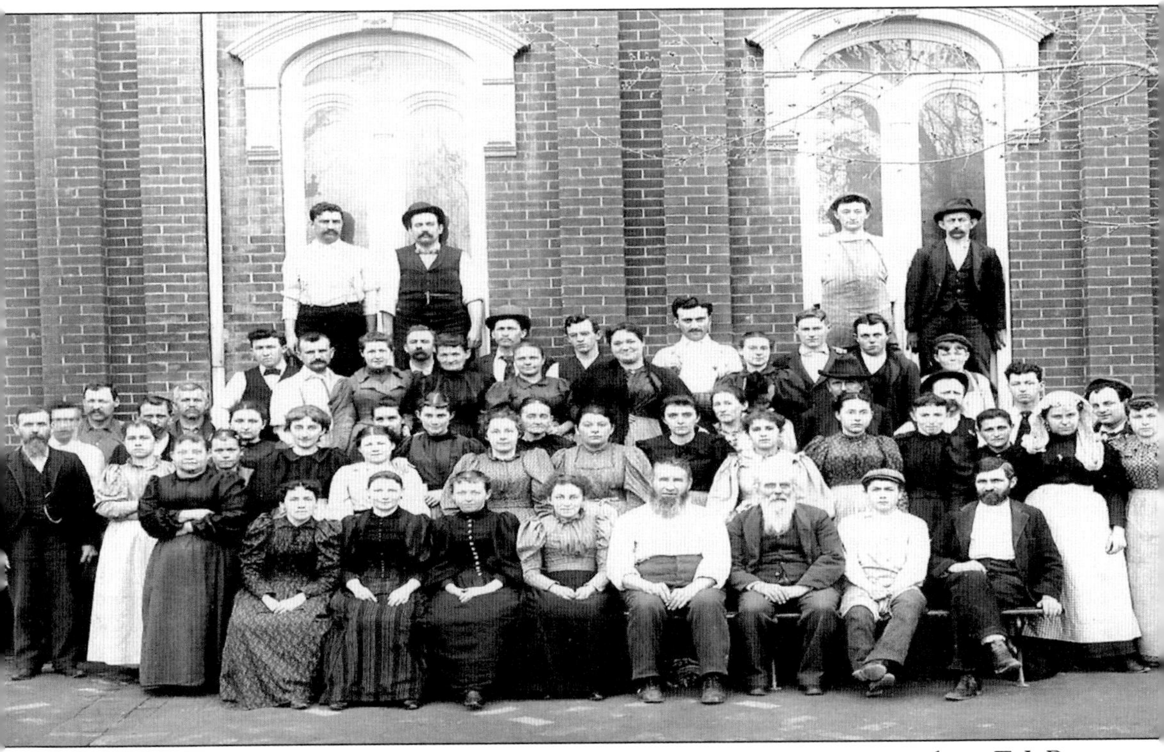

Workers at the cigar factory on South Franklin Street in Boyertown are seen here. T. J. Dunn and Company moved its cigar making operations to South Franklin Street after moving from its first building at Fifth and Walnut Streets. Later the Hayman's Cigar Company moved into the South Franklin Street building. It was in turn succeeded by Eisenlohr's. The cigar industry was a flourishing industry at one time. The town was dotted with "buckeyes," which were little one-man operations conducted in homes or in conjunction with cigar stores.

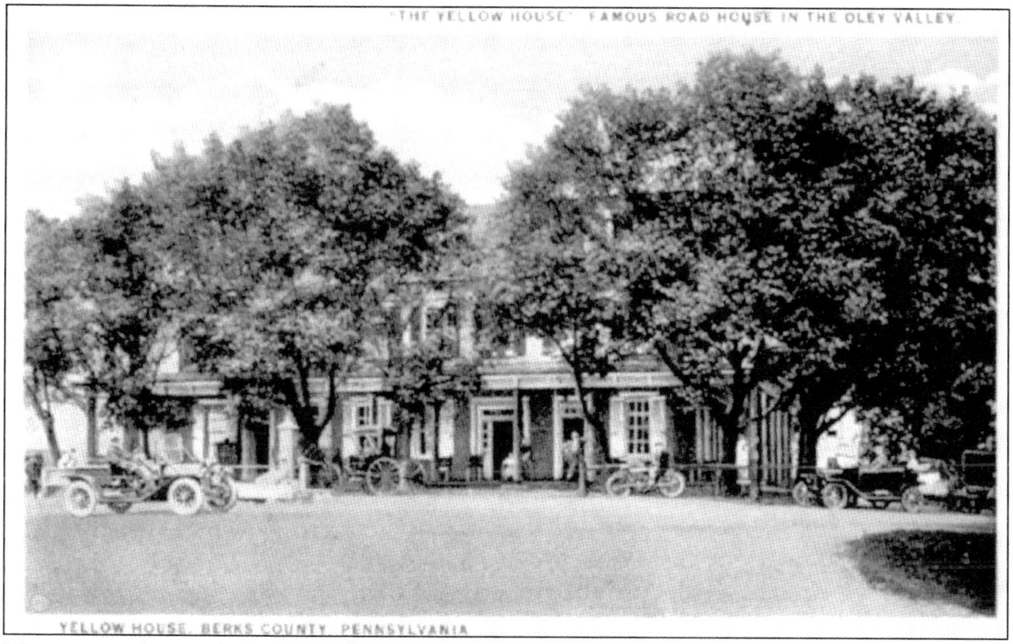

This postcard view shows the Yellow House Hotel.

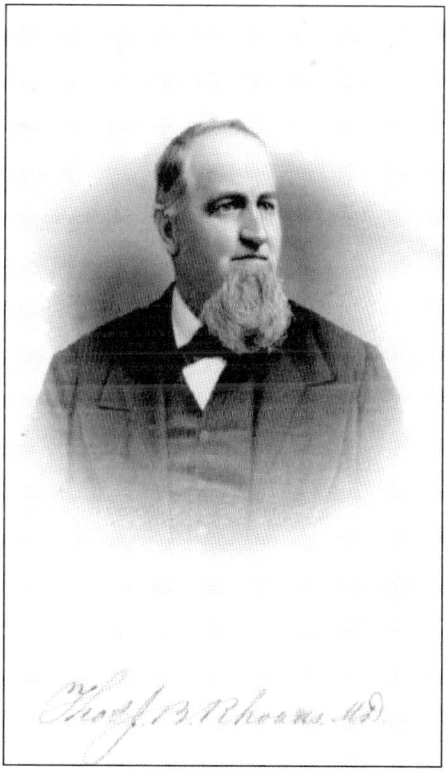

Dr. Thomas Rhoads of Boyertown is shown here. He was the owner of the Rhoads Opera House and was among the Boyertown residents who perished in the 1907 fire.

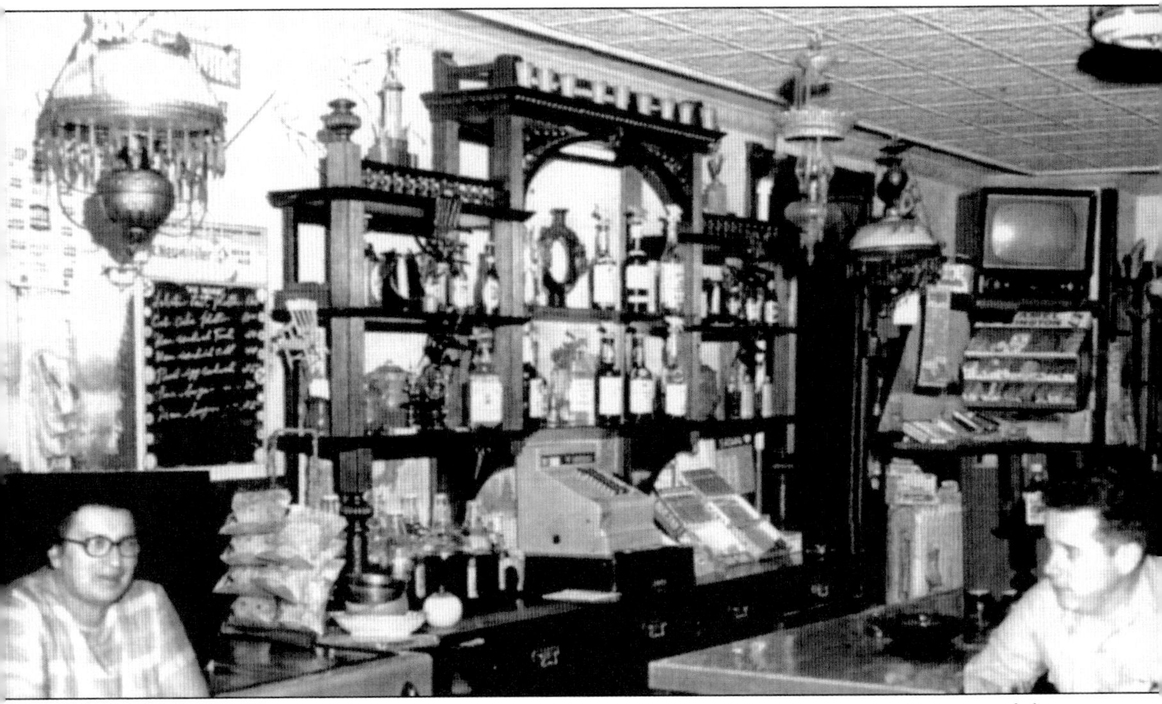

This is the interior of the barroom where Alma and Russell Stahl are seen. Women of the area were known as excellent Pennsylvania Dutch cooks, and Alma was no exception. She would serve foods such as pig stomach, which is filled with smoked sausage and potatoes, and she would bread and fry mushrooms, found locally, drenched with butter and serve them as a sandwich. Homemade soups and barbeque sandwiches, along with oyster sandwiches, were also favorites.

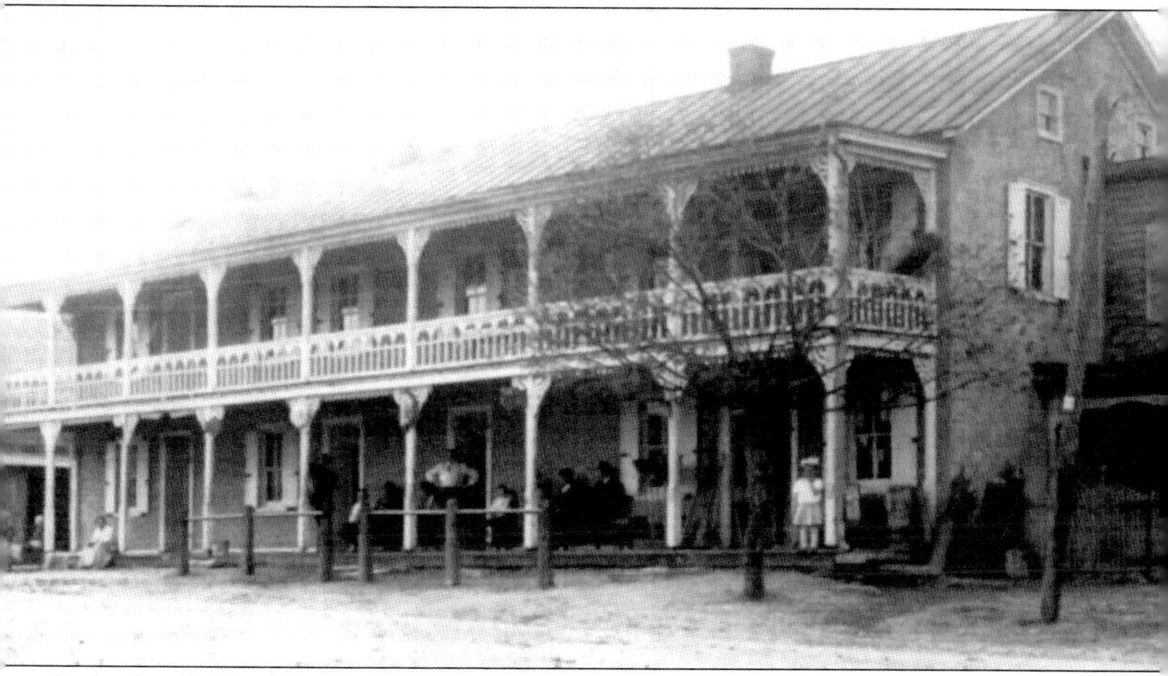

Fredericksville Hotel is shown here around the early 1900s. Friendships were made while spending time on the weekends at various local taverns, and the Fredericksville Hotel was no exception. The author remembers visiting the hotel as a youngster with family, when one heard the Pennsylvania Dutch or Pennsylvania German dialect spoken, which was typical of the time. Growing up in the area, children learned how to understand the dialect; however, many parents insisted the children learn proper English. It is sad that the Pennsylvania German language is swiftly fading with time.

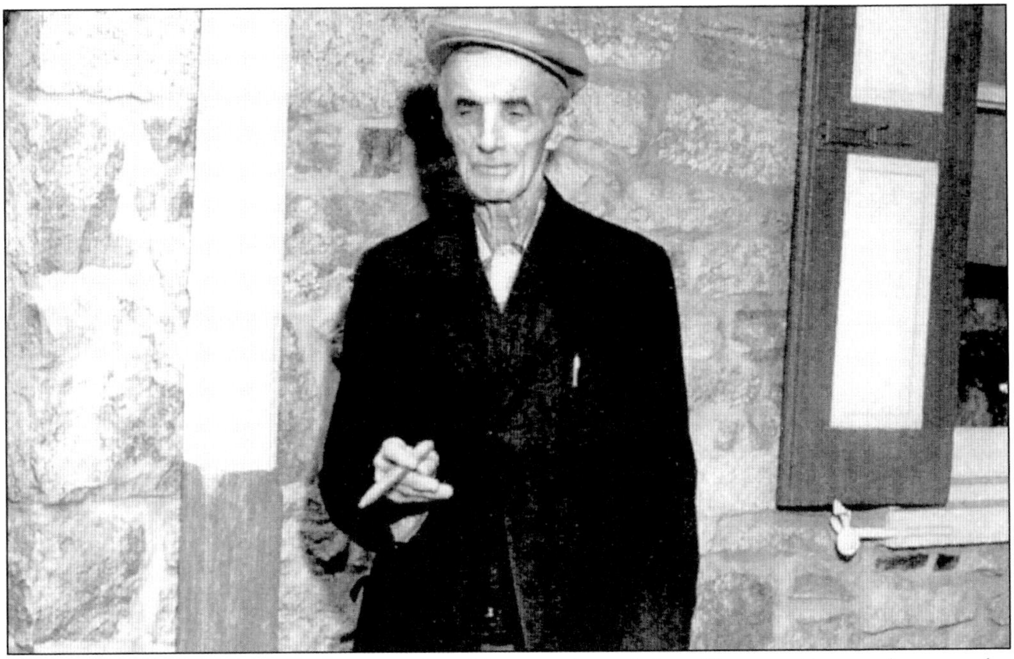

Allie Dey, a regular at the tavern, was the oldest resident of the village and is seen here on the front porch of the tavern at the Seisoltzville Hotel. Alma Stahl would purchase all her meats from the local butcher, Willis Shupp, who lived just a short way from Alma's father's farm in Bally up Crow Hill, and Allie loved to accompany Alma on her trips.

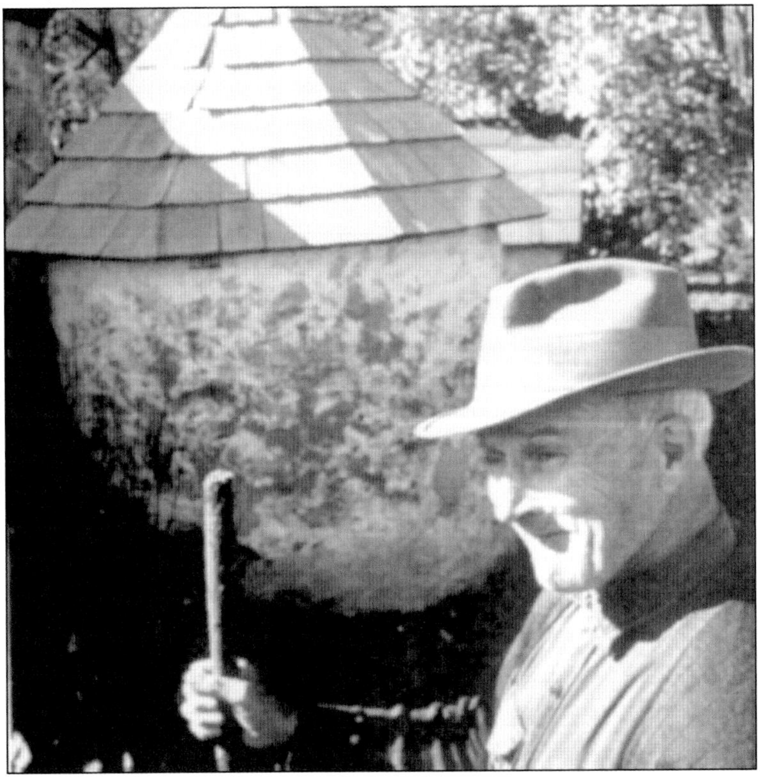

Charlie Dey lives a short distance from the Frederickville Hotel, and he is seen here along the road in front of an ancient, circular smokehouse. The Dey family was comprised of three brothers, Allie, Uni, and Charlie. The author did not know these men; however, Allie's grandson, Carl, was employed for many years at Bally Case and Cooler. So the Dey family goes on, along with the decedents of the Isaac Stahl family, as shown in a family picture included in this book.

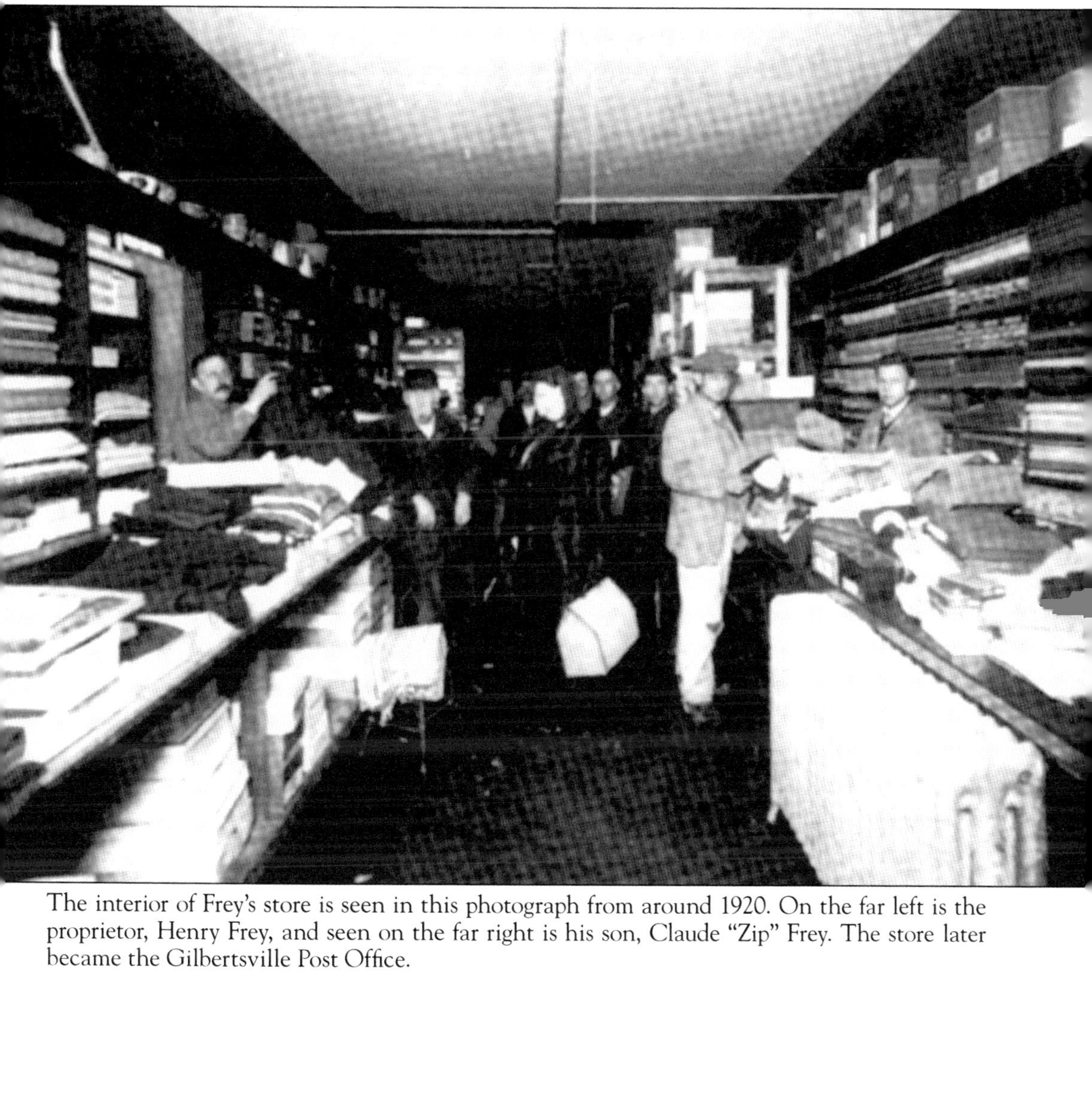

The interior of Frey's store is seen in this photograph from around 1920. On the far left is the proprietor, Henry Frey, and seen on the far right is his son, Claude "Zip" Frey. The store later became the Gilbertsville Post Office.

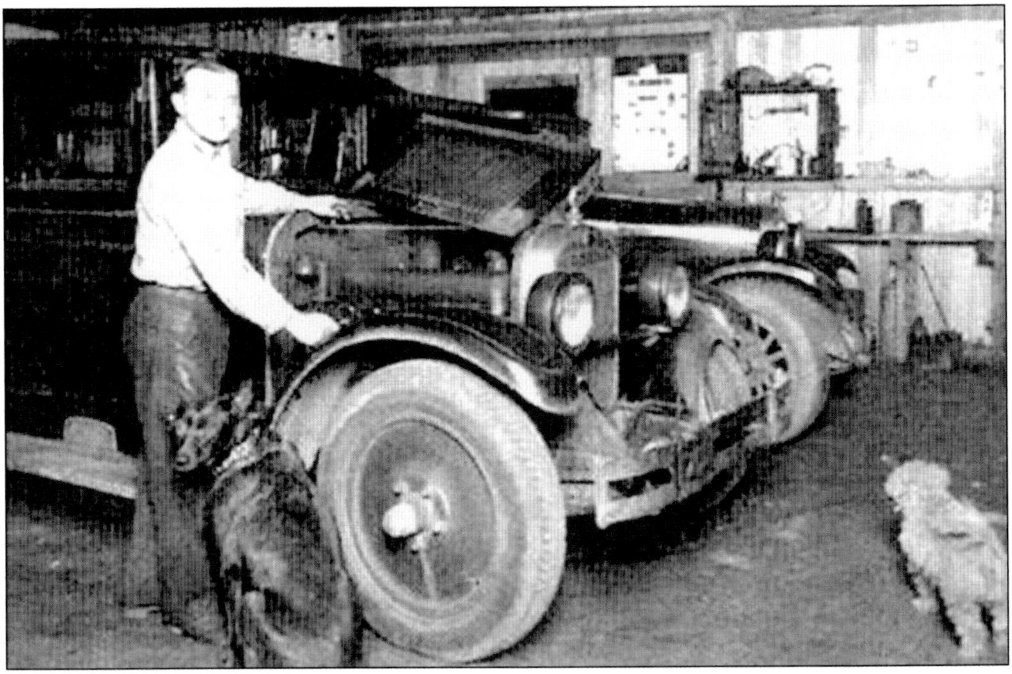

Jake Krupp operated the Clayton Garage, which was the local source for repairs. The garage was originally built by Henry Schultz, a local resident. Prior to Krupp's ownership, Anderson cars were first sold at this site by Schultz, who happened to be the brother-in-law of Joe Quigley of Bally, co-owner with his brother, William, of the first Ford sales named Quigley Ford on Main Street.

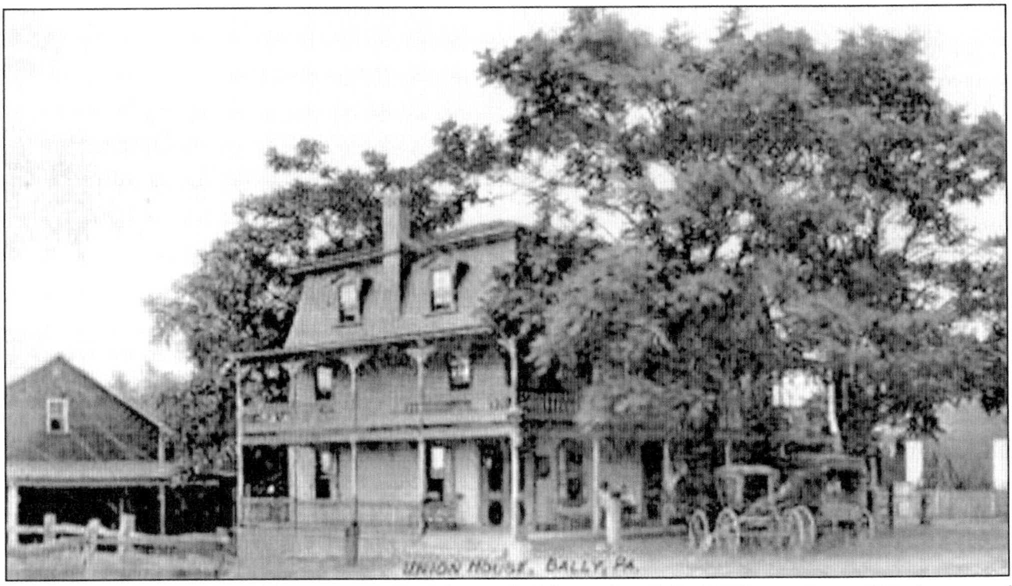

The first meeting of Bally's town council was held on April 3, 1913, in the public house of Horace Quigley on Main Street. Hall rental cost 50¢ per meeting. Five mills was the first tax levy passed in 1914, which was collected from homes by the tax collector, Henry Leh. Henry Eddinger was the chief burgess, appointed in June 1913, Horace Quigley was treasurer, and John Gehringer was president.

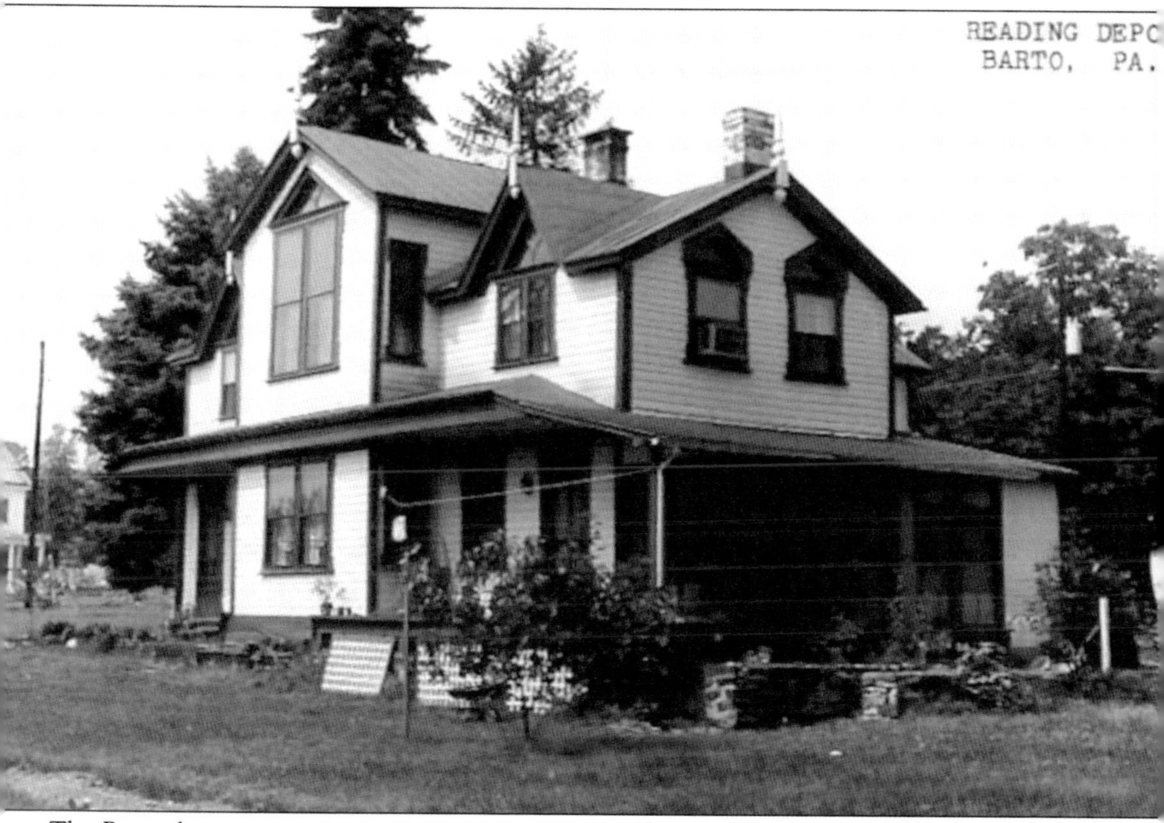

The Barto depot was an impressive structure, and local residents relied heavily on using the train services from Barto.

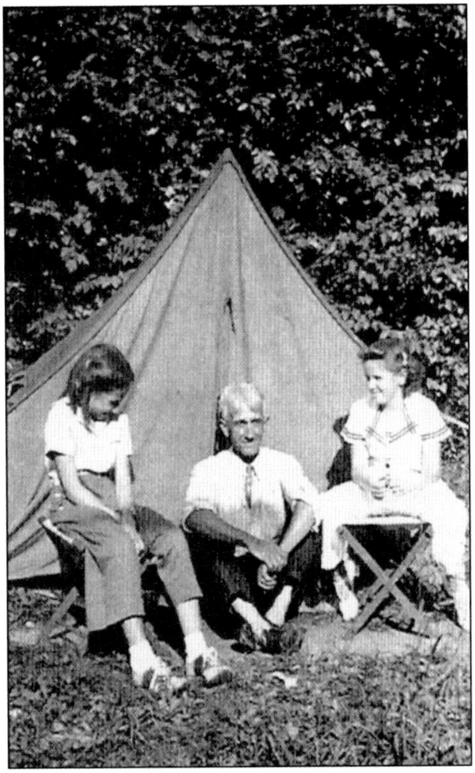

Two local Camp Fire girls, Janet Bechtel (left) and Miriam Smith (née Kulp), enjoy their campouts at Larkland and the friendship of Ralph Berky. These two girls from Bally, along with the other Camp Fire girls, helped deliver the Bally newsletter to local residents, which was written by local women and Ralph Berky (center) for the World War II servicemen.

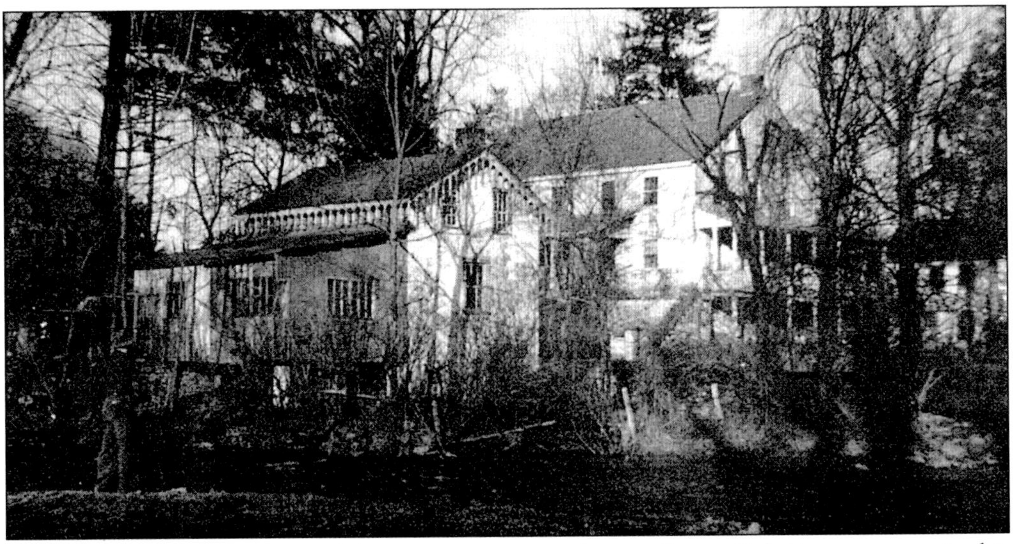

Schall Home and the remains of the company store and post office at Dale Forge are seen in this photograph from around 1955. This was the home of Capt. William A. Schall. He was captain of Company G, 167th Pennsylvania Regiment, and was mustered in for nine months of service on October 20, 1862. The company of soldiers from Washington Township included 24 Catholics who were members of Fr. Augustin Bally's church. Captain Schall saw service at Yorktown, Richmond, and Gettysburg. Discharged in August 1863, he began farming at the Dale Forge farm in 1872. He also had a coal, lumber, and grain business at Barto.

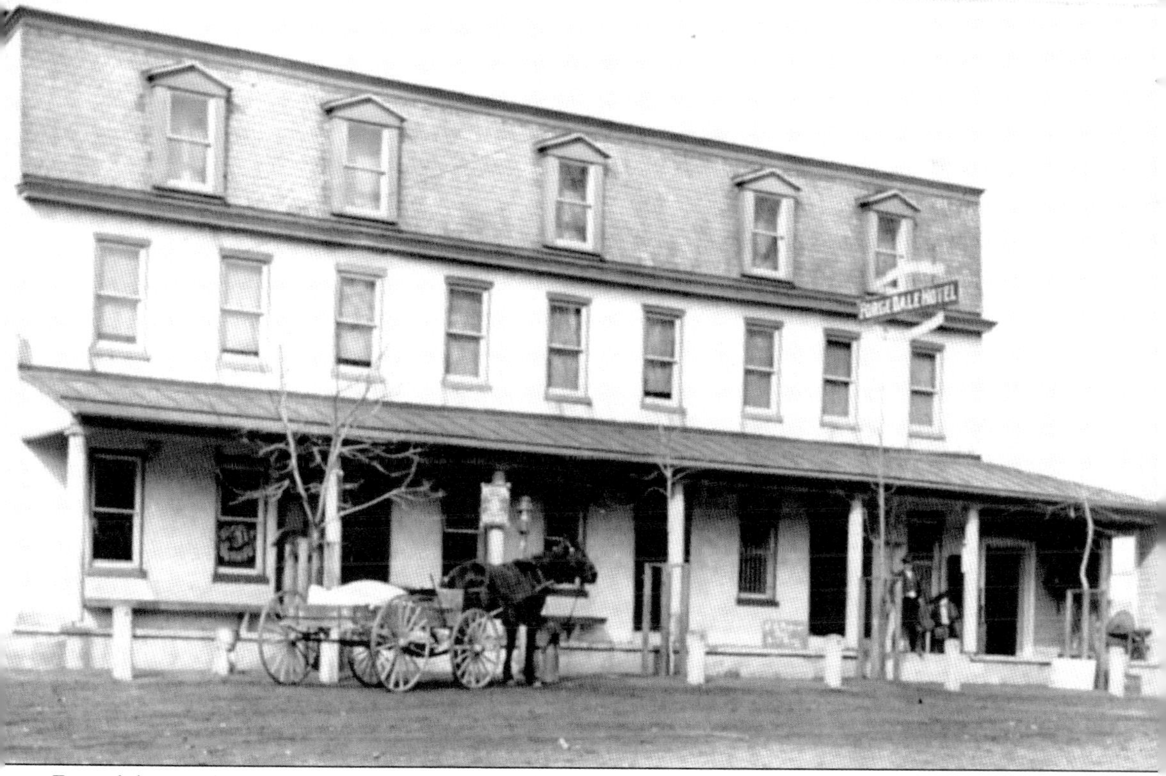

Forgedale Hotel was a popular meeting place. It dates back many years, but the author's memory dates back to the early 1950s when it was owned by George Sanders. It was both a country store and a hotel, each separate areas so women and children could obtain the groceries without having to go into the bar area. Early memories are of buying ice cream called Dixie cups and collecting the lids; when one lifted off the lid and looked underneath, there were photographs of cowboy actors such as Gene Autry, Roy Rogers, and others.

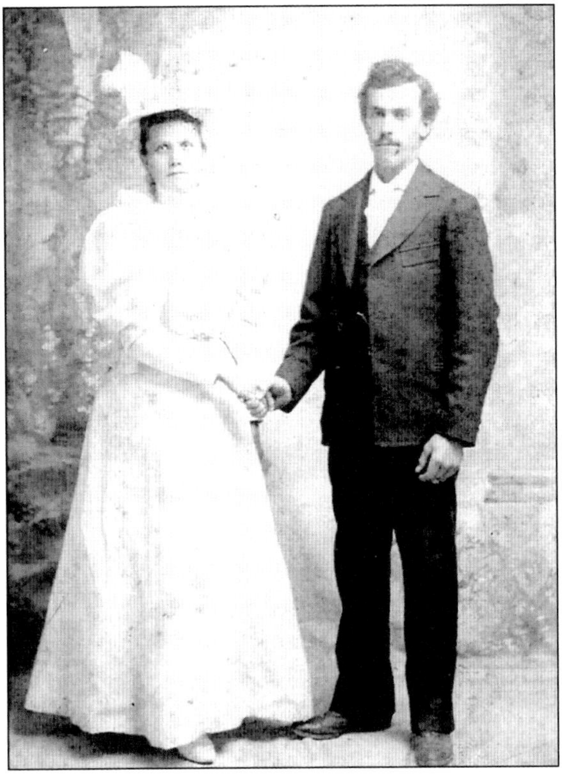

This wedding photograph from the late 19th century is of Henry and Elizabeth Bauman from Washington Township. The couple later resided in Bally, and they were the great-grandparents of the author. Their children were Helen Fox (née Bauman), Harvey Bauman, Rachel Miller (née Bauman), George Bauman, and several others who died at an early age.

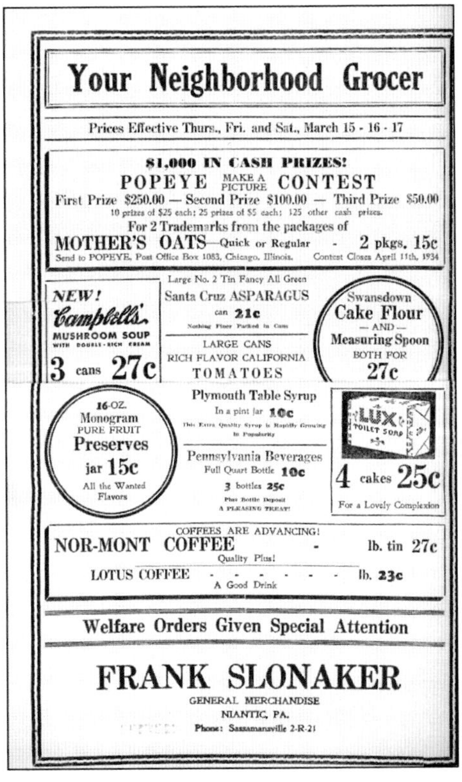

Your Neighborhood Grocer

Prices Effective Thurs., Fri. and Sat., March 15 - 16 - 17

$1,000 IN CASH PRIZES!
POPEYE MAKE A PICTURE CONTEST
First Prize $250.00 — Second Prize $100.00 — Third Prize $50.00
10 prizes of $25 each; 25 prizes of $5 each; 125 other cash prizes.
For 2 Trademarks from the packages of
MOTHER'S OATS—Quick or Regular - 2 pkgs. 15c
Send to POPEYE, Post Office Box 1083, Chicago, Illinois. Contest Closes April 11th, 1934

NEW! Campbell's MUSHROOM SOUP WITH DOUBLE-RICH CREAM
3 cans 27c

Large No. 2 Tin Fancy All Green
Santa Cruz ASPARAGUS
can 21c
Nothing Finer Packed in Cans

LARGE CANS
RICH FLAVOR CALIFORNIA
TOMATOES

Swansdown Cake Flour — AND — Measuring Spoon
BOTH FOR 27c

16-OZ. Monogram PURE FRUIT Preserves
jar 15c
All the Wanted Flavors

Plymouth Table Syrup
In a pint jar 10c
This Extra Quality Syrup is Rapidly Growing in Popularity

Pennsylvania Beverages
Full Quart Bottle 10c
3 bottles 25c
Plus Bottle Deposit
A PLEASING TREAT!

LUX TOILET SOAP
4 cakes 25c
For a Lovely Complexion

COFFEES ARE ADVANCING!
NOR-MONT COFFEE - lb. tin 27c
Quality Plus!
LOTUS COFFEE - - - - - - lb. 23c
A Good Drink

Welfare Orders Given Special Attention

FRANK SLONAKER
GENERAL MERCHANDISE
NIANTIC, PA.
Phone: Sassamansville 2-R-21

This sales flyer is from the Niantic store when the proprietor was Frank Slonaker. The prices are very attractive now, but back in that era, pennies relate to current-day dollars.

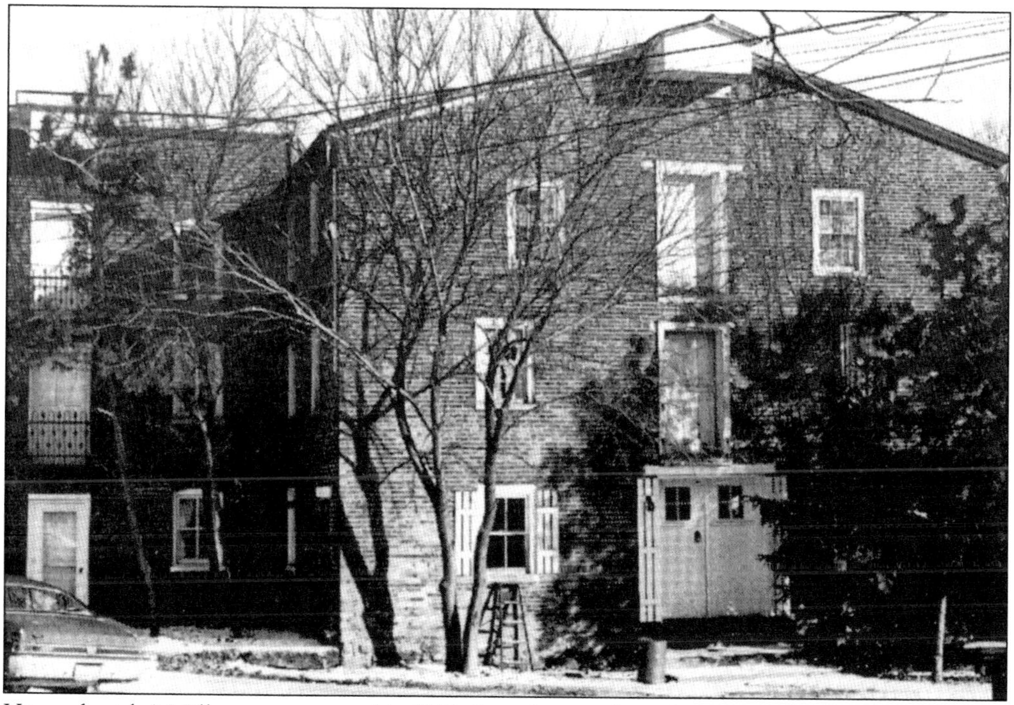

Himmelwright's Mill was constructed in 1840 along the west branch of the Perkiomen. This mill was formerly the focal point for farmers in the Niantic area and was located on Himmelwright Road.

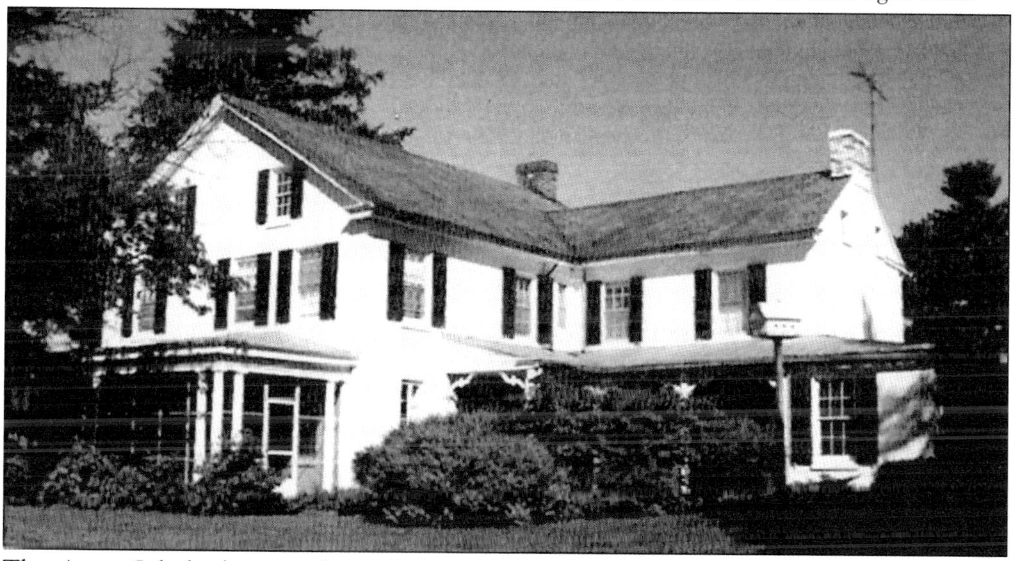

The Amos Schultz home is located along Niantic Road. Amos Schultz (1809–1895) was a builder, farmer, and investor. At age 24, Schultz moved to the Niantic area to live with his uncle, Joseph Schultz. He was born and raised a Schwenkfelder and was one of the first to advocate the publication and give support to the Corpus Schwenkfeldianorum. For many years, he served as a justice of the peace, being one of the first to receive his commission under the new constitution of 1838. In politics, he was a Whig and, subsequently, a Republican. The career of Amos Schultz is a notable example of the result of preservation, industry, and rigid adherence to high principles. In all Amos's ventures and years of community services, he was loyally supported by his wife.

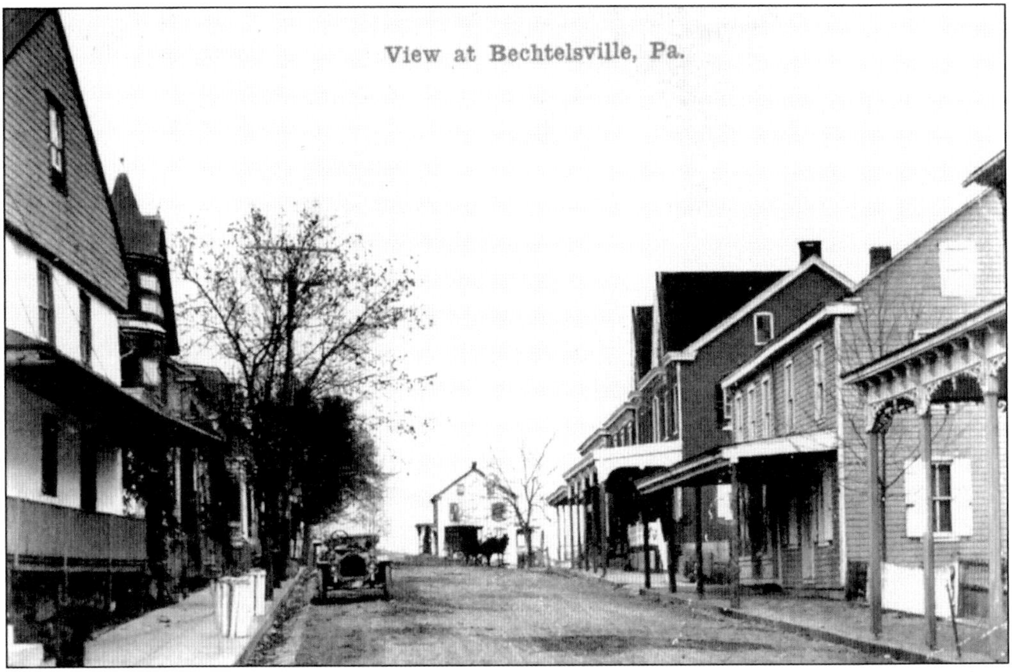

This is a postcard view from the early 1900s, traveling through Bechtelsville toward Eshbach.

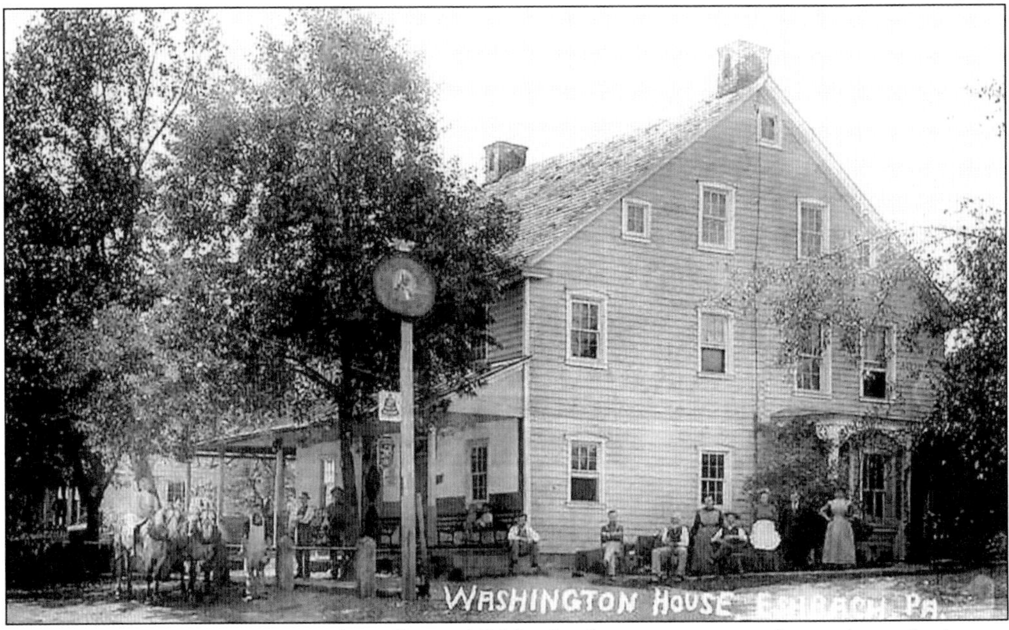

Along old Route 100, entering the village of Eshbach, this vintage view shows the early days at the Washington House, yet another meeting place for local residents. Establishments such as this were the places where neighbors could get together, enjoy a delicious Pennsylvania Dutch meal, play cards, and just talk about what was happening in the area. The building still stands and has had many owners since this early photograph.

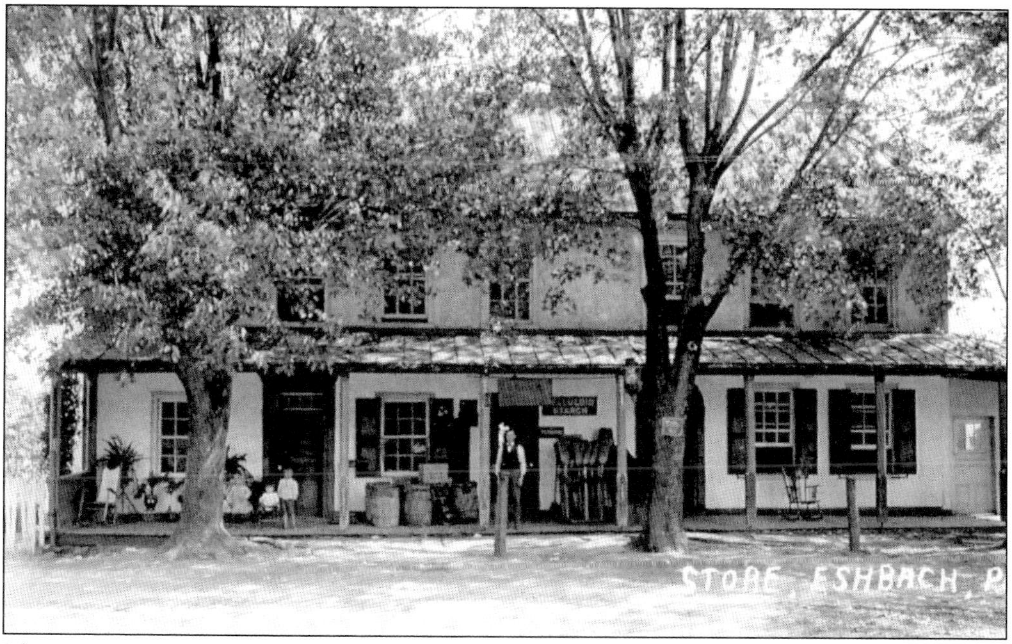

The general store was located directly across the street from the Washington House in Eshbach. Throughout the years, it has served as the store, post office, a floral store, and a carpet store. The town of Eshbach was actually known as Eshbach Crossing in Washington Township.

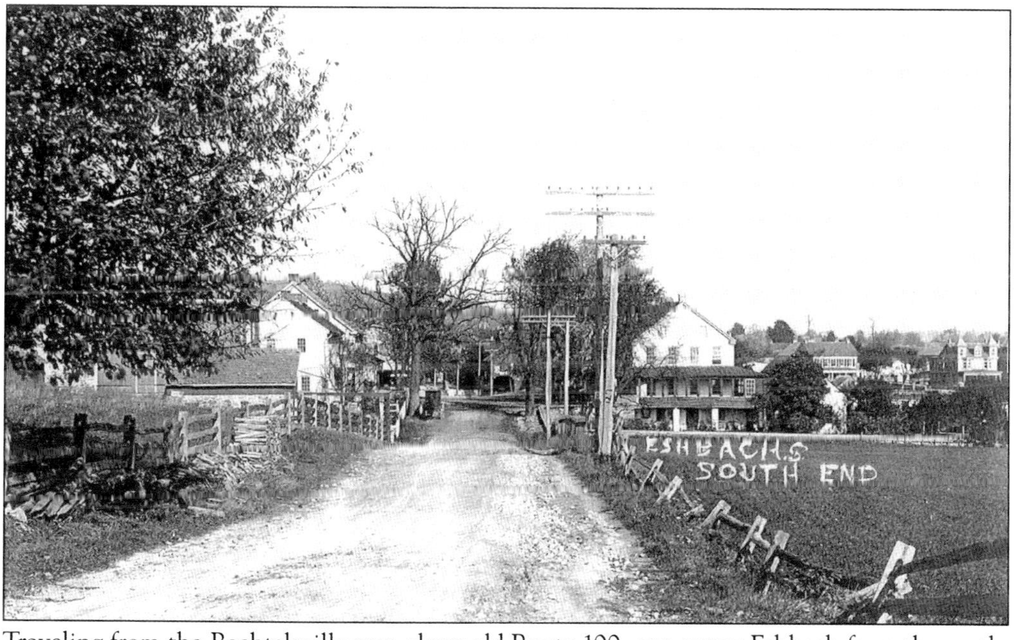

Traveling from the Bechtelsville area along old Route 100, one enters Eshbach from the south. The Washington House would have been on the left and the general store on the right. Just a stone's throw from the establishments, one crossed over a little bridge at the curve in the road. Continuing on this road, one would then enter Barto.

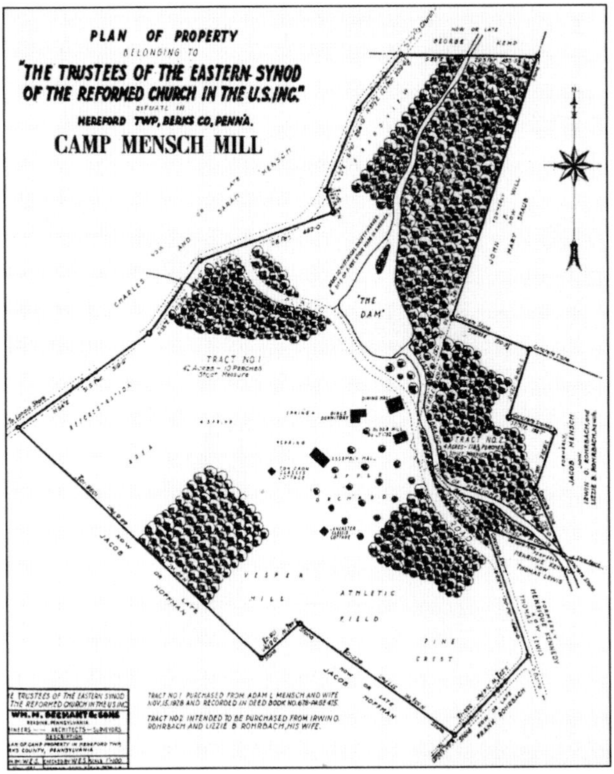

This map shows the proposed layout of the Camp Mensch Mill.

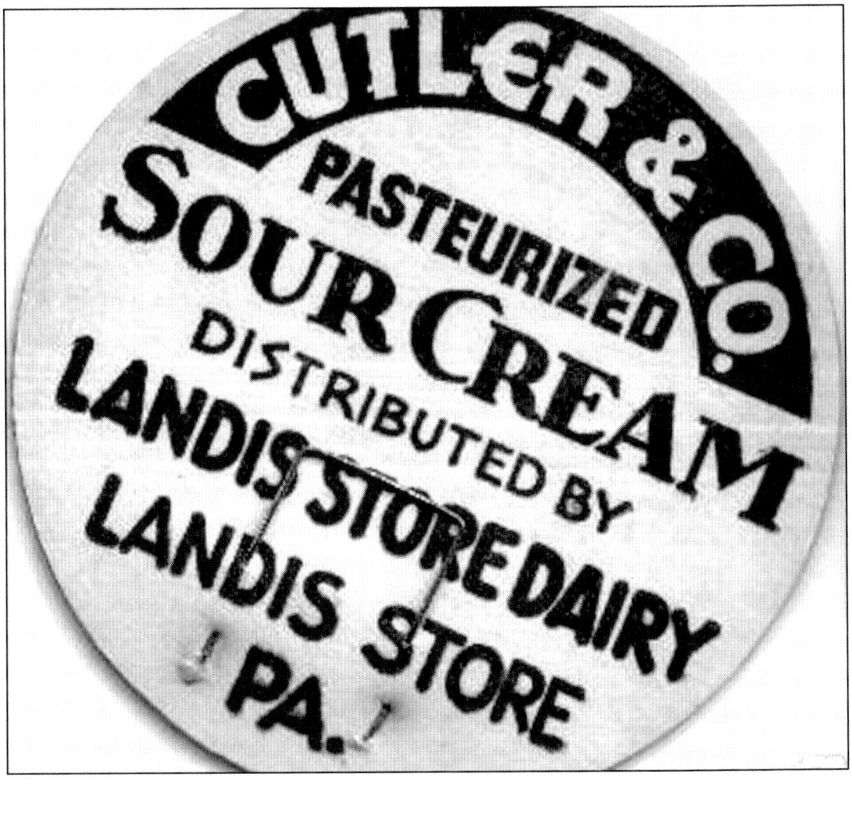

This is the sour cream lid from the Landis Store Dairy.

Mr. and Mrs. Adam L. Mensch, shown here, owned the property where the historic Mensch mill is located. It covers over 43 acres and was the most ideally located site for the church camp, and yet it was readily accessible from many locations. The Camp Mensch Mill dates back to approximately 1925.

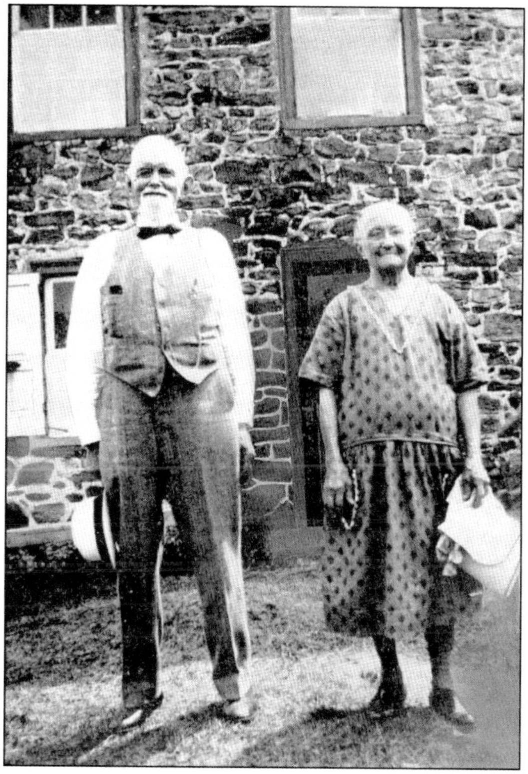

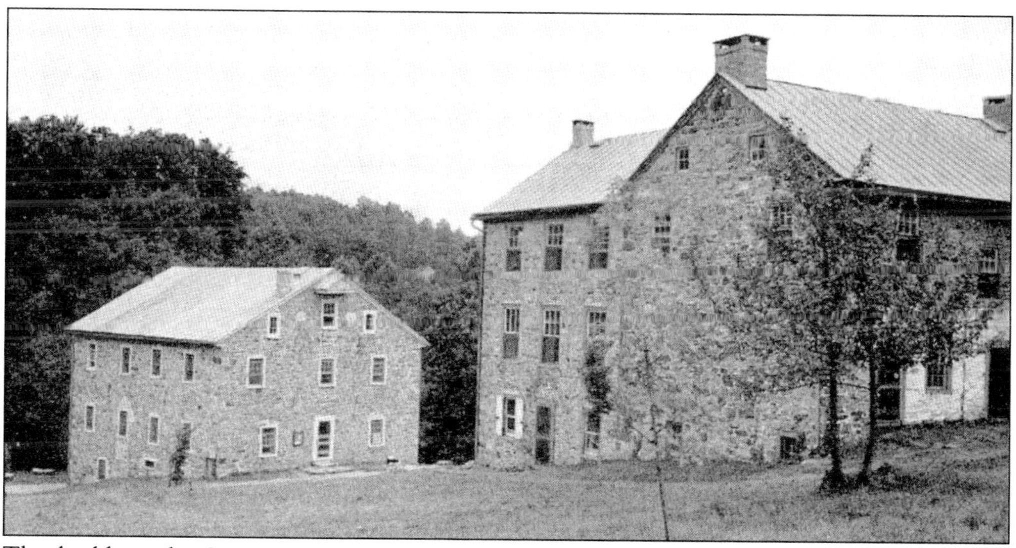

This building, the Camp Mensch Mill, was photographed here in 1933.

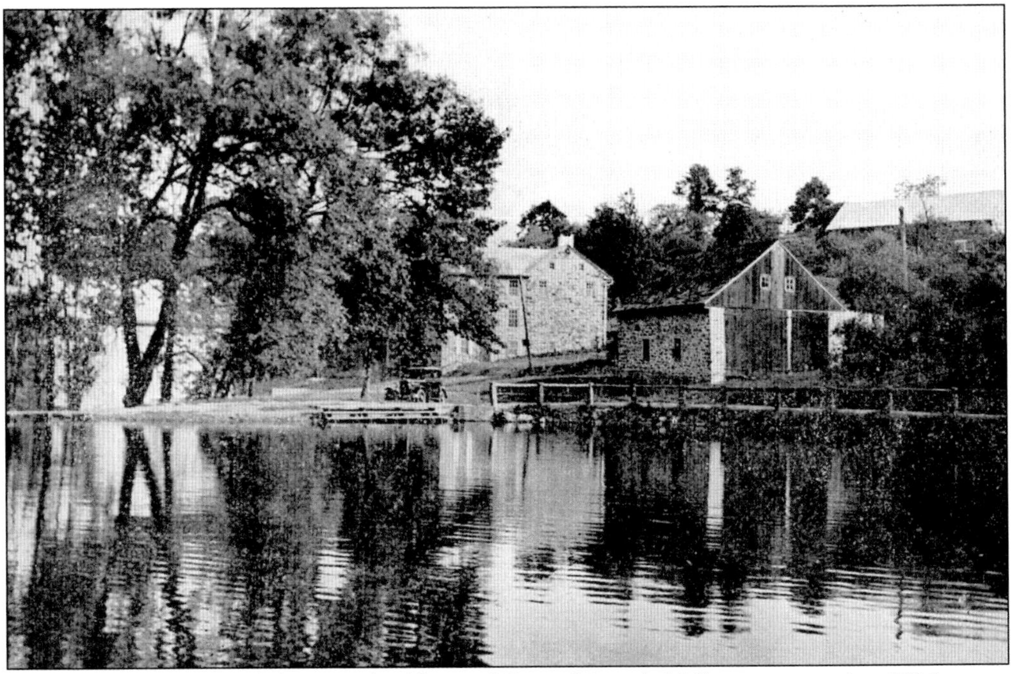

This picturesque view of the main buildings of Camp Mensch Mill was captured in 1936.

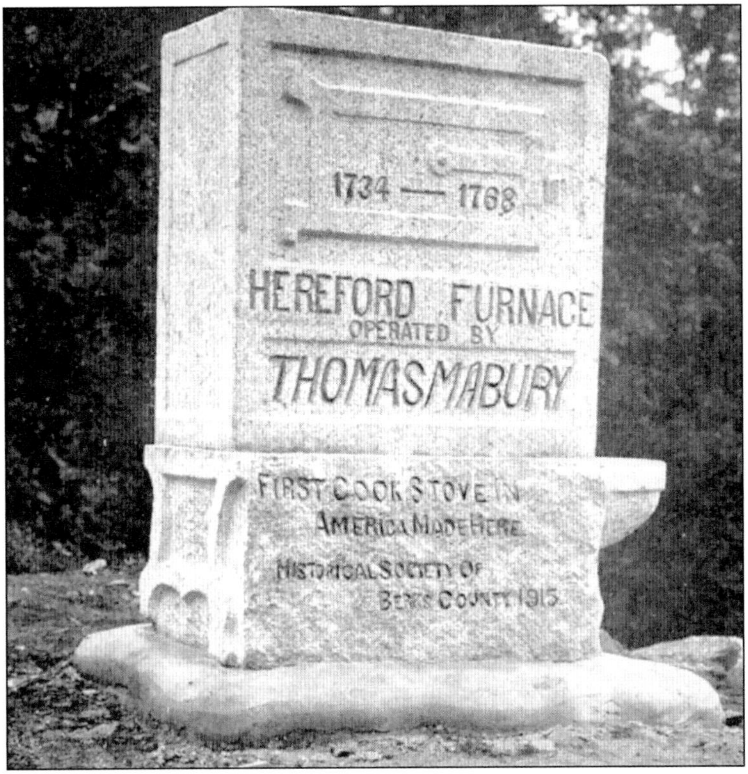

Thomas Maybury's company was known as Hereford Furnace. The walls in the chapel at Camp Mensch Mill were constructed of the same stones used by Maybury in the building of the Hereford Furnace.

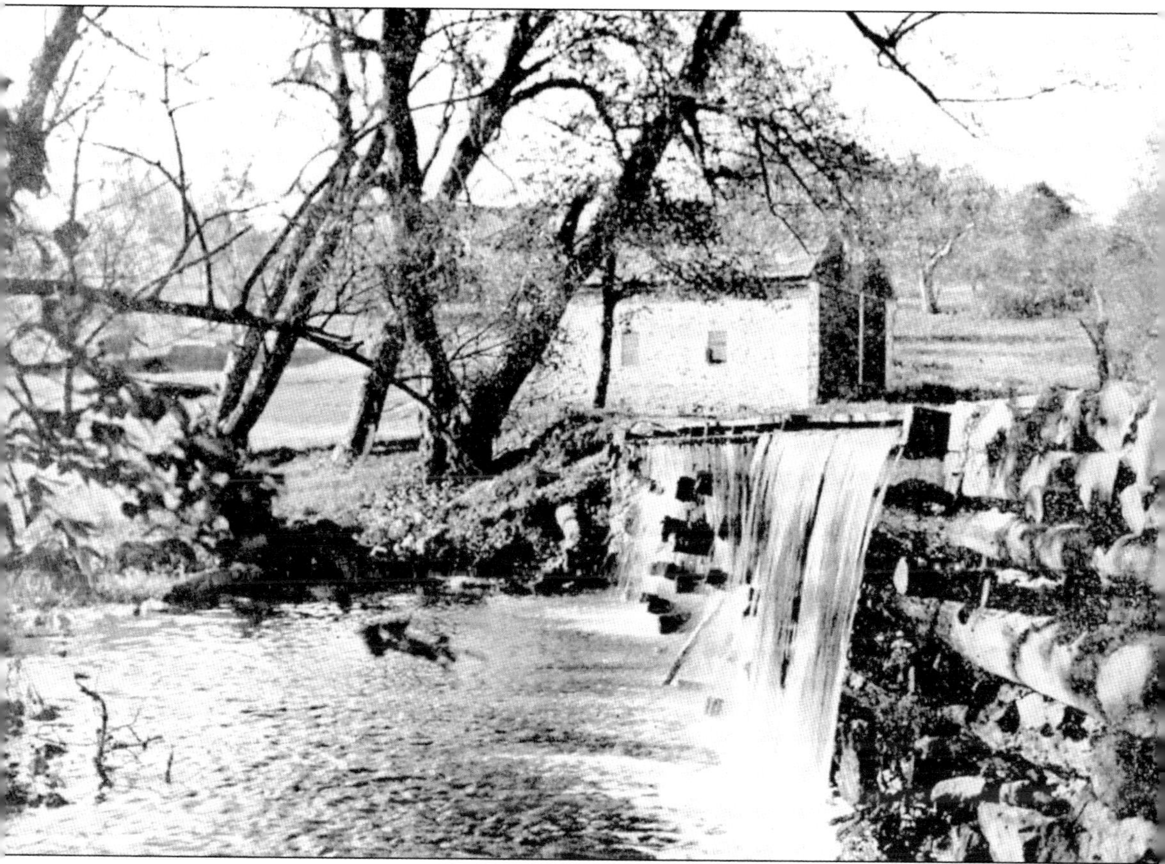
This log breast was replaced by stone in 1940 at Camp Mensch Mill.

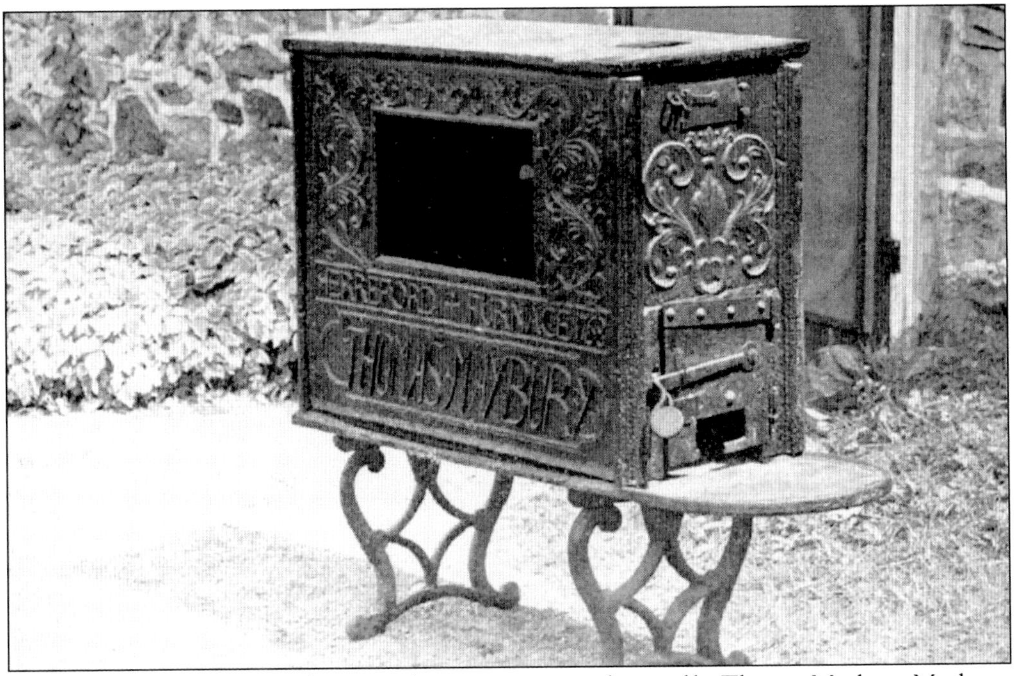

The oldest wood-burning cookstove in America was manufactured by Thomas Maybury. Maybury, his son, and grandson operated a charcoal furnace as early as 1753. During heavy manufacturing times, they employed anywhere from 50 to 100 men, and they were woodchoppers, teamsters, and charcoal burners. Historical records show Maybury was at one time a very rich and generous man, but he died in poverty. Maybury is buried just two miles from Camp Mensch Mill in the woods to the northwest.

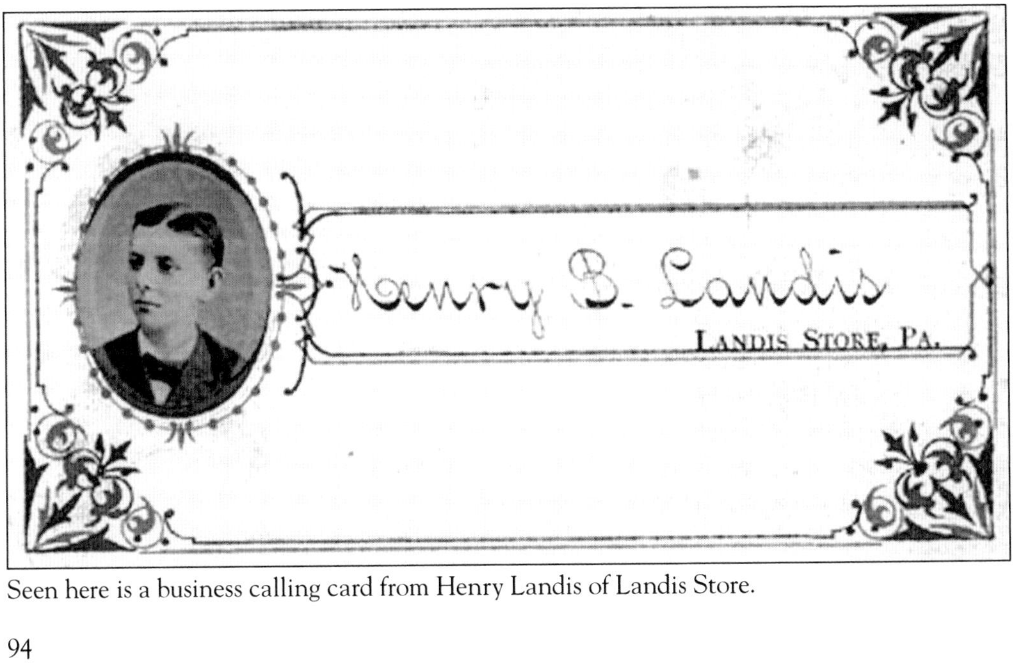

Seen here is a business calling card from Henry Landis of Landis Store.

Five

EDUCATION

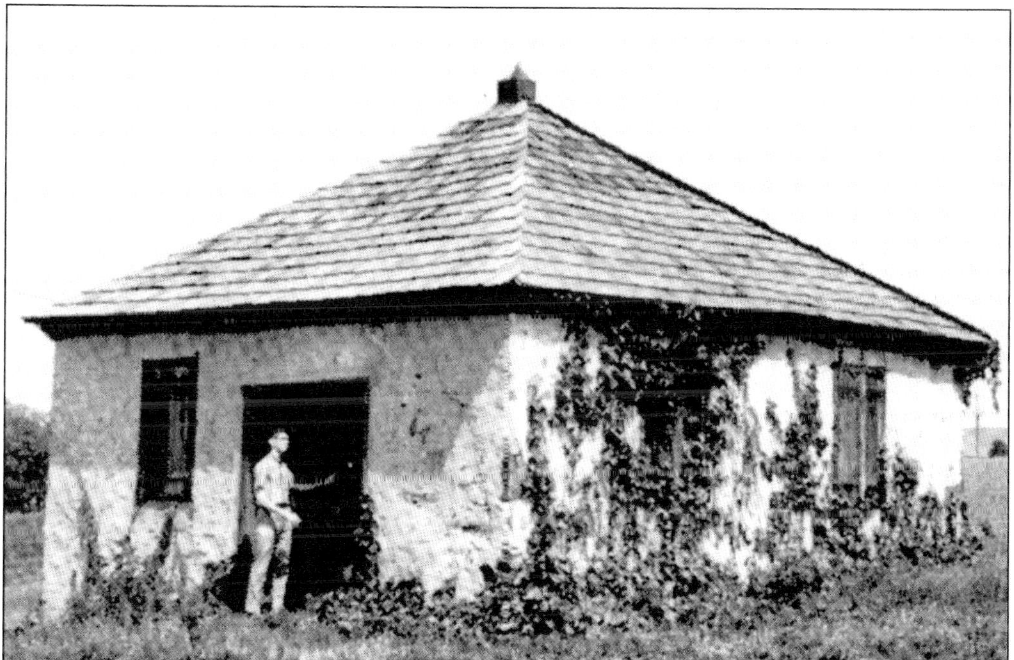

Constructed in 1846, this old schoolhouse is located along Hoffmansville Road, west of Congo. It operated as a private, or "subscription," school before being absorbed into the township school system in 1851.

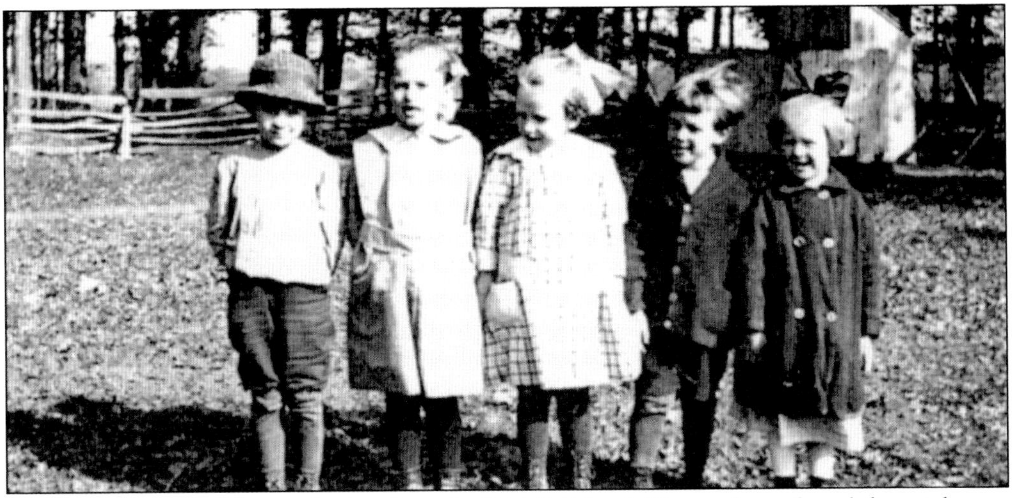

Seen here is the 1920 first-grade class from the Diehl's School. The students, from left to right, are Melvin Gehman, Mary Kriebel, Alverda Fronheiser, Orlando Brand, and Verna Latshaw.

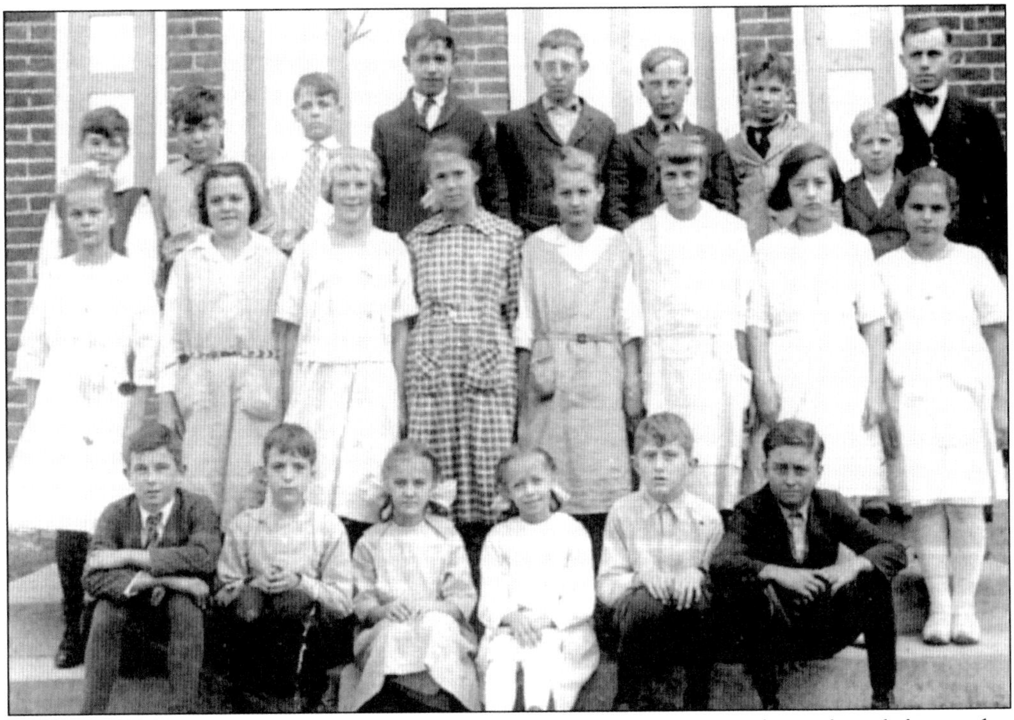

The 1921 class from the Diehl's School pose for a photograph. The students, from left to right, are as follows: (first row) Elwood Bolton, Enos Gehman, Marie Heffentrager, Mary Kulp, Albert Hillegas, and Tony Miller; (second row) Rose Mutter, Lottie Kemp, Helen Clemmer, Elizabeth Kulp, Vena Fox, Beulah Schell, Gertrude Quigley, and Mae Latshaw; (third row) Waldo Brand, Matthew Mengel, Harlan Edge, Austin Ames, Irwin Schantz, unidentified, Earl Kehs, Willie Mickel, and Raymond Leeser (teacher).

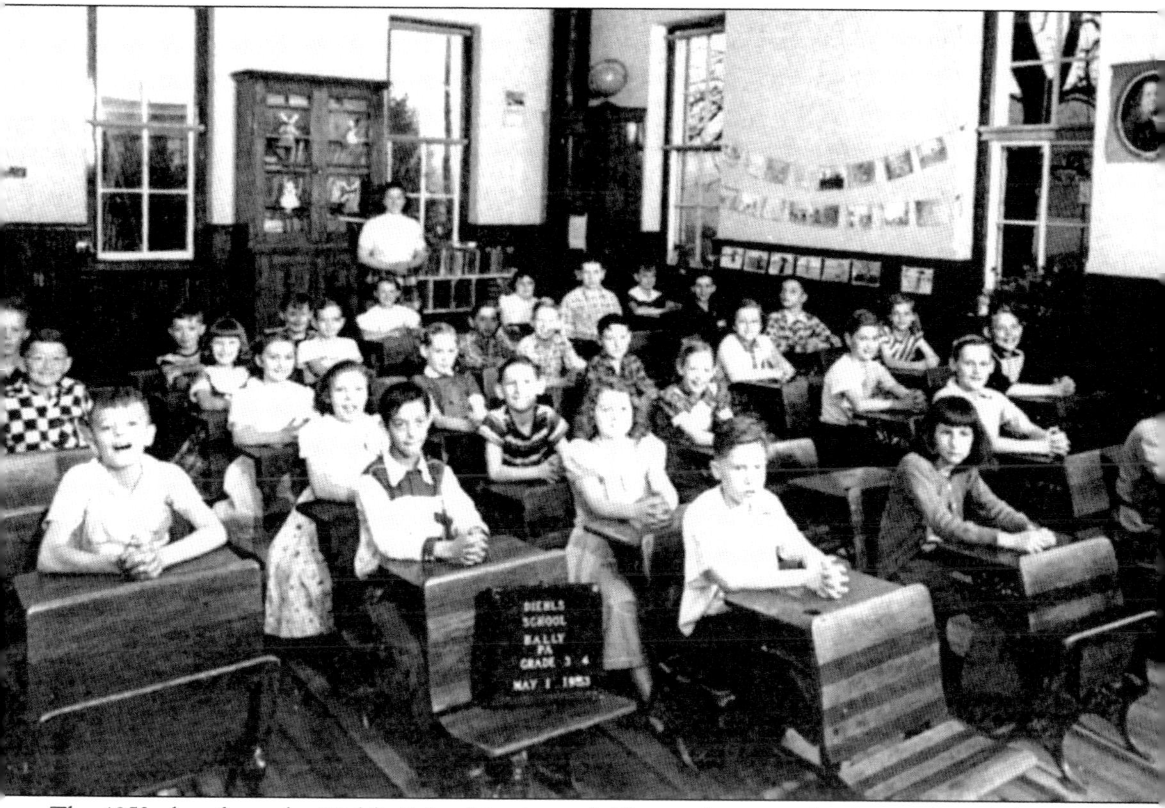

The 1953 class from the Diehl's School is pictured. The students in school rows, from left to right, are as follows: (first row) Gerald Leh, John Ehrst, and Norman Hill; (second row) Herb Bender, Virginia Kemp, Janis Sheetz, Sandy Forsyth, and Carl Eline; (third row) Paul Gerhart, Ruth Moyer, Richard Gehman, Dolores Hoffman, unidentified, and John Strauss; (fourth row) Sylvia Moon, Ada Gehman, Roy Hoffman, Ted Eck, Tom Updegrove, and Cheryl Moll; (fifth row) Marsha Hazlet, George Sibalic, Walton Gehman, Linda Fronheiser, Eugene Yerger, and Kathy Eddinger; (sixth row) John Heffner, unidentified, Fred White, Daniel Nester, and Sandra Glaser; (standing) teacher Violet Frey.

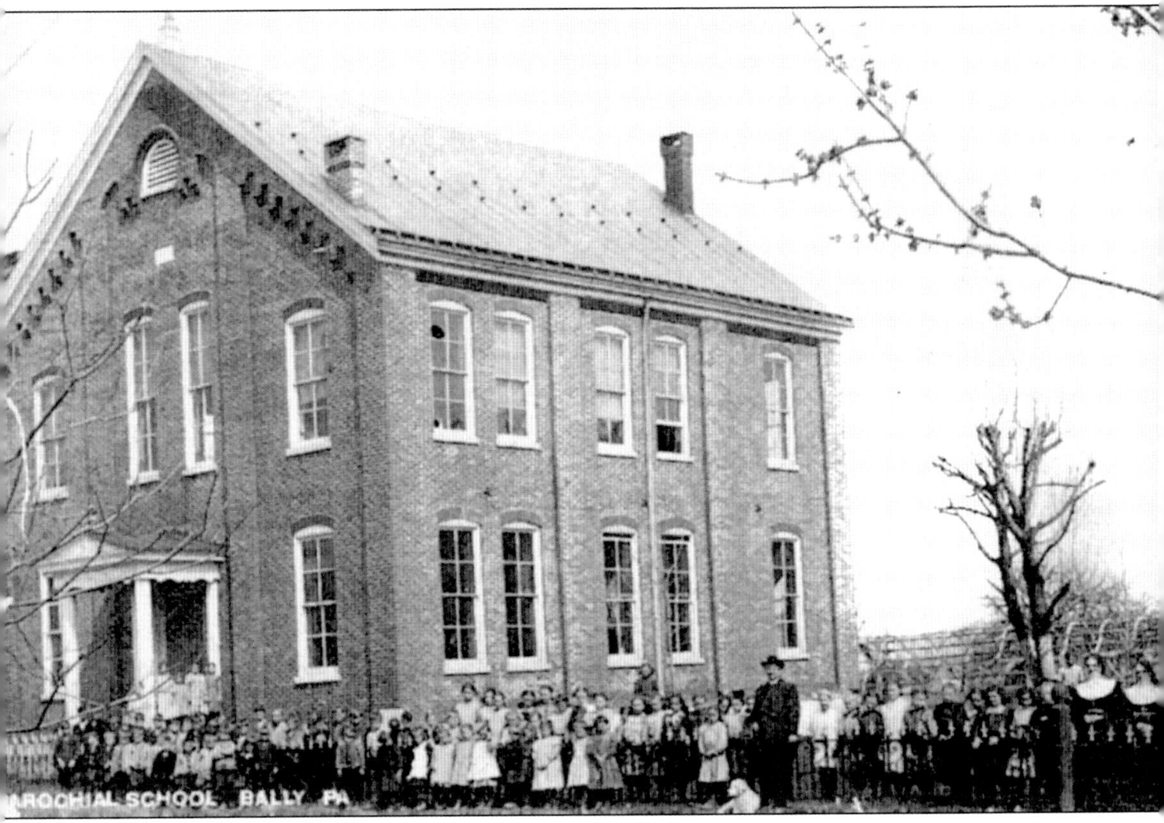

This very early view shows the Catholic school in Bally.

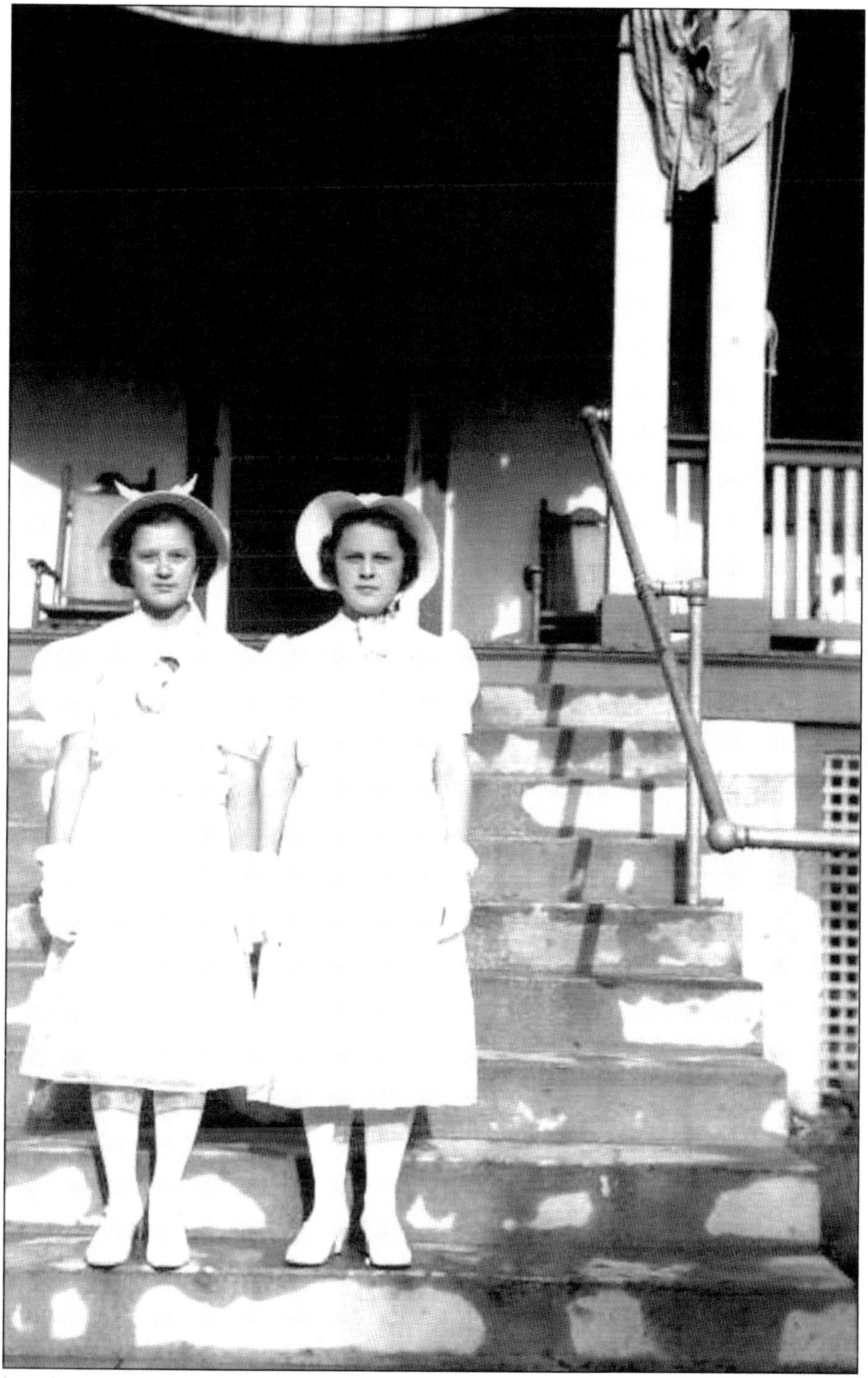

Two friends and classmates, from left to right, Helen Stompf (née Benfield) and Helena Riegner (née Kelsch), in 1937 graduate from Most Blessed Sacrament School in Bally. They attended the freestanding school building between the rectory and the convent, often referred to as "the old school." Stompf is the mother of the author, and Riegner is the mother of Luanne (Riegner) Zambanini.

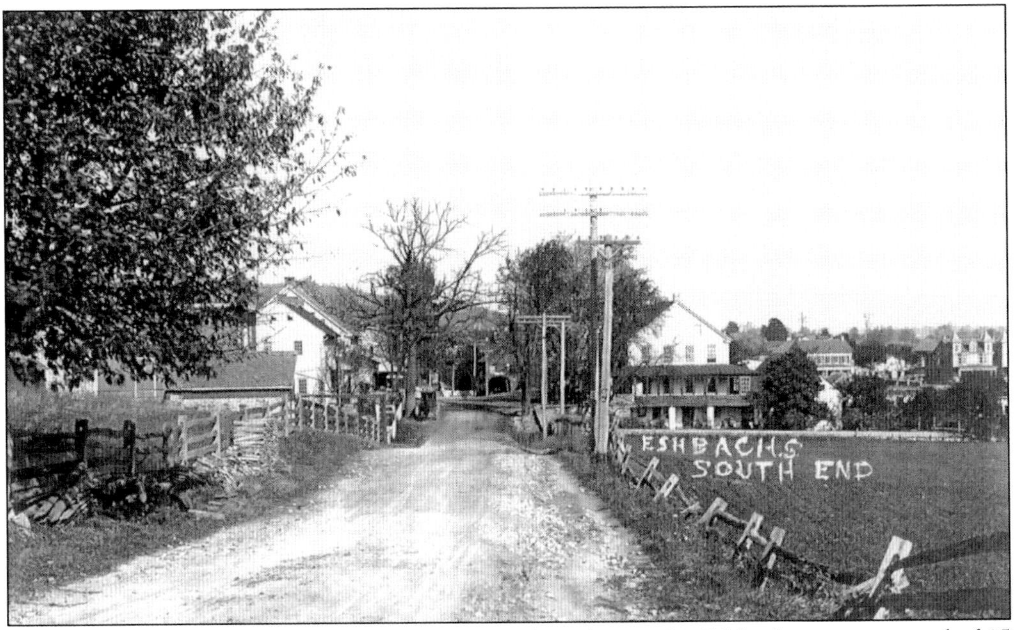

The village of Eshbach is seen here from the south end. In 1858, Eshbach was comprised of 15 homes according to the *History of Berks County* by Morton Montgomery, written in the late 1800s. Throughout the years, Eshbach still remains a small village of homes even though the industries have all left the area, as is the case in the majority of this Berks County area.

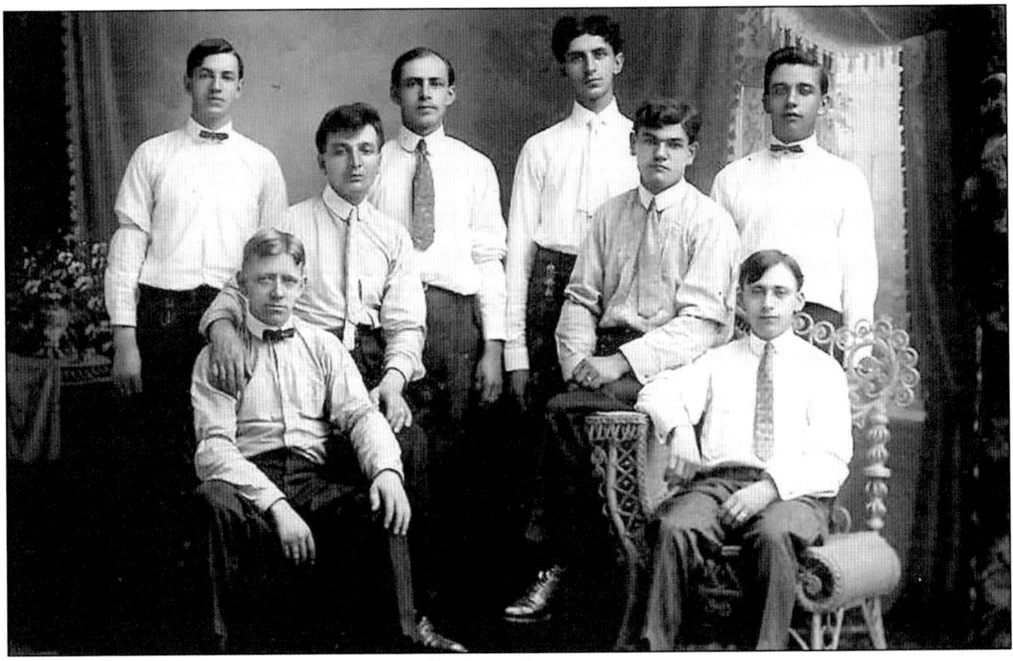

This photograph depicts eight distinguished gentlemen.

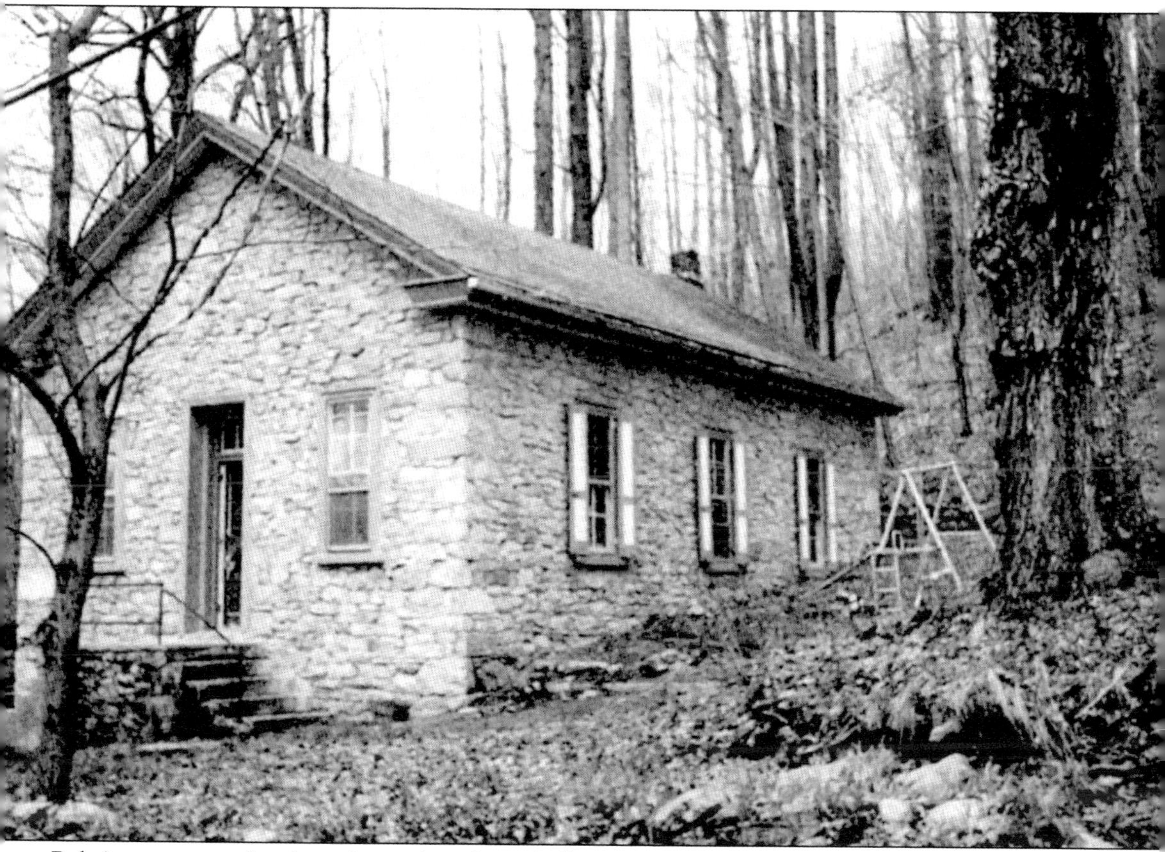

Rehr's one-room school was located on Crow Hill approaching Forgedale. Aaron Rohrbach was the teacher of the 1937–1938 class, which included 26 students.

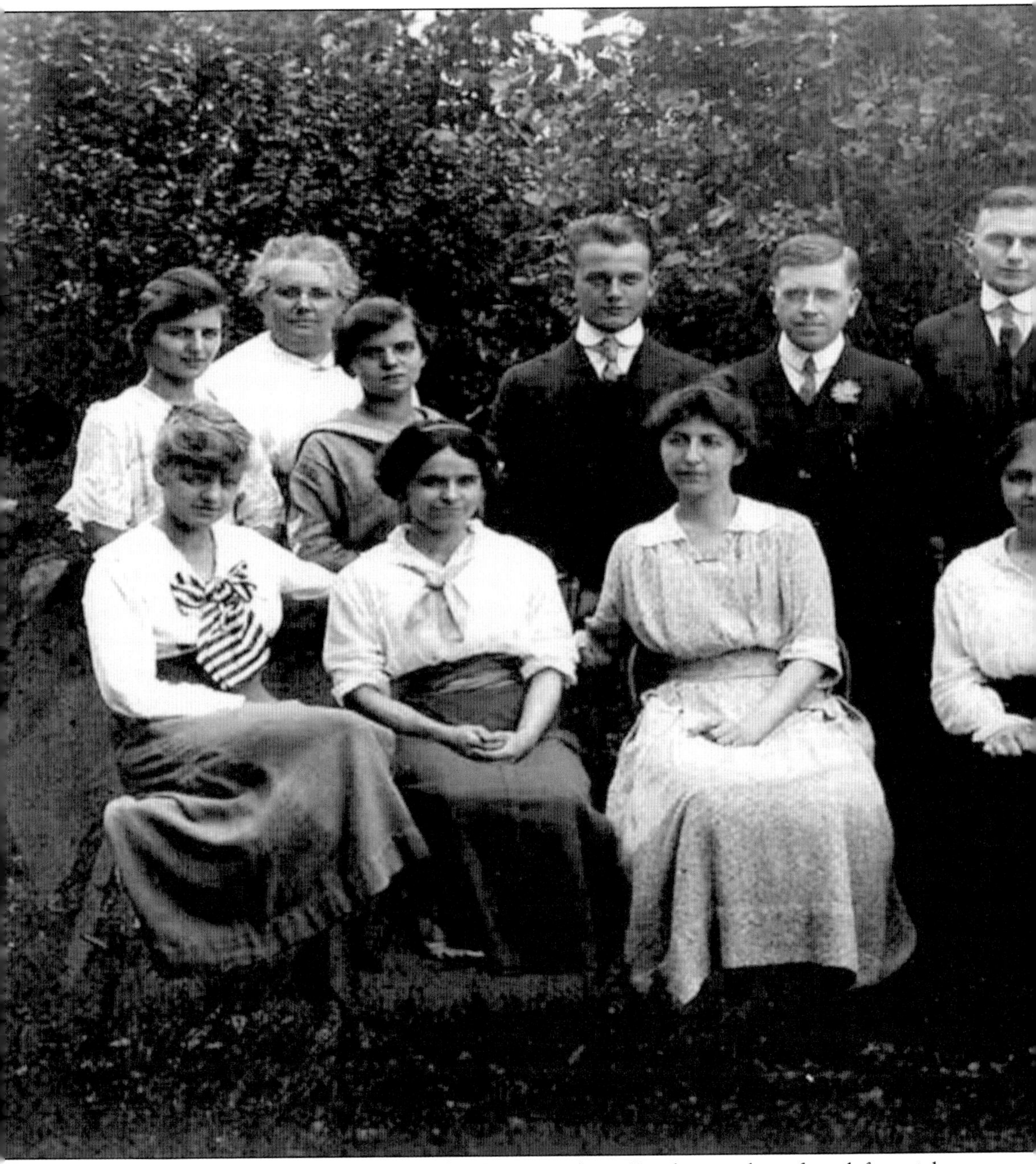

The 1914 Boyertown School District faculty is seen here. Faculty members, from left to right, are as follows: (first row) Lillian Matheys Reidenauer, Eva Brunner, Ida Reinert, Margaret Gottshall Stauffer, Lucia Beeker, Carrie Lorah, and Helena Guldin Miller; (second row) Edna Yoder

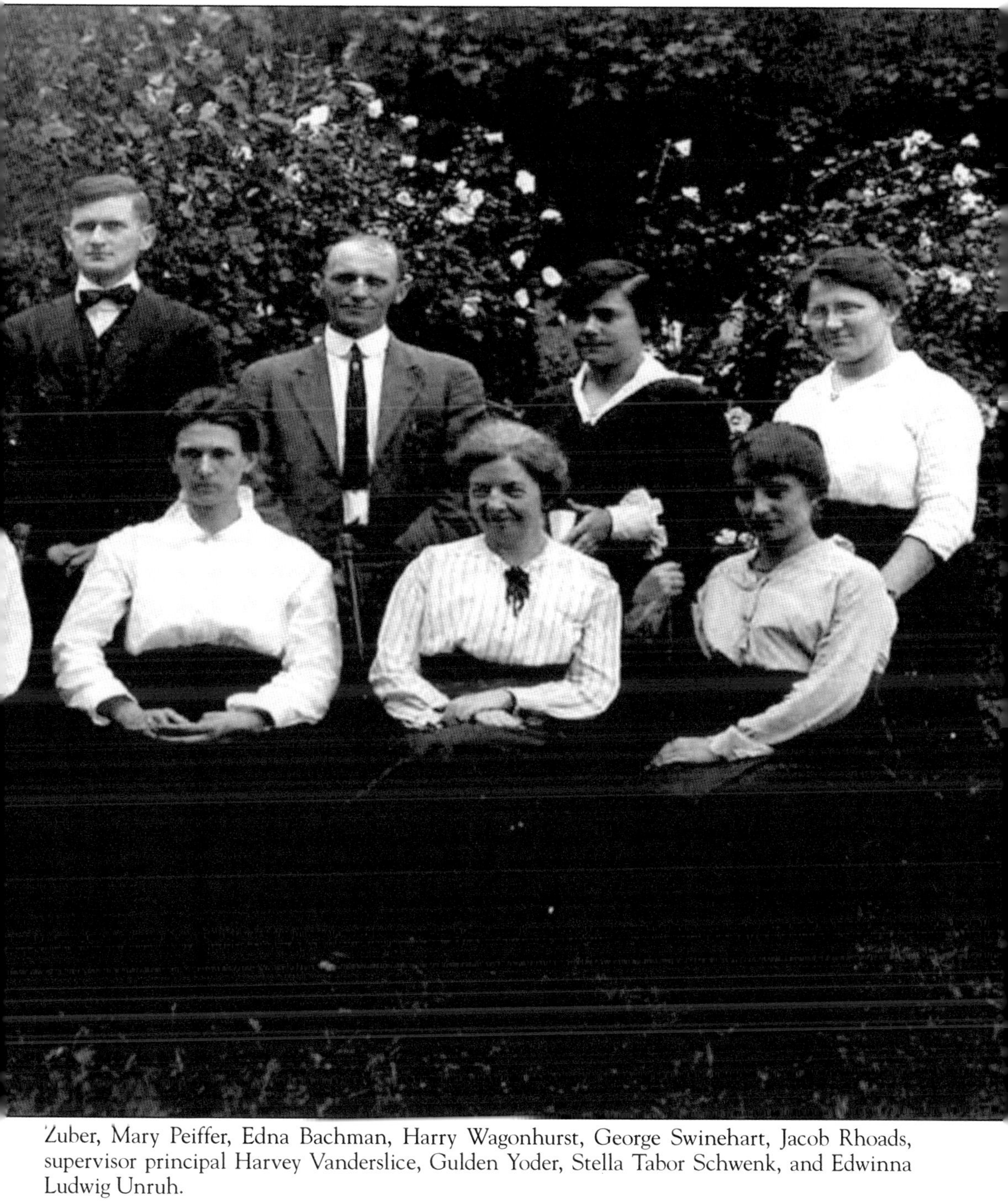

Zuber, Mary Peiffer, Edna Bachman, Harry Wagonhurst, George Swinehart, Jacob Rhoads, supervisor principal Harvey Vanderslice, Gulden Yoder, Stella Tabor Schwenk, and Edwinna Ludwig Unruh.

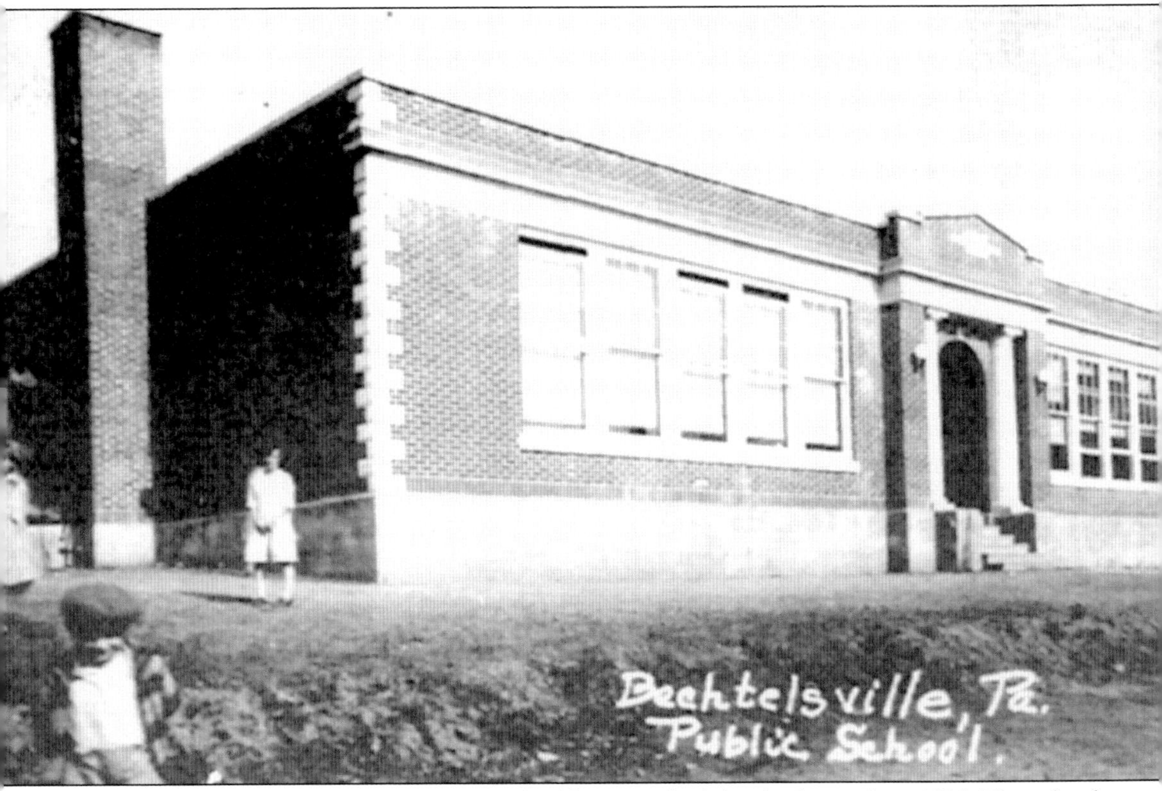

Bechtelsville Public School, a one-story building, was built by the borough in 1890. The school, located on West Chestnut Street, had the first classes in the town. The grades 1–3 met in one room and at the same time, grades 4–6 met on the second floor of the fire house, and grades 10–12 rode the train to Boyertown Senior High School. In 1925, a new school was built and grades 1–8 attended at the end of West Chestnut Street. Grades 9–12 were transported to Boyertown Senior High School. It was later closed in the 1960s due to overcrowding. The building was sold and is now a residential home.

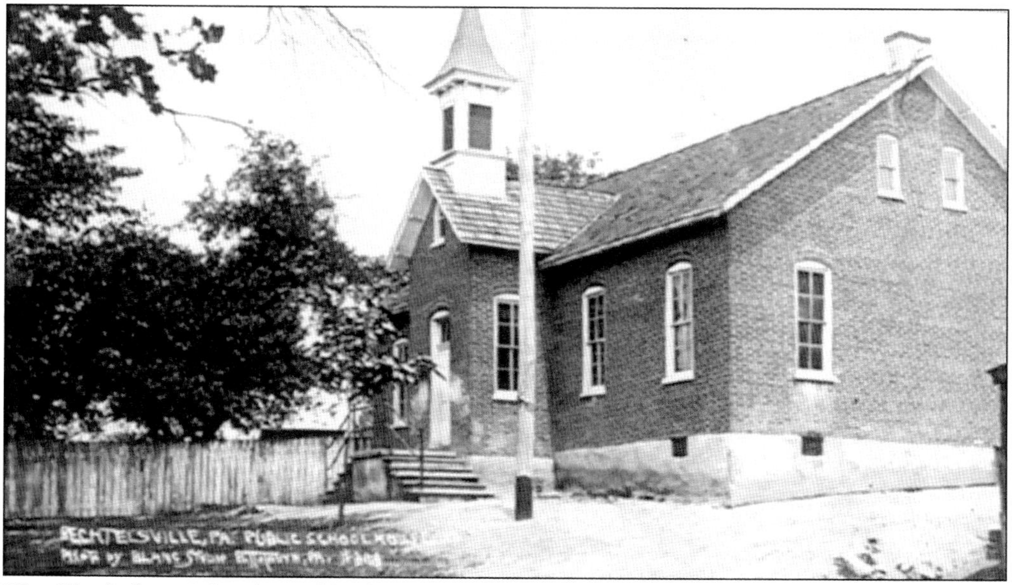

The Oberholtzer School in Eshbach is pictured here around 1910.

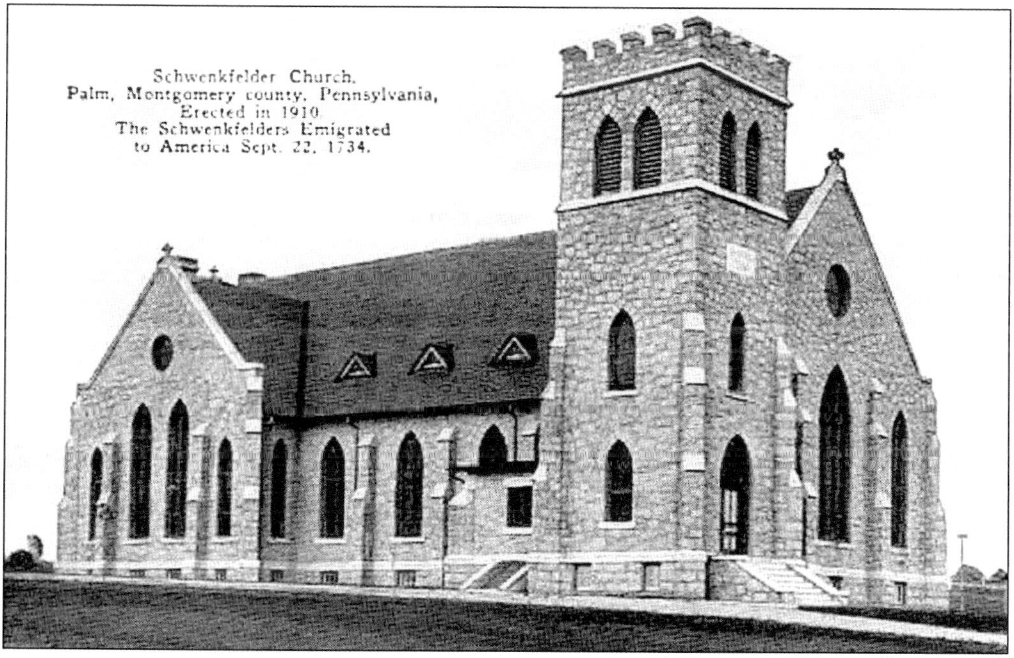

This postcard shows the Palm Schwenkfelder Church. The Schwenkfelders were one of the first religious sects to live in the Route 100 area, along with the Mennonites and Catholics.

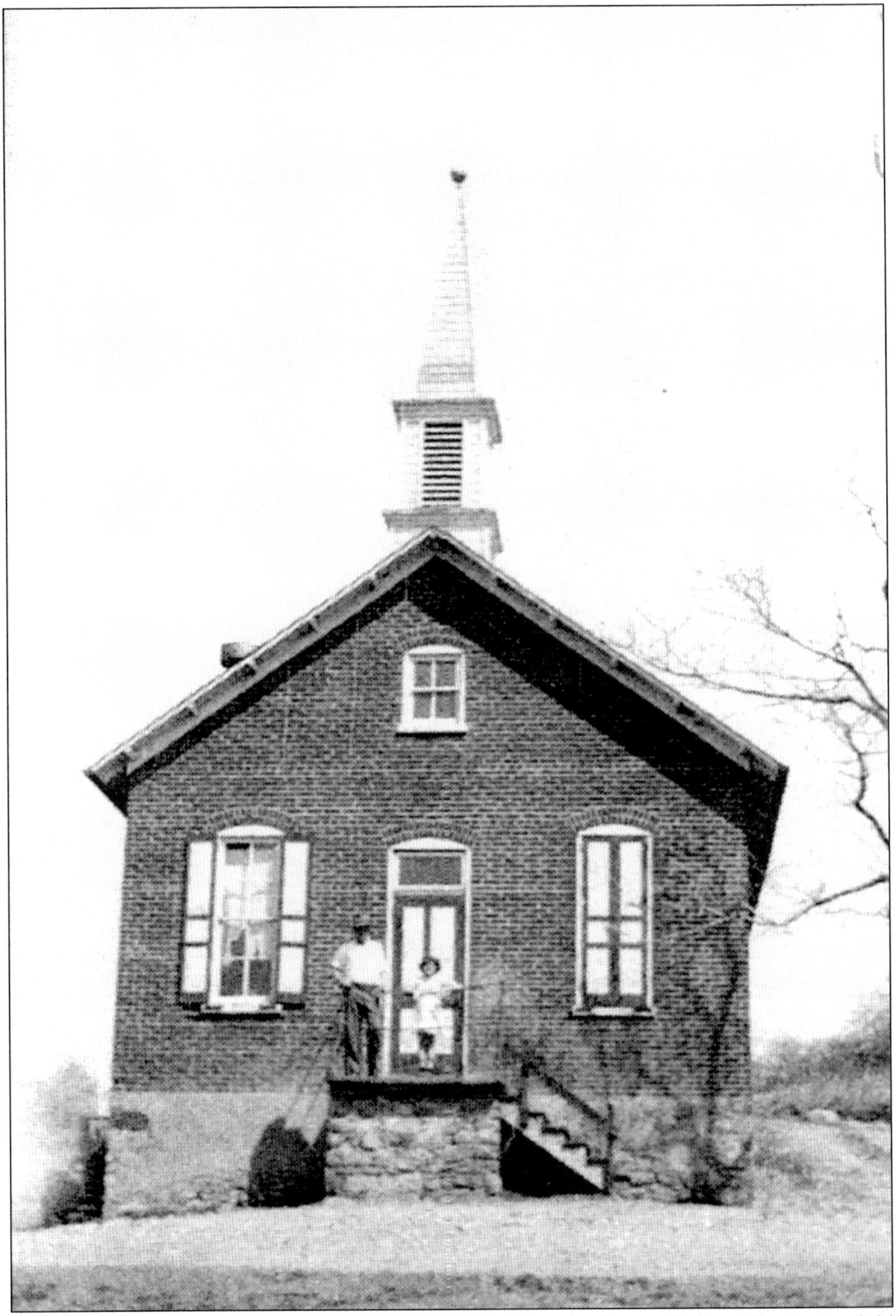

Heydt's School above Bechtelsville was attended by the author's grandfather Charles Benfield and his siblings. The school first opened in June 1894.

Six

Stahl Pottery

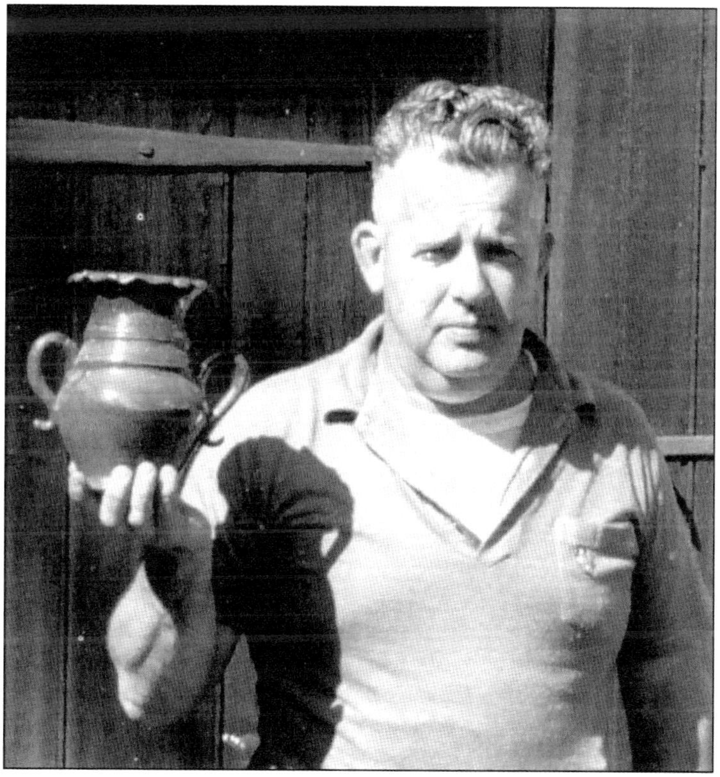

Russell Stahl displays one of his collectible clay pitchers.

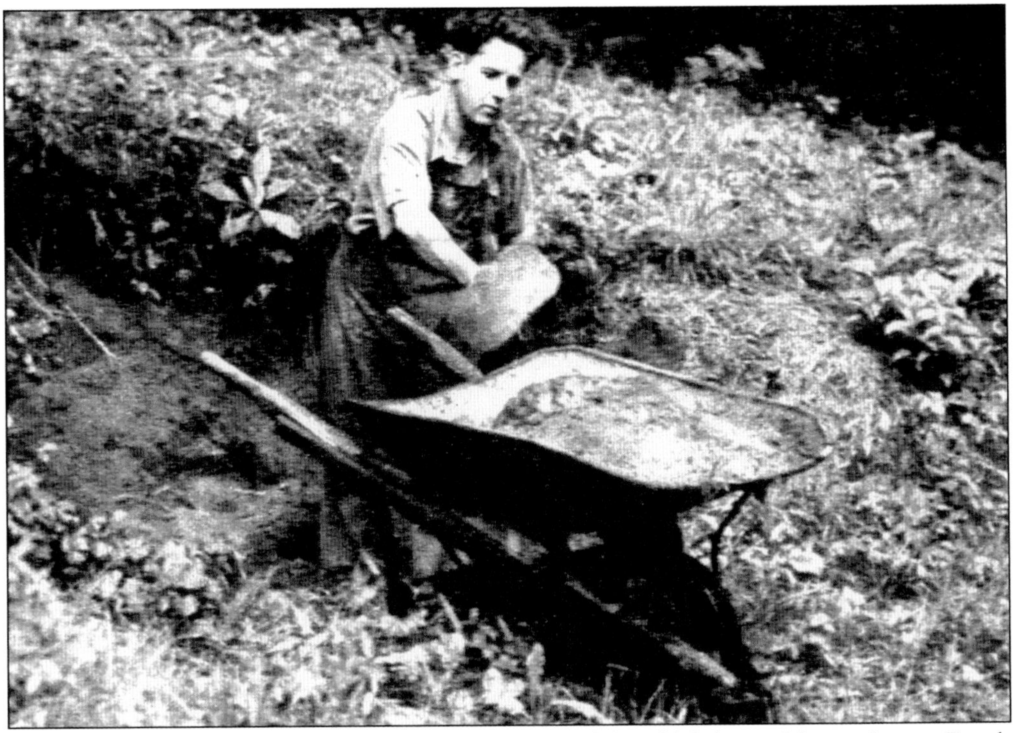

The Stahl family operated what is said to be the last of the old-fashioned Pennsylvania Dutch potteries. Close by the pottery was an inexhaustible supply of clay. Russell Stahl would dig his own clay, and the two favorite colors—red and green—were obtained by digging at different places. The pottery was located in a small settlement in Powder Valley near Hosensack.

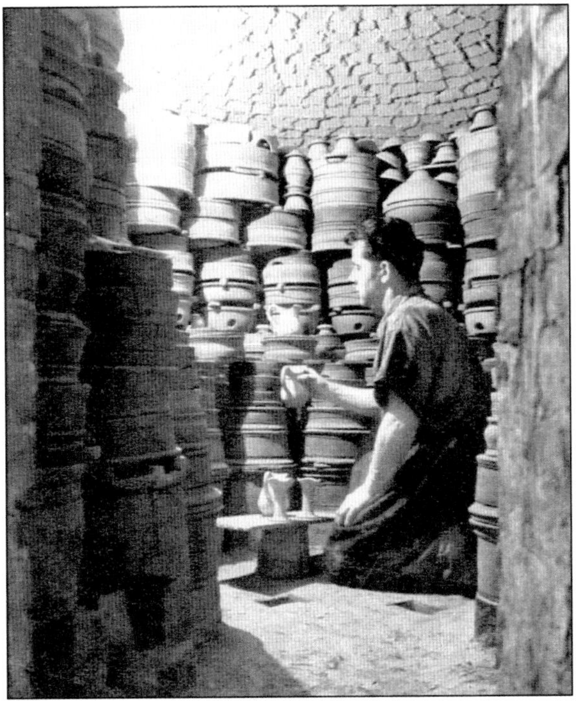

Difficult aspects of the craft come in making an even bottom to a jug, vase, or plate, as an off-center bottom cracks when fired. Decorations or moldings have to be applied so the object does not become misshapen. Pieces are dried for at least three weeks, placed bone-dry in the kiln.

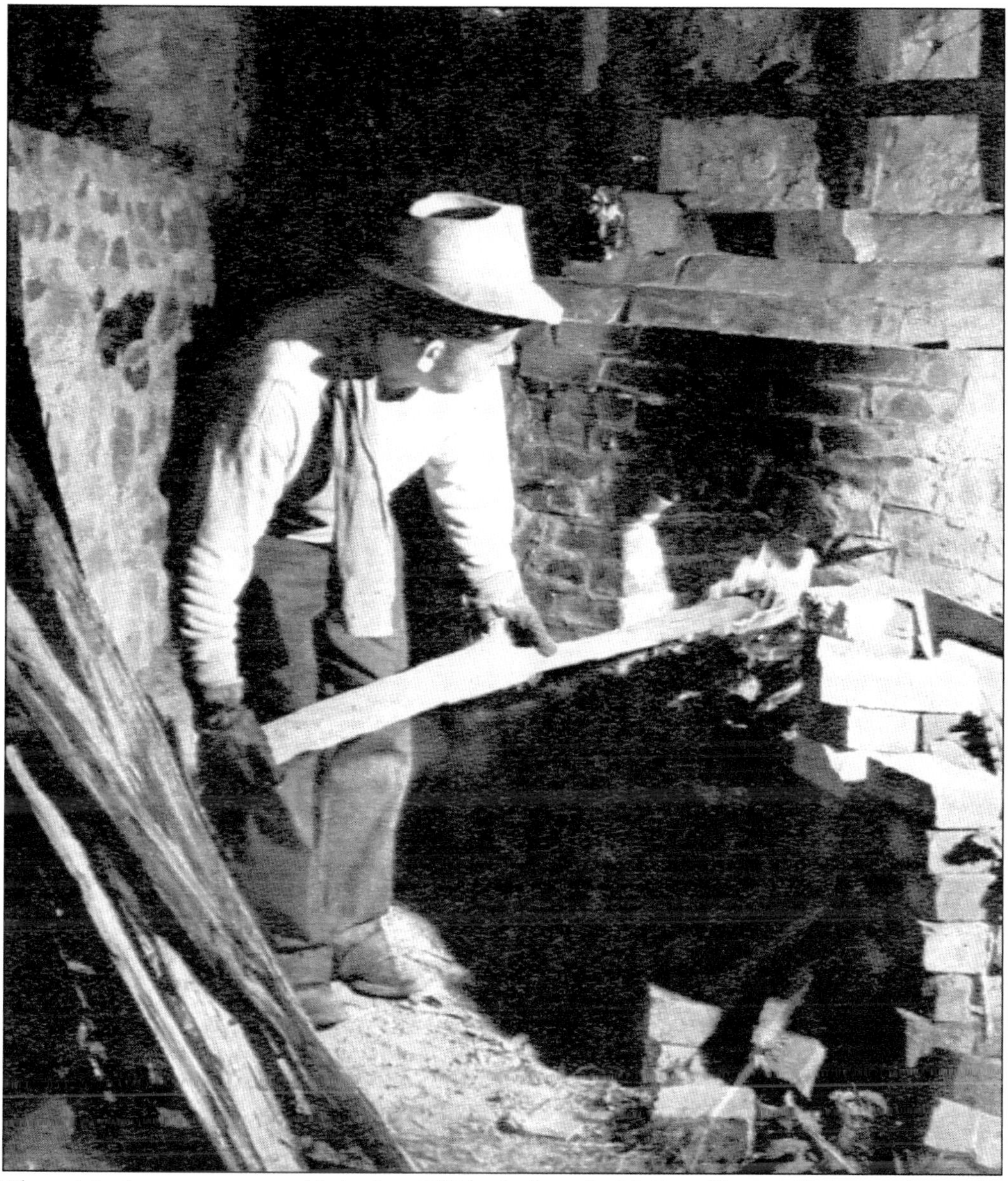

The original pottery was established in 1874 by Ludwig Stahl, Russell's grandfather, and Russell's methods were retained by his father, Issac Stahl. Russell fired the great wood-fed kiln once a year.

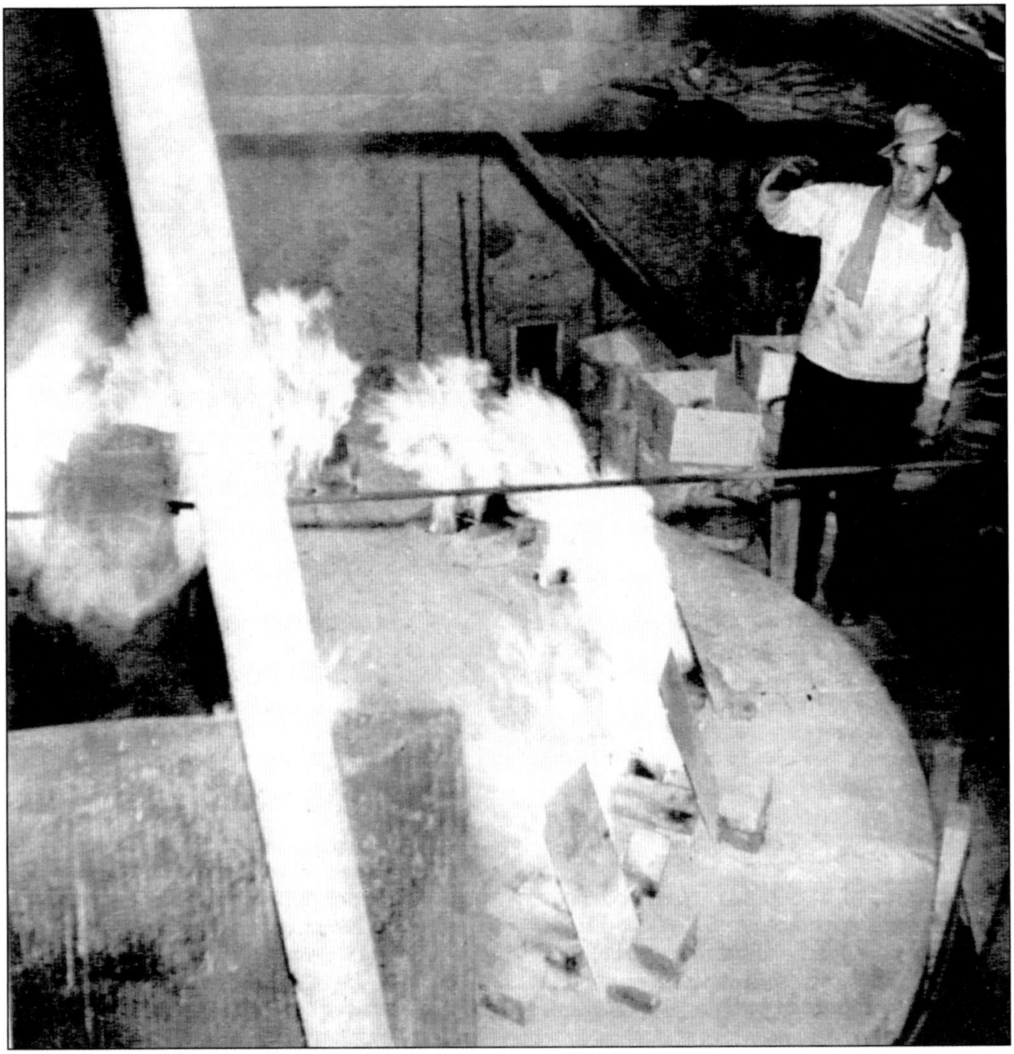

For the firing, Russell Stahl himself cut about seven cords of wood, which, like the clay, was abundant in the area, then he called for outside help in feeding the four furnace holes. After a cooling period of two weeks, he started to unload the kiln, and customers began coming for their pieces.

Seven

WORSHIP

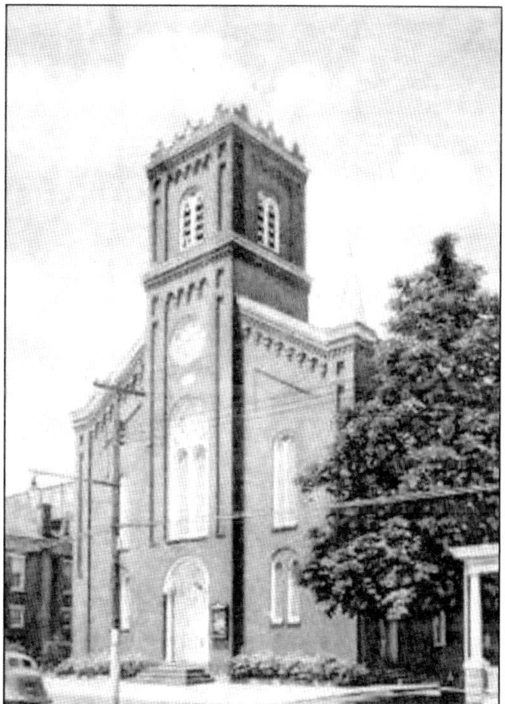

St. John Lutheran Church, located in Boyertown, is shown here around 1930.

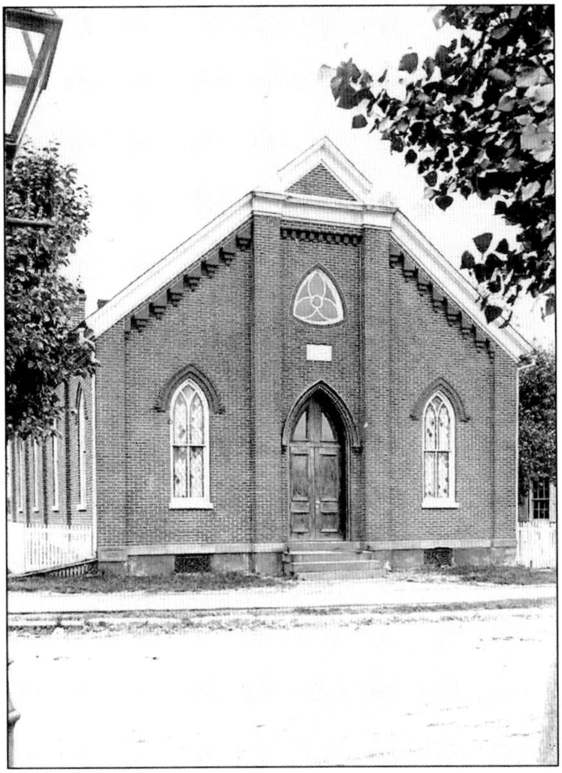

The Ebenezer Methodist Church is pictured here.

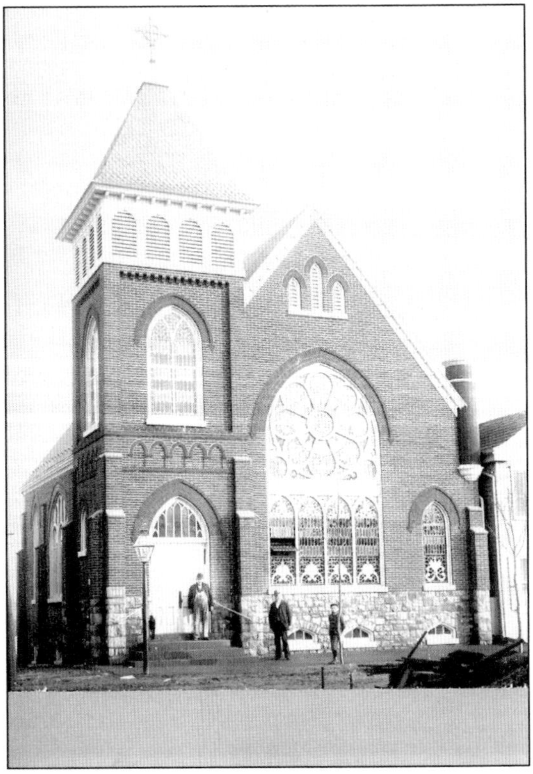

Evangelical Congregational Church, seen here, is located at South Washington Street in Boyertown.

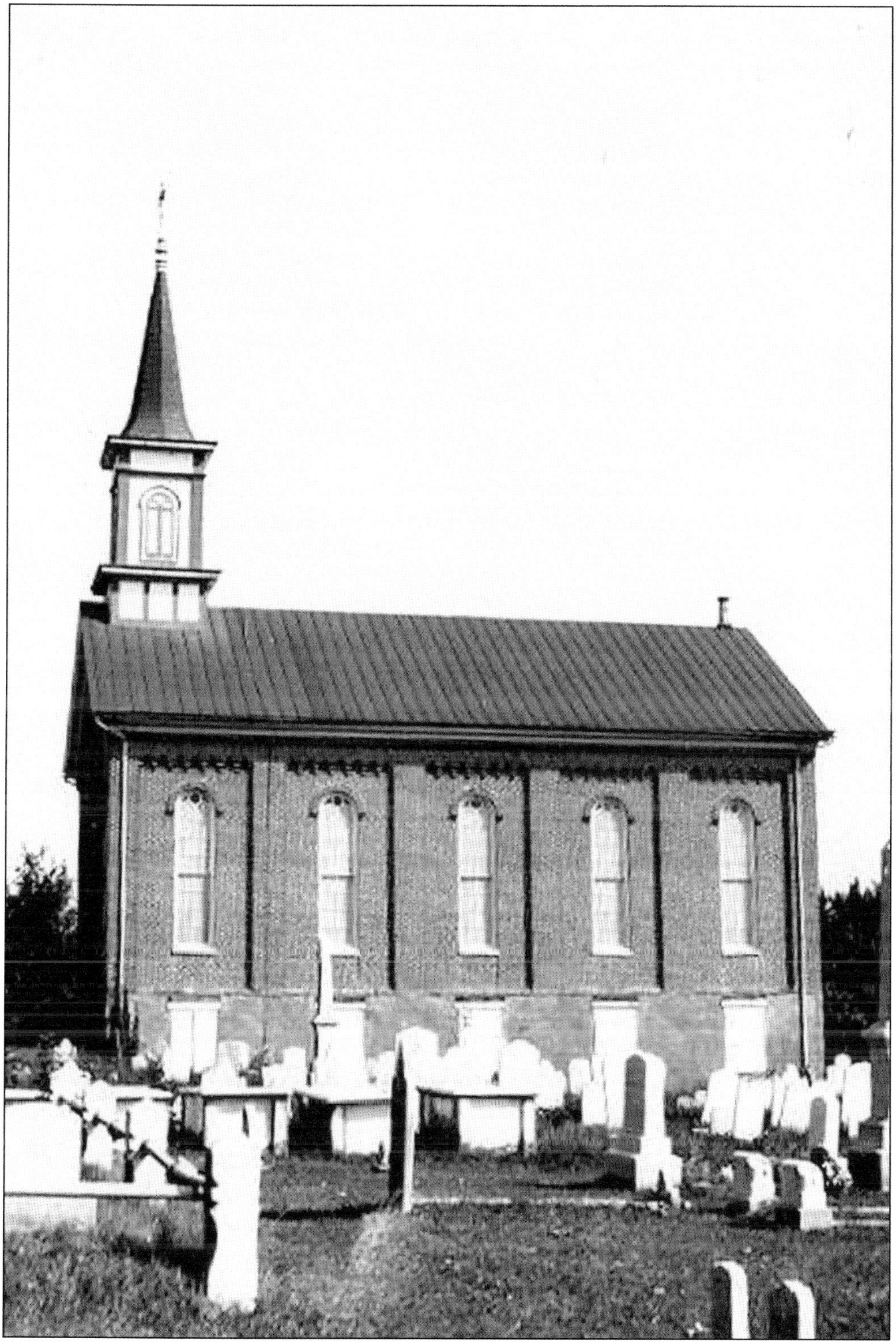

Huber's Church, which is pictured here, is located on Niantic Road in the village of Niantic.

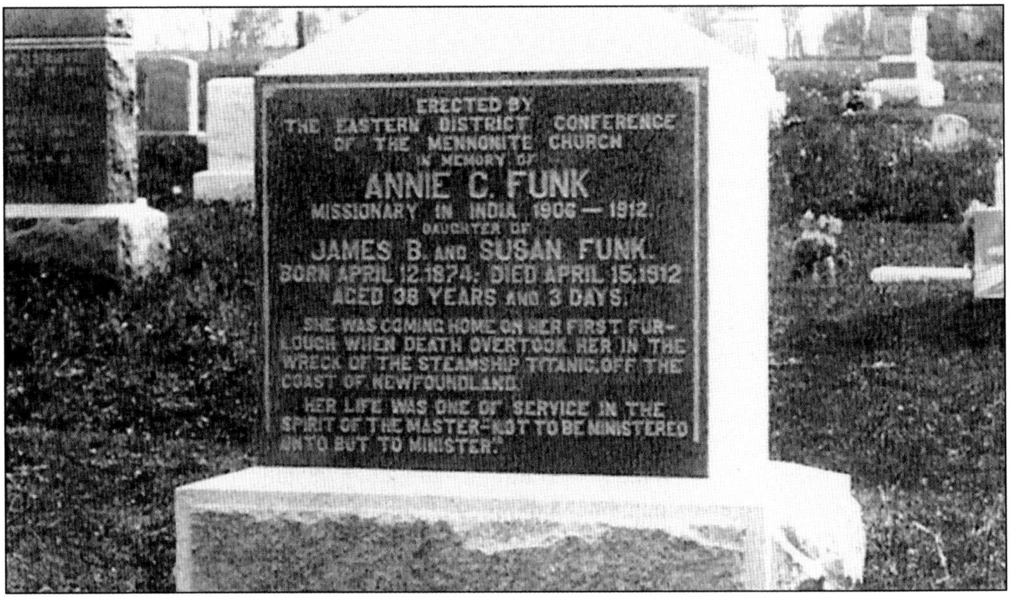

The memorial at Hereford Mennonite Cemetery was unveiled in May 1913, as a tribute to missionary Annie Funk. At the services, more money was collected than required for the memorial, and the balance was donated to the fund to erect an Annie C. Funk Memorial School for girls in India. Funk perished April 15, 1912, on what was called the unsinkable ship, the *Titanic*. Visitors still come pay tribute to Funk at the cemetery located along Route 100 upon entering Bally.

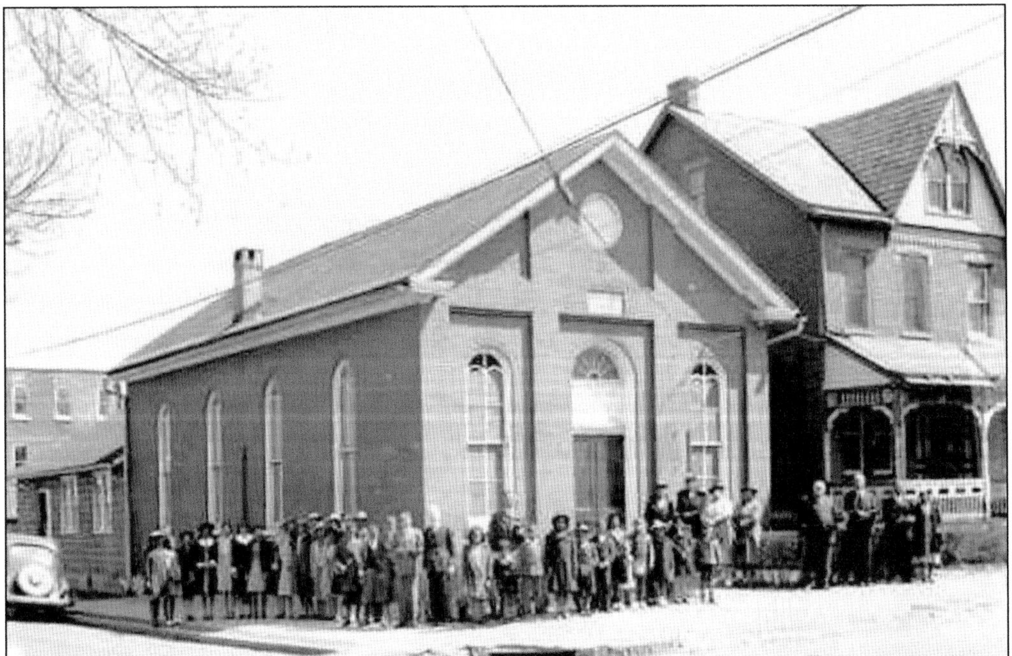

This photograph of the Bethel African Methodist Church was taken in 1940. This congregation was formed and the church erected in 1871. The church still stands on the corner of Beech and Franklin Streets.

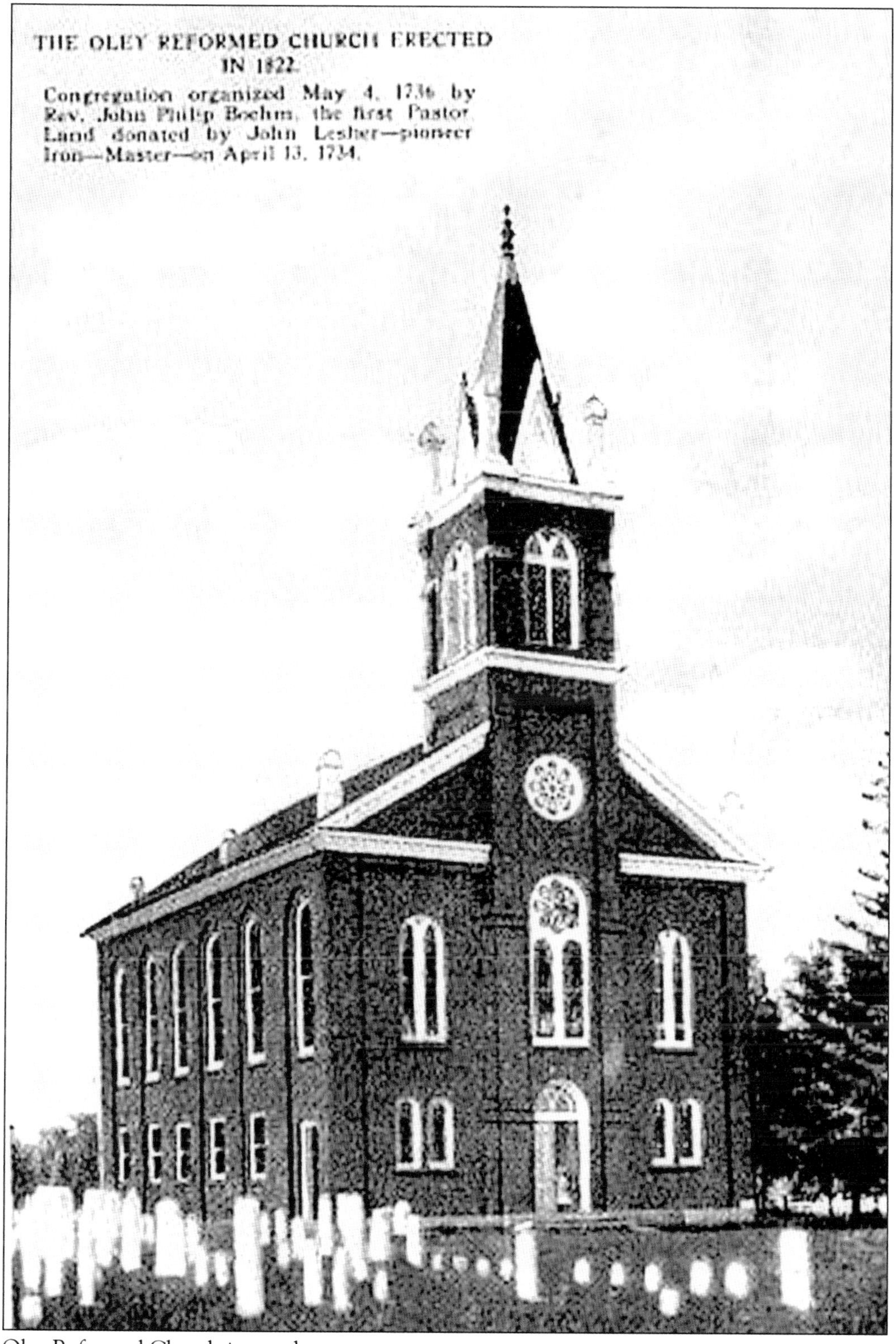

Oley Reformed Church is seen here.

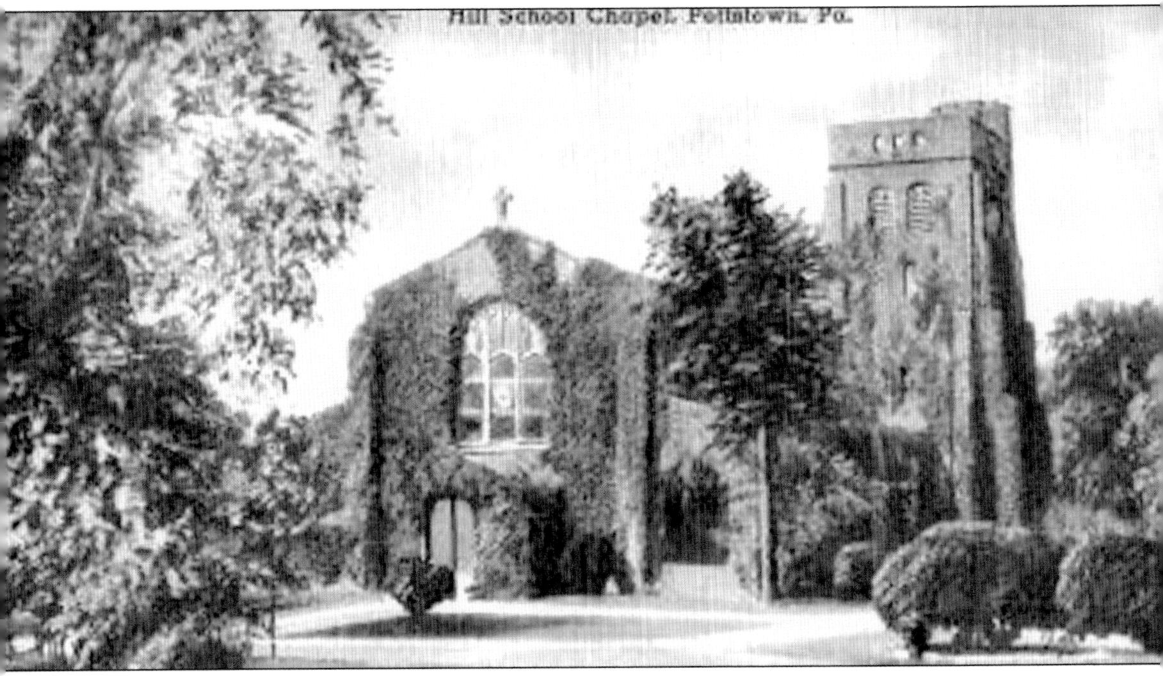

The chapel at the Hill School in Pottstown is pictured here.

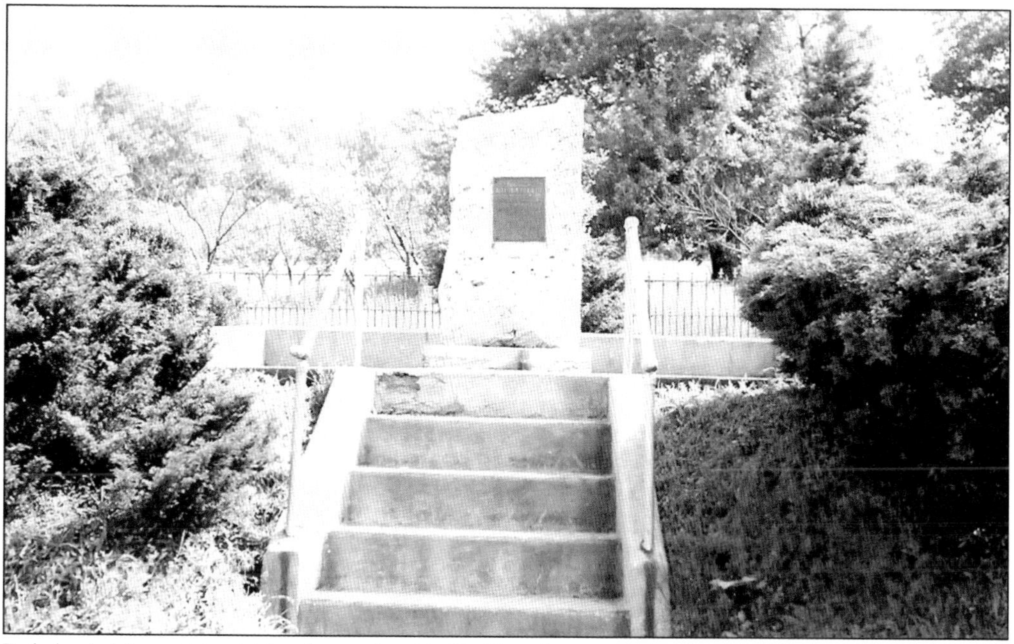

Rohrbach Memorial, which is housed at Huff's Church west of Route 100 and Clayton, is seen here.

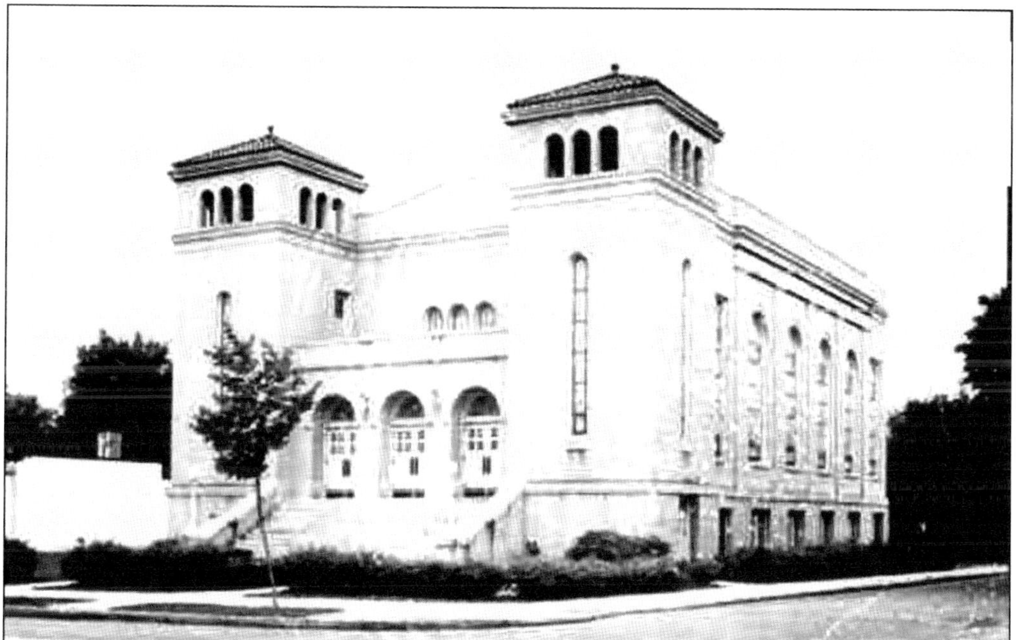

Mercy of Truth Synagogue was erected in 1925 at High and Warren Streets. It was the second building for the congregation. It was razed in the 1970s, and a new building was built on North Keim Street.

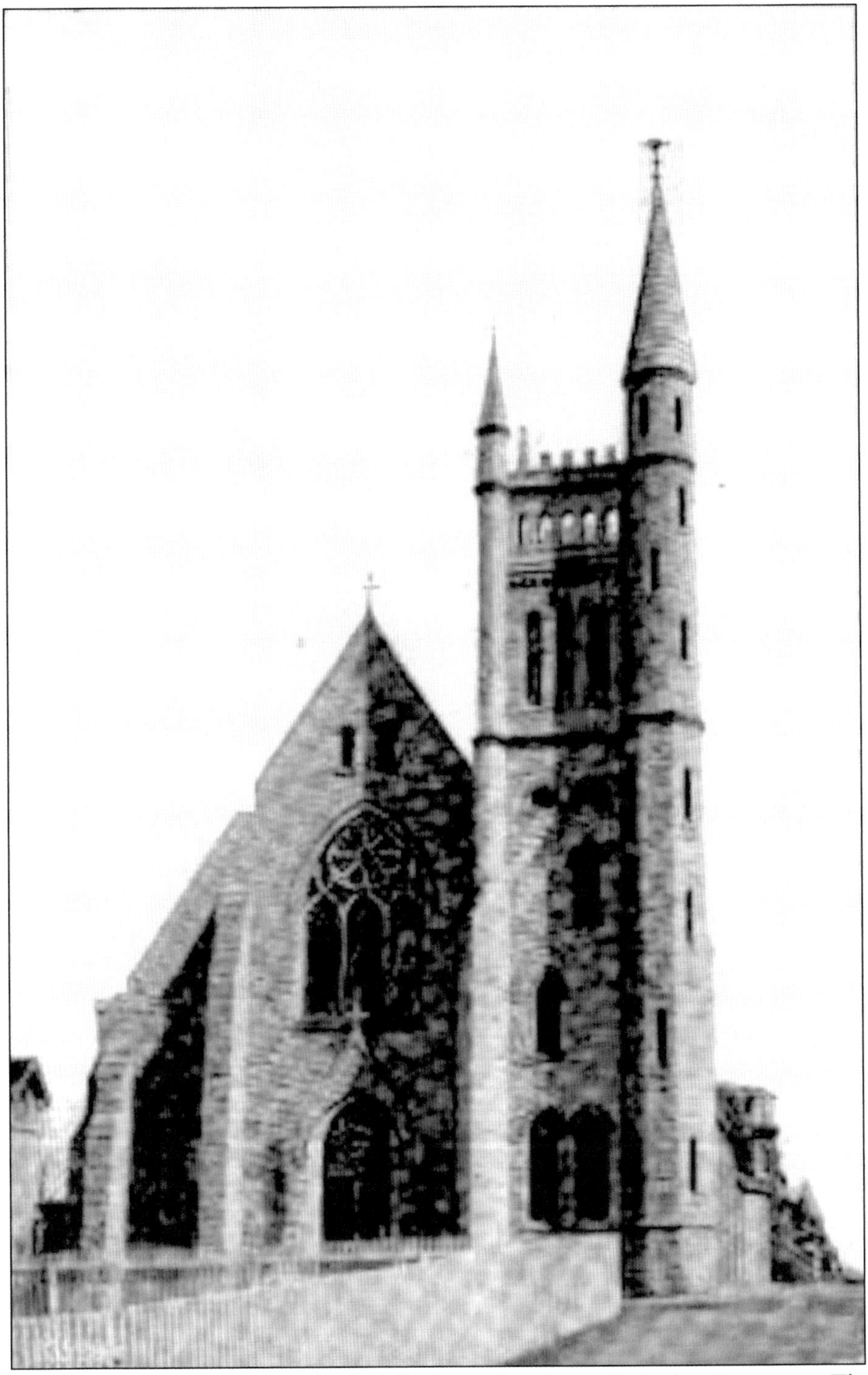

St. Aloysius Catholic Church was the first Catholic church established in Pottstown. The first church building was dedicated in 1856. The current church building was dedicated in December 1891. The cornerstone of St. Aloysius School was laid in January 1913, and the present rectory was constructed in the early 1900s after a fire destroyed the original.

Eight

Areas of Interest

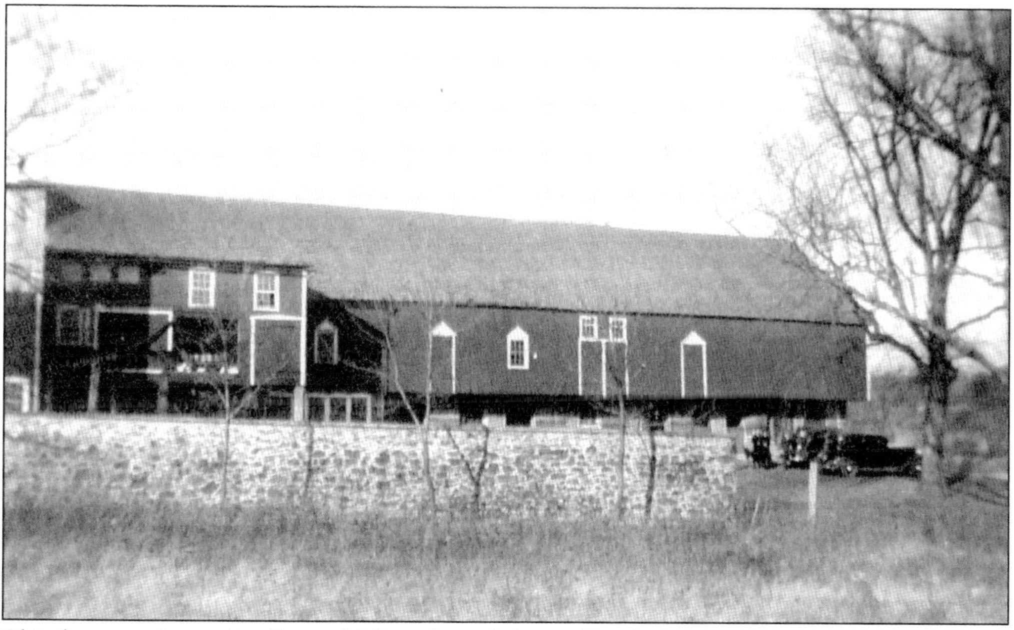

This farm was located in Butter Valley along Gehman Road.

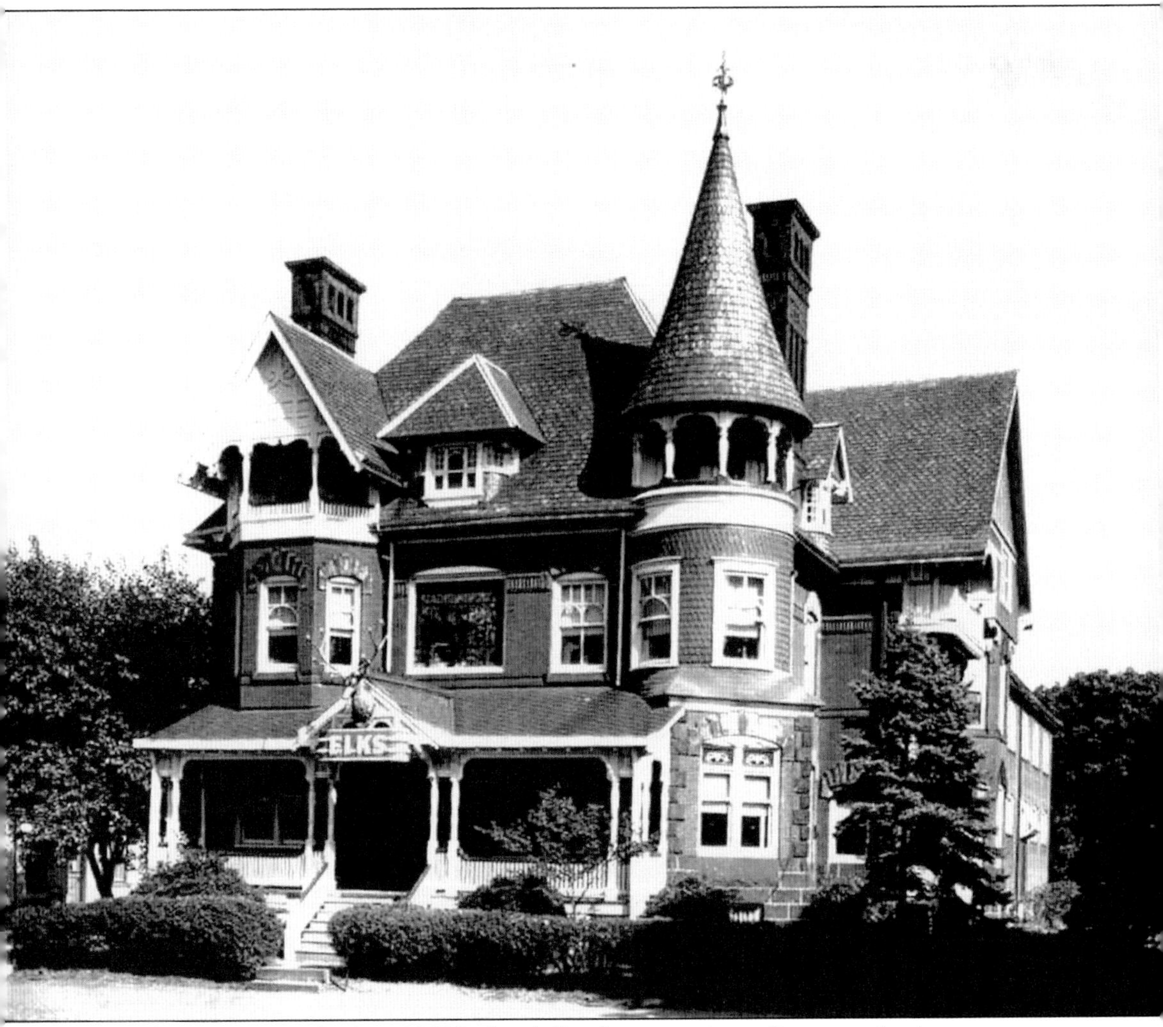

Fegely Mansion was built in 1887 by Jacob Fegely, a prominent Pottstown businessman.

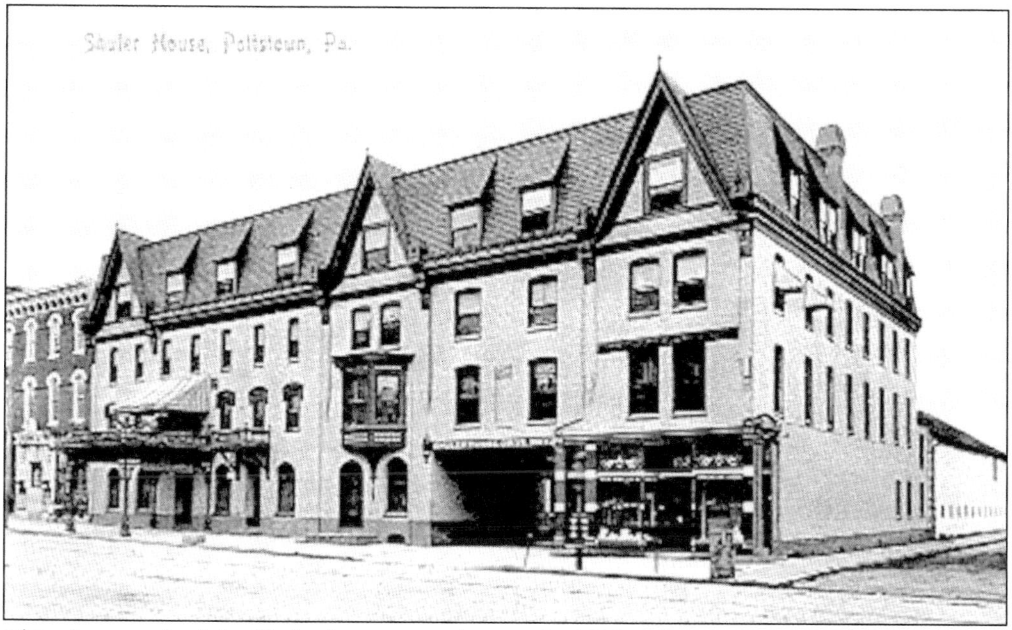

This photograph of the Shuler house was taken in the 1920s. The 1880s-enlarged Farmers Hotel can be seen in the photograph. The Shuler family owned the house from 1870 to 1910.

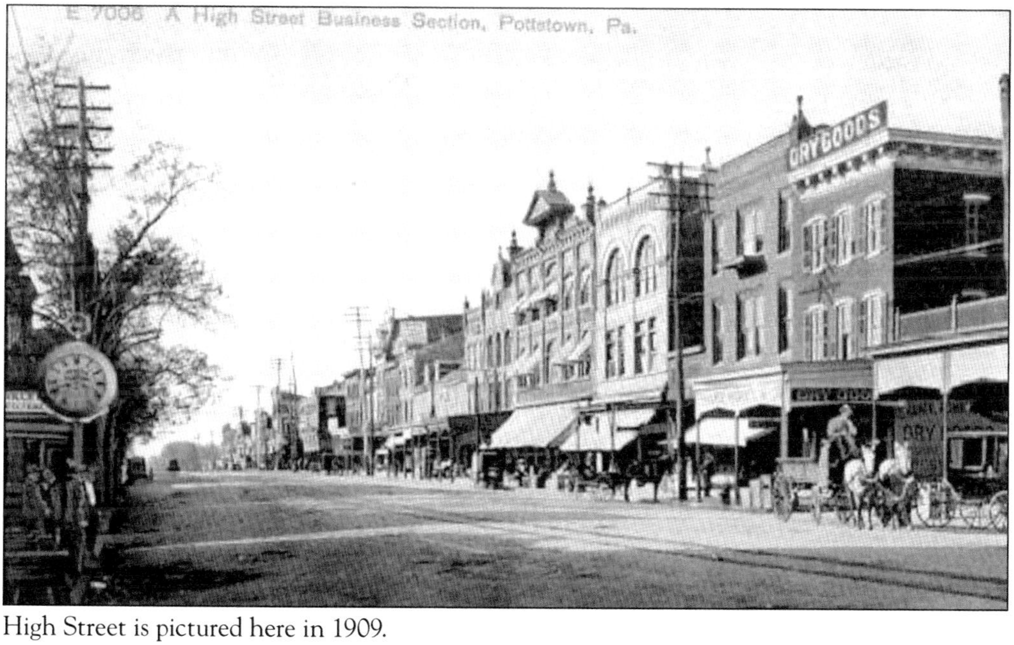

High Street is pictured here in 1909.

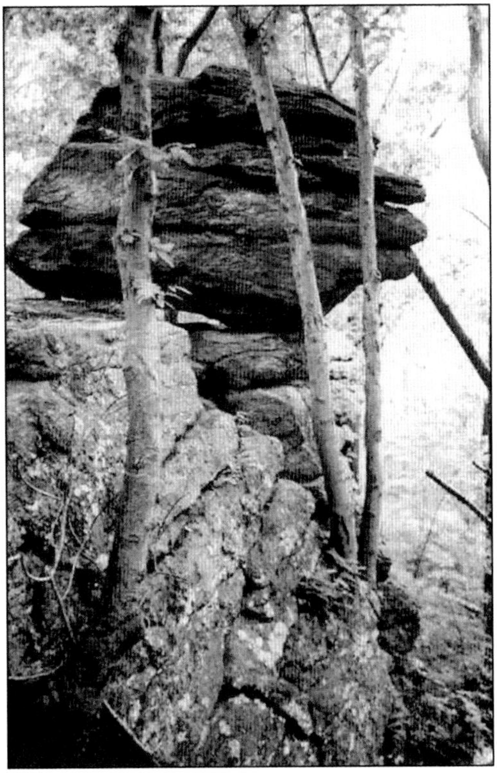

The face of Poshta Yokel can be seen hidden behind trees along Forgedale Road. There are many versions of whom or what this is; however, it is believed to be a large boulder balanced on the top of the hillside. Photographs such as this one, which was taken in the 1930s, give a clear view over Forgedale toward Thomas Mayberry's Hereford Furnace.

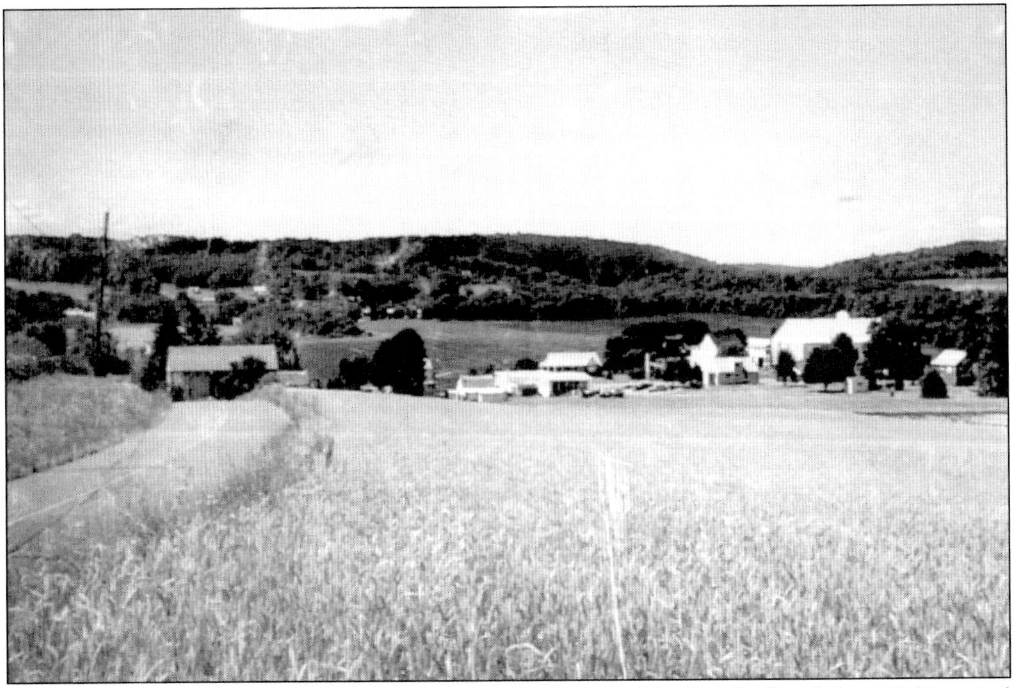

From the top of Gehringer Road, one can witness the beauty of the farmland and the rich historical villages along Route 100. This particular view looks directly over what was Schultzville (Barto).

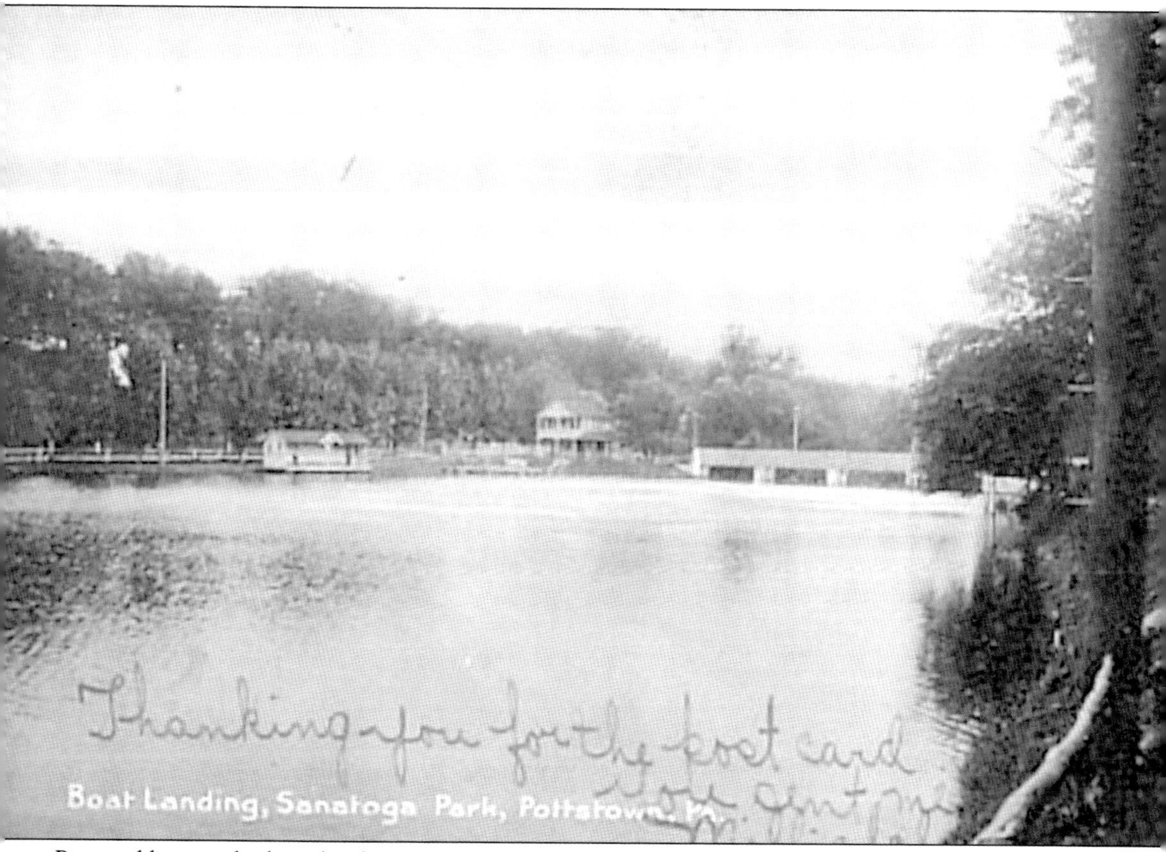

Pictured here is the boat landing at Sanatoga Park.

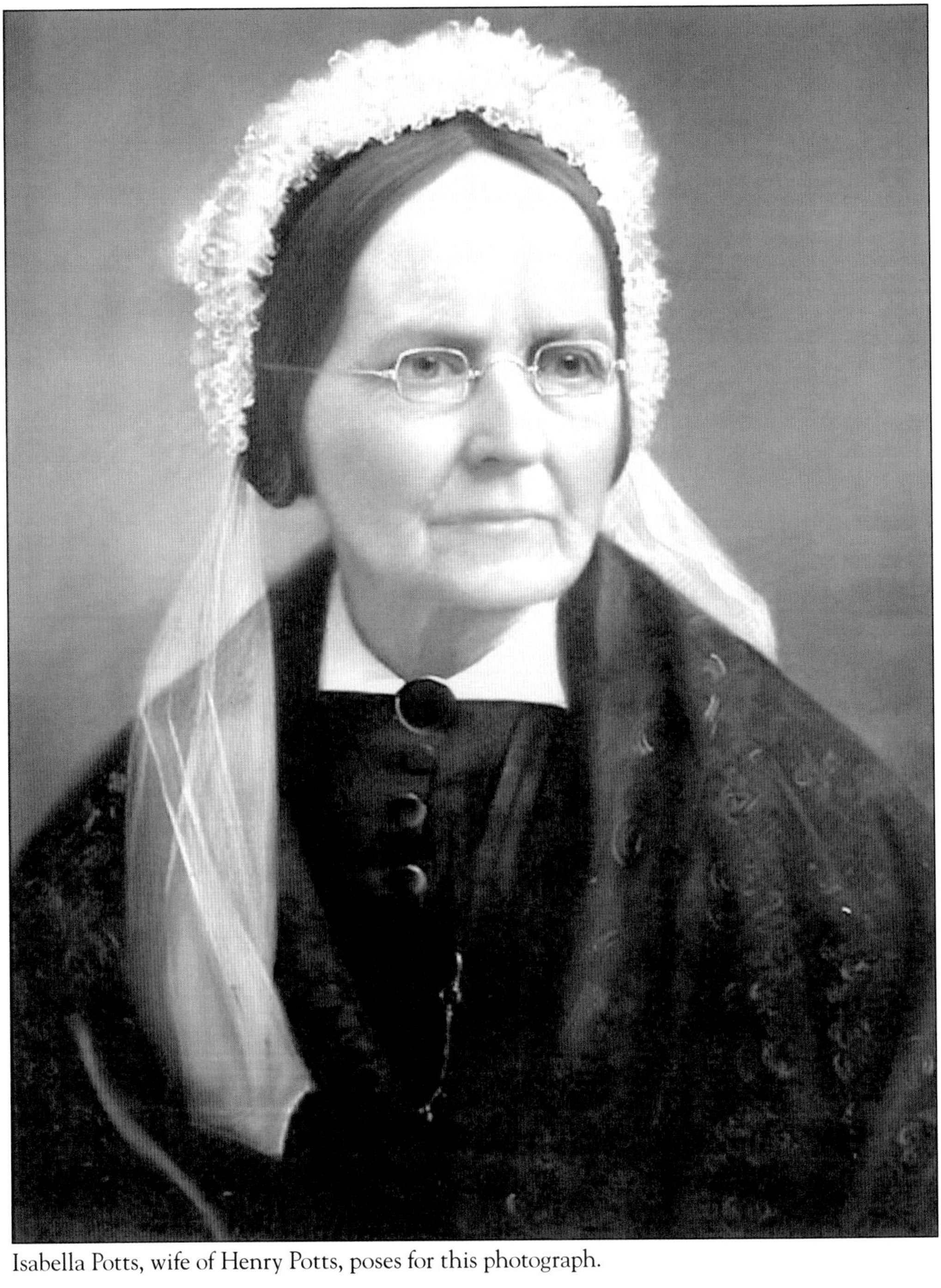

Isabella Potts, wife of Henry Potts, poses for this photograph.

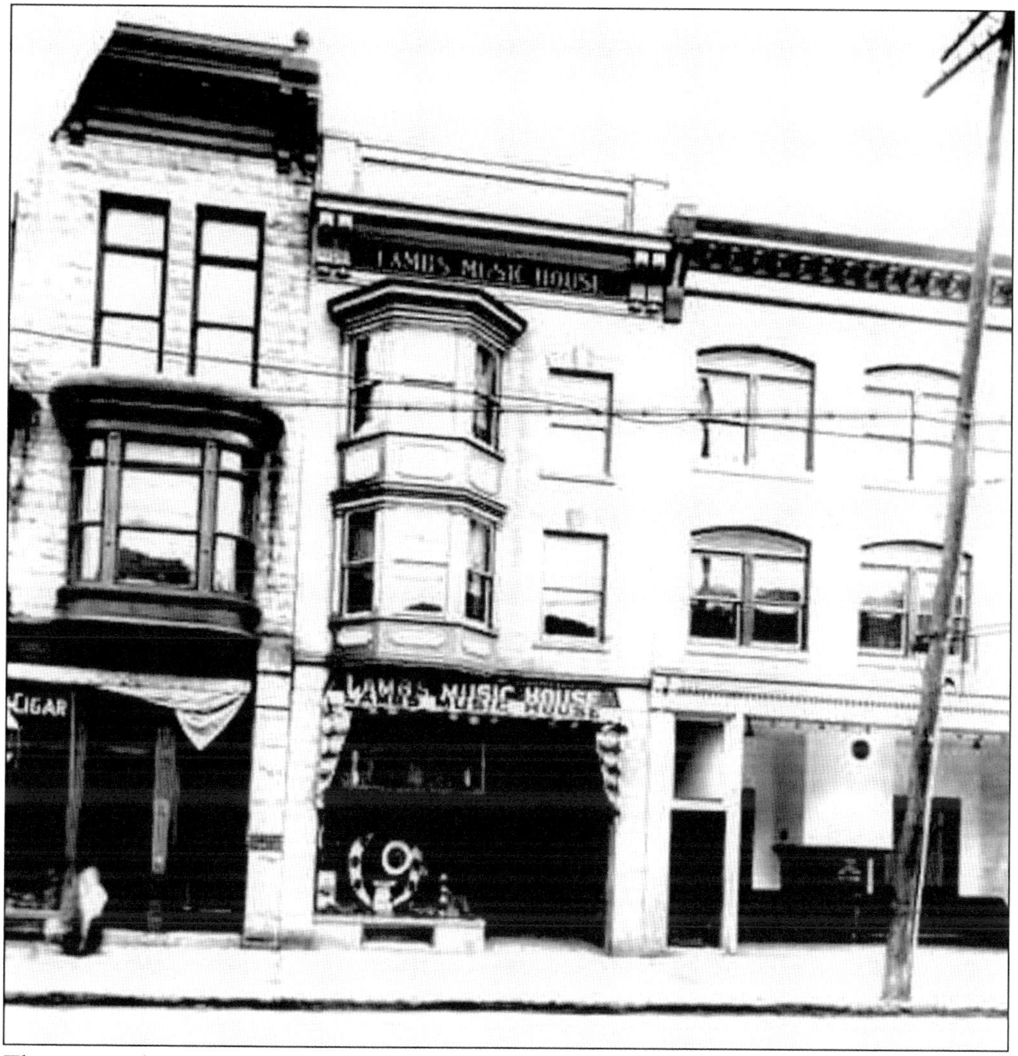

This is an early-1900s view of Lamb's Music Store, which was located in the business district of High Street in Pottstown. Pottstown has been fortunate to preserve many of the old historical buildings.

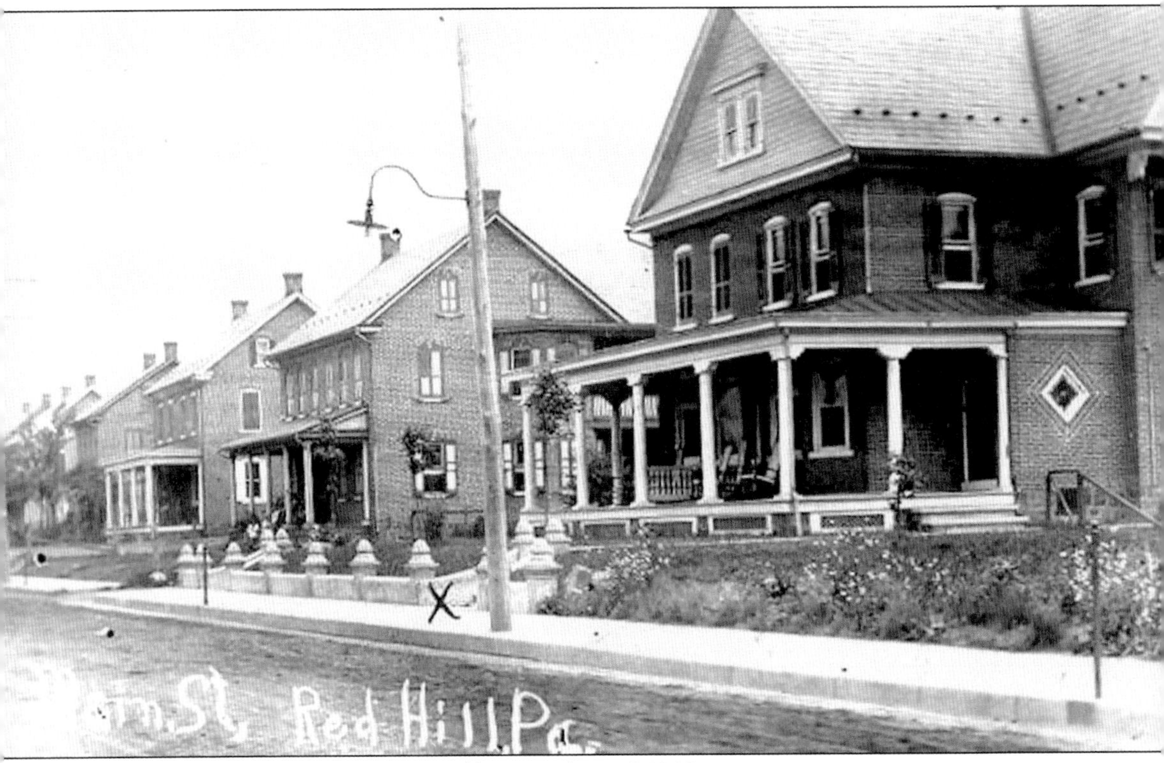

Main Street in Red Hill is pictured here in the mid-1900s.

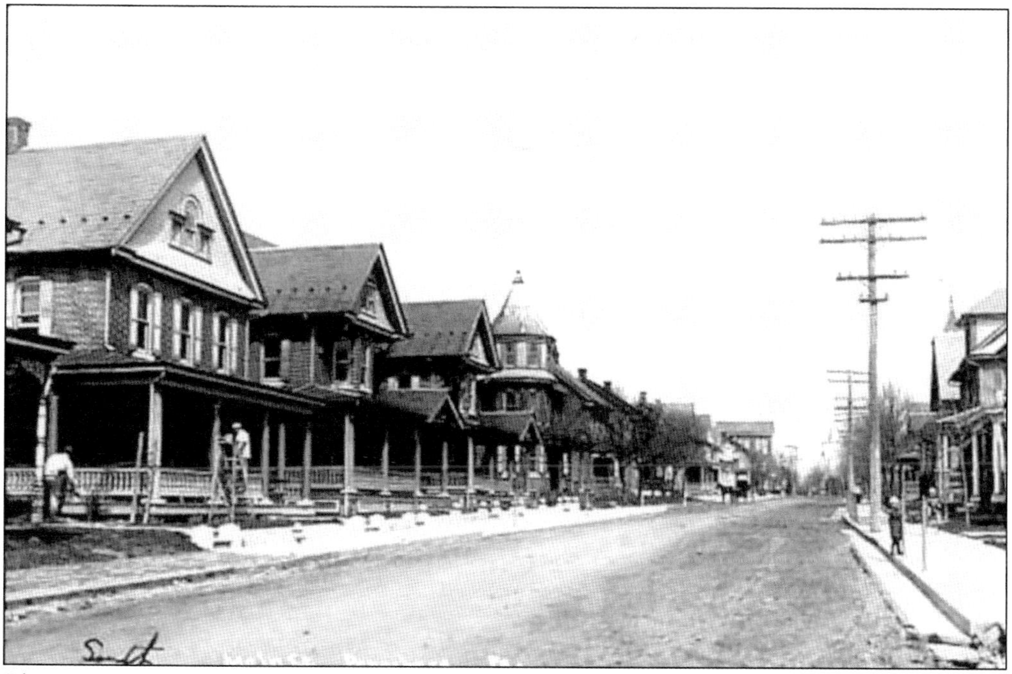

This postcard view shows South Main Street in Pennsburg.

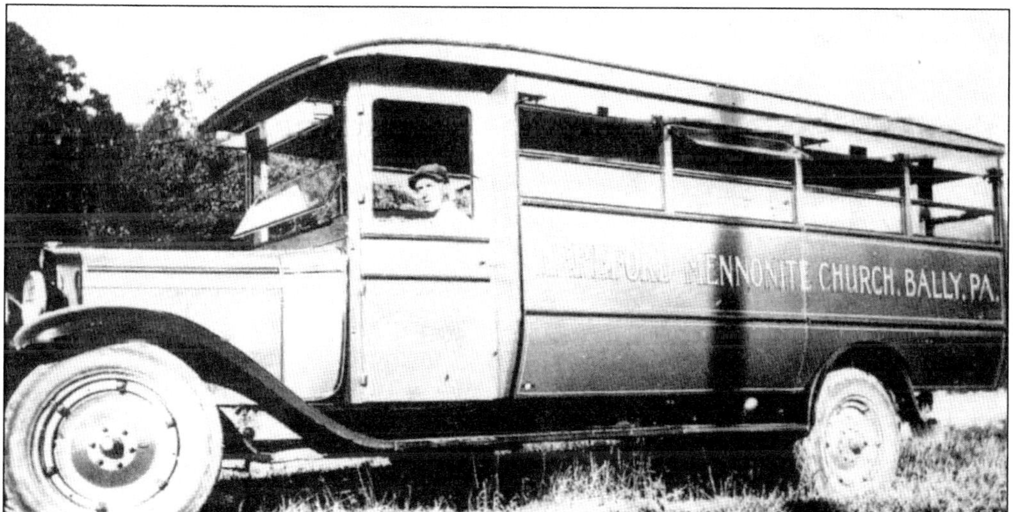

Charles Snyder of Barto is seen driving the first Sunday school bus at the Mennonite church in Bally.